Paul Robinson

Freud

University of California Press

Berkeley   Los Angeles   Oxford

University of California Press
Berkeley and Los Angeles, California

University of California Press, Ltd.
Oxford, England

LIBRARY OF CONGRESS CATALOGING-IN-PUBLICATION DATA

Robinson, Paul A., 1940–
    Freud and his critics / Paul Robinson.
        p.   cm.
    Includes bibliographical references and index.
    ISBN 0-520-08029-7 (alk. paper)
    1. Freud, Sigmund, 1856–1939.   2. Sulloway, Frank J.—Views on
psychoanalysis.   3. Masson, J. Moussaieff (Jeffrey Moussaieff),
1941–   —Views on psychoanalysis.   4. Grünbaum, Adolf—Views on
psychoanalysis.   5. Psychoanalysis—Philosophy—History.   I. Title.
BF109.F74R64   1993
150.19'52—dc20   92-12935
                                                                            CIP

Printed in the United States of America
9 8 7 6 5 4 3 2 1

For
Dr. Carlos Esquivel
Dr. Paul Nakazato
and
Dr. Barry Levin

who gave me a new liver
but left me my old spleen

Contents

I would like to thank the Stanford Humanities
Center and the Institute for Advanced Study in
Princeton for supporting my work on this book.

Introduction:
The Anti-Freudian Mood

Everybody knows that Freud has fallen from grace. Whenever I have told someone that I was writing a book about him, the response has almost invariably been the same: "Hasn't he been disproved?" Or I have been asked about the latest scandal from the newspapers: "Wasn't he a cocaine addict?" "Didn't he lie about his patients being sexually abused?" "Freud's Reputation Shrinks a Little" read a recent front-page headline in the *San Francisco Chronicle*, introducing an account of Freud's American patient Dr. Horace Frink, whom Freud apparently urged to divorce his wife and marry a former patient. In the same article Frank Sulloway is quoted: "Each of Freud's published cases plays a role in the psychoanalytic legend. But the more detail you learn about each case, the stronger the image becomes of Freud twisting the facts to fit his theory."[1] Hardly a month seems to pass without a story or a comment of this sort, whether in the popular press or in scholarly writings and reviews.

The tide had already begun to turn in the 1970s. The first hint that Freud's reputation was in trouble came from

---

1. *San Francisco Chronicle,* March 6, 1990.

the new feminists. The year 1970 itself was particularly
rough, when, in separate books, Kate Millett, Germaine
Greer, Shulamith Firestone, and Eva Figes all took Freud
to task for his reactionary views on women.[2] 1970 also
witnessed the publication of Henri Ellenberger's massive
study *The Discovery of the Unconscious,* with its irreverent
chapter on Freud; a few years later Paul Roazen's *Freud and
His Followers* continued in a similar vein. Ellenberger and
Roazen were significant precursors of the more full-
blooded criticism of the 1980s, but in retrospect they seem
relatively mild and conventional. The past decade, by
comparison, has brought an avalanche of anti-Freudian
writings, their tone ever more hostile. Undeniably,
Freud's reputation has undergone a sea change.

The contrast with the 1950s and 1960s, when I first read
Freud, could hardly be greater. In the wake of Ernest
Jones's three-volume biography, published between 1953
and 1957, the American intellectual community seemed to
have reached a consensus that Freud was not only the most
important thinker of the twentieth century but one of the
giants in the history of thought. The year 1952 saw him installed as the author of the final volume in Robert May-
nard Hutchins's *Great Books of the Western World,* placing
him in the company of the immortals. In *Freud and the Crisis of Our Culture* (1955), Lionel Trilling, the voice of the
liberal intellectual establishment, pronounced him the
prime mover of modernism, and he was accorded a similar
dignity, a decade later, in Richard Ellmann and Charles

---

2. Millett, *Sexual Politics;* Greer, *The Female Eunuch;* Firestone, *The
Dialectic of Sex;* and Figes, *Patriarchal Attitudes.* In "Freud and the Feminists" (*Raritan* 6, no. 4 [Spring 1987], pp. 43–61) I try to assess Freud's
feminist critics, like Millett and Greer, as well as his feminist defenders,
like Juliet Mitchell and Nancy Chodorow.

Feidelson's widely used anthology, *The Modern Tradition*. Philip Rieff's *Freud: The Mind of the Moralist* reflected perhaps most perfectly the stature he had attained by the year of its publication, 1961. Freud, Rieff argued, was the great moral intelligence of the century and the virtual creator of the modern conception of the self. Steven Marcus—who, with Lionel Trilling, edited a one-volume abridgment of Jones's biography—summed up the mid-century consensus just as it was about to dissolve:

As the twentieth century moves through its last two decades, it becomes increasingly evident that the figure of Sigmund Freud remains as one of a very small handful of intellectual presences who have presided over the complex courses that Western thought and culture have taken throughout the entire epoch. His reputation and place in the history of the modern world have never stood higher or enjoyed a firmer security than they do today.[3]

Writing a couple of years before Marcus, Frederick Crews more accurately sensed the winds of change that were about to buffet Freud's creation. "Psychoanalysis," Crews predicted, "will fade away just as mesmerism and phrenology did, and for the same reason: its exploded pretensions will deprive it of recruits."[4] Unquestionably, the collapse of Freud's reputation in the 1980s—not unlike the simultaneous collapse of Marx's reputation—was an extraordinarily dramatic reversal of fortune.

In one respect, Freud might seem to be alive and well in the contemporary intellectual world. I am thinking of the

3. Steven Marcus, *Freud and the Culture of Psychoanalysis* (Boston, 1984), p. 1.

4. Frederick Crews, "Analysis Terminable," *Commentary*, July 1980, pp. 33–34.

prestige that psychoanalysis still enjoys in literary studies, particularly those influenced by his French disciple Jacques Lacan. But analytically inclined literary critics have been largely uninterested in Freud himself, and, in any event, the Lacanian version of psychoanalysis favored by many literary critics is a very different intellectual animal from the Viennese original, lacking both Freud's strong clinical base and his devotion to lucidity. One might even argue that the airy extravagance of recent literary theory—psychoanalytic or otherwise—has actually contributed to the pervasive sense of Freud's disgrace: to many, the bad intellectual manners on display in deconstruction bear more than a family resemblance to the interpretive habits fostered by analysis. Frederick Crews, for one, is as dismissive of contemporary literary theory as he is of Freud, and for similar reasons. Crews's fellow critic Nina Auerbach observes of Freud's popularity in the literary community: "No sadder proof exists of the rift between literature and science than this new adherence to a Freudianism that is rapidly losing authority outside the circle of literary theory."[5] The boom in psychoanalytic literary studies, then, seems to have at best ambiguous implications for Freud's reputation as a thinker.

For some time I have pondered how to respond to the new anti-Freudianism—how to take the measure of it, how to offer a corrective to its obvious excesses. If I thought of trying to chart the shift in all its manifestations, I was confronted with an embarrassment of riches: there were too many naysayers to choose among. Inevitably, however, some of them were more interesting and impres-

5. Nina Auerbach, review of *Charles Dickens and the Romantic Self*, by Lawrence Frank, *The New York Times Book Review*, March 17, 1985, p. 43.

sive than others, and eventually I hit on the tactic that has led to the present book: I would look very closely at the critics who offered the most systematic, original, and disturbing (if not always the most hostile) reinterpretations of Freud's life and thought. These, I quickly became convinced, were precisely the three figures whose views of Freud I examine in the following chapters: the historian of science Frank Sulloway, the Sanskrit scholar and sometime psychoanalyst Jeffrey Masson, and the philosopher of science Adolf Grünbaum. Sulloway, Masson, and Grünbaum can hardly be said to constitute a school, because their interpretations of Freud are so utterly unlike. Nor do they appear to have influenced one another's thinking. What they share is simply a marked hostility to Freud, as well as the talent and industry to have created counterviews whose weight and ingeniousness require that they be taken seriously.

Frank Sulloway studied with the sociobiologist Edward O. Wilson. His *Freud, Biologist of the Mind,* published in 1979, aims to place Freud within the tradition of evolutionary thought leading from Darwin to Wilson. The book argues that Freud's psychoanalytic biographers fundamentally misrepresent his achievement when they portray him as a psychological thinker. This misrepresentation, Sulloway believes, was intended to create an image of Freud as an embattled innovator carrying on a lonely and heroic campaign against organic determinism. *Freud, Biologist of the Mind*—whose subtitle is *Beyond the Psychoanalytic Legend*—is thus as much an attack on the hagiographic proclivities of traditional scholarship on Freud as it is a revisionist interpretation of the psychoanalytic revolution. Freud's ideas, Sulloway insists, are simply an offshoot of the Darwinian paradigm that has dominated biological thought from the late nineteenth century to the present.

Jeffrey Masson is the best known of my three critics, mainly because in 1983 he was the subject of a withering *New Yorker* profile by the journalist Janet Malcolm, whom he subsequently sued for malicious misrepresentation (in a case that recently reached the Supreme Court). While employed as a professor of Sanskrit at the University of Toronto in the 1970s, Masson obtained analytic training and eventually rose within the Freudian establishment to become the editor of the Freud-Fliess correspondence. His highly visible defection from analysis in 1981 and the publication, in 1984, of *The Assault on Truth: Freud's Suppression of the Seduction Theory* made him the most famous analytic renegade since Carl Jung. His book argues that the psychoanalytic revolution was based on Freud's cowardly cover-up of his discoveries about the sexual abuse of children. In Masson's view, moreover, the entire history of psychoanalysis has been corrupted by the original lie on which the profession was founded: analysts have excused the abusive behavior of parents by blaming psychological disorders on the erotic imagination of children. Freud emerges from *The Assault on Truth* as perhaps the greatest moral failure of the century. Whether intentionally or not, Masson stands Philip Rieff's Freud on his head.

By comparison, Adolf Grünbaum's critique of Freud seems decidedly sober and academic. But if Grünbaum is less irreverent than Sulloway or Masson, his indictment far surpasses theirs in philosophic weight. Many commentators seem to feel that his *Foundations of Psychoanalysis,* also published in 1984, is the most impressive piece of philosophical criticism to which Freud has yet been subjected. Grünbaum's interpretation is complex, and his attitude toward Freud more nuanced than either Sulloway's or Masson's. In essence, though, his book (like the numerous articles that preceded it) amounts to a prolonged and detailed argument that Freud's theories are inadequately supported by evidence. Freud, Grünbaum suggests, was a failed scientist, even if his failure was more honorable than the enemies of psychoanalysis have generally allowed.

Other critics have made more spectacular charges. Peter Swales, for example, claims that Freud had an affair with his own sister-in-law, Minna Bernays, and that he plotted to murder Wilhelm Fliess, while E. M. Thornton has written a book purporting to show that Freud's ideas were the "direct outcome" of his use of cocaine.[6] Still others have developed Freud-bashing into a finer rhetorical art, notably the literary critic Frederick Crews, himself once a true believer but now a violent apostate. Yet the rival candidates have been unable to elaborate their complaints into a systematic revision. None of them has produced the kind of serious, full-scale reinterpretation of Freud offered by Sulloway, Masson, and Grünbaum.

In the chapters that follow I have found myself burdened with what might seem contradictory responsibilities. The first has been to provide a clear exposition of the views of my three chosen critics. In the case of two of them, Frank Sulloway and Adolf Grünbaum, this expository task has been unusually difficult because their own writings are extremely dense. Sulloway's book is so cluttered with detail that its main lines of argument often remain elusive; Grünbaum writes in a unique philosophical jargon that is surpassingly intricate and pedantic. I doubt that many readers will have had the fortitude to persevere to the end with either Sulloway or Grünbaum. So my initial duty, ironically, has been to render their ideas as plain as possible without doing violence to their inherent complexity. Jeffrey Masson, by contrast, is a clear and vivid

6. E. M. Thornton, *The Freudian Fallacy* (New York, 1984), p. ix.

writer, but he makes up in deviousness what he lacks in density, so that in his case, too, the job of exposition has not been easy.

Beyond exposition, however, I have been eager to mount a critique of the critics. Indeed, my interest in Sulloway, Masson, and Grünbaum stems most deeply from the conviction that they fundamentally misrepresent Freud. If Freud himself were not such an overwhelming intellectual presence—if he were a lesser figure in the history of thought—it would be hard to justify conducting such a close and (some might think) protracted argument with my three subjects. But I hope that both the exposition of their views and my animadversions will serve to shed useful light on Freud himself, even though he appears in these pages largely refracted through their hostile lenses. Sometimes I have worried that my enterprise might seem rather scholastic, as I cite chapter and verse from my authorities and then seek to counter them by noting failures of logic or evidentiary malfeasance. More than once I have had to remind myself (as I now remind the reader) that Freud is too important a figure to allow Sulloway's, Masson's, and Grünbaum's interpretations to go unchallenged, even at the risk of an unseemly argumentativeness. In this respect, the book is unlike anything I have written before: a labor not of love, but of duty.

■   ■   ■

Inevitably one must wonder what has caused Freud's fall from grace. What does it mean? We should not discount the banal possibility that, in some respect, it is nothing more than a reaction against the uncritical celebration of his ideas in the 1950s and 1960s. There is an unwritten law in the history of reputations according to which too much enthusiasm inexorably inspires the urge to revise and deflate. The law holds not just for thinkers but for artists, scientists, and politicians as well. Even figures whose greatness might seem beyond dispute must submit to the stock market effect in the history of renown: every bull brings its bearish counterpart, as inflation and deflation follow one another in an endless cycle. If Johann Sebastian Bach has been subjected to the yin and yang of historical evaluation—widely ignored, if not actually denigrated, until Mendelssohn's famous revival of 1829—we can hardly be surprised that Freud should receive the same treatment. Perhaps at a deeper level this process betrays the need to find our heroes flawed. The literature on the *trahison des clercs,* from Edmund Burke through Julien Benda to Paul Johnson, suggests that ambivalence toward intellectual innovators is one of the constants of modern history.

But two considerations set Freud's case apart. The first is the peculiar insult that he represents to familiar and deeply held ideas—ideas about the self, about reason, about propriety. Freud himself often cited the insulting nature of his thought to explain the hostility it inspired; he had, he said, disturbed the sleep of the world. Of course, there is a danger in this line of argument, which in psychoanalytic theory has been given the doctrinal label of resistance: objections to analytic ideas are not to be judged on their intellectual merits but to be exposed as psychic defenses, rationalistic fig leaves used to conceal embarrassing emotional truths. Here is Freud explaining why so many people reject his teachings:

Psycho-analysis is seeking to bring to conscious recognition the things in mental life which are repressed; and everyone who forms a judgement on it is himself a human being, who possesses similar repressions and may perhaps be maintaining them with difficulty. They are therefore bound to call up the same resistance in him as in our patients; and that resistance finds it easy to disguise itself as an intellectual rejection and to bring up arguments like those which we ward off in our patients by means of the fundamental rule of psycho-analysis.[7]

The only proper response to this kind of reasoning is to insist that it is entirely out of bounds: it undermines the very possibility of intellectual life and, if taken seriously, would lead to a dismissal of psychoanalysis itself as nothing more than a projection of Freud's neuroses. Ad hominem arguments—of which the appeal to resistance is a classic example—simply have no place in reasoned debate. That having been said, one must also concede that, empirically speaking, Freud was probably right: his ideas disturb us as do those of no other important thinker, and many of our objections to them, whatever their intellectual validity, spring from deep emotional sources. We of the late twentieth century are perhaps less inclined to take offense than were Freud's contemporaries, but he nonetheless refuses to fade gracefully into the historical woodwork. Rather, he continues to be a rebarbative figure of contemporary debate, and there remains, I'm convinced, an underground reservoir of resentment to his troublesome ideas. Granted, this perennial anti-Freudian sentiment cannot alone explain the specific criticisms of Frank Sulloway, Jeffrey Masson, and Adolf Grünbaum. But it assures them of a receptive audience. Apparently there are always people eager to believe the worst about Freud. I know of no other

7. Freud, *Five Lectures on Psycho-Analysis,* in *The Standard Edition of the Complete Psychological Works of Sigmund Freud,* translated from the German under the general editorship of James Strachey (London, 1953–74), vol. XI, p. 39.

thinker who occupies a similarly unlovely place in the collective imagination.

The second factor setting Freud apart is his creation of a professional movement that is still very much with us. In the United States today there are some four thousand practicing psychoanalysts, who look to Freud as their founding intellectual authority and the first (and greatest) practitioner of their therapeutic art. As individuals these professionals may not know or care a great deal about Freud, and their ideas may deviate considerably from the original dispensation. But no one can doubt that Freud's reputation is bound up with the estate of contemporary analysis. In this respect he is very much like Marx—also at once an intellectual innovator and the conscious founder of a movement that sought to realize his ideas in the world. Just as Marx's reputation has suffered from both the questionable successes and (more recently) the undeniable failures of communism, so Freud's suffers from the prevailing sense that the profession of psychoanalysis has grown stale and bureaucratized (and not a little greedy), and that its intellectual habits are sclerotic, perhaps even moribund.[8] The analogy must not be pushed too far, because Freud's disciples have been vastly more decent, humane, and indeed sensible than Marx's. There is also much to be said for the proposition that, whatever its shortcomings, psychoanalysis remains the best therapeutic game in town. Nonetheless, one often senses that attacks on Freud disguise highly personal and perhaps legitimate grievances

8. In *Psychoanalysis: The Impossible Profession* (New York, 1981) Janet Malcolm paints an unglamorous and dispiriting portrait of analytic practice in the 1980s—a gray, routinized medical subdiscipline that seems light-years removed from the adventurous, eventful therapeutic world conjured up in Freud's famous case histories.

against the contemporary analytic profession. Jeffrey Masson makes this connection explicit in his autobiography, *Final Analysis,* which recounts his harrowing experiences as a psychoanalytic trainee. We need not conclude, with Masson, that psychoanalysis is an abusive scam to recognize that Freud has been hurt by the failures, the excesses, and, above all, the plain mediocrity of his followers. Although it is legitimate to distinguish between a thinker and the movement that invokes his authority, I also believe that a thinker cannot be entirely exonerated of the crimes and misdemeanors committed in his name. This is true even for a figure like Friedrich Nietzsche, who apparently entertained no plans to bring his ideas to life in the world of politics and institutions but who nonetheless managed to say things that inspired (or misled) others to regrettable political acts. It is true in spades for the likes of Marx and Freud, both of whom labored mightily to embody their ideas in concrete, institutional form.

The perennial resentment aroused by Freud's uncomfortable ideas and the liabilities attending his association with a slightly weary therapeutic profession will not of course explain why he came under such sharp attack precisely in the 1980s. To account for the aggressive anti-Freudianism of recent vintage we must look to more specific historical factors. Once again, two considerations impress me as paramount: the first is the renaissance of feminism during the past quarter century, and the second is what might be called the neopositivist intellectual backlash of the 1980s, which lent to the assault on Freud a distinctly reactionary flavor.

I have already suggested that the disenchantment with Freud can be traced to the revival of feminism. Betty Friedan's chapter "The Sexual Solipsism of Sigmund Freud" in *The Feminine Mystique* (1963), Kate Millett's characterization of psychoanalysis as "The Reaction in Ideology" in *Sexual Politics* (1970), and Germaine Greer's dismissal of "The Psychological Sell" in *The Female Eunuch* (1970) all excoriated Freud as a principal font of modern misogyny. Their diagnoses had been anticipated two decades earlier by Simone de Beauvoir's *The Second Sex* (1949), whose chapter "The Psychoanalytic Point of View" already identified the particular analytic ideas that feminists found most invidious. Pride of place in this litany of abuse belongs to Freud's theory of penis envy: the notion that women's psychology is based on a feeling of genital inadequacy, from which follows their inclination to passivity, narcissism, and masochism. The theory condemned women to perpetual inferiority (because "anatomy is destiny"), representing them as castrated males whose lives were dominated by efforts to compensate for this fundamental defect. In the 1970s the attack on Freud's ideas about women established itself as a fixture of neofeminist discourse, rehearsed in countless books, articles, and reviews. I have no doubt that it provided a firm base of sentiment and opinion—a kind of ideological substructure—upon which the more comprehensive criticisms of the past decade were to build. One might say that the feminist critique created a specially aggrieved interest group within the general ranks of Freud's detractors.

But feminism served only as a backdrop to the intensified anti-Freudianism of the 1980s. The specifics of Freud's female psychology play no role in the writings of Sulloway, Masson, and Grünbaum. Perhaps the case against it had been so thoroughly aired in the 1970s that nothing further needed to be said. Alternatively, the notion of penis envy may have impressed the new critics as too marginal in Freud's thought, or just too preposterous, to bother with. By the 1980s even many of Freud's defenders were inclined to dismiss his ideas about women as the expendable residue of a long-standing cultural prejudice. Nevertheless, in Jeffrey Masson's effort to rehabilitate the seduction theory one detects an unmistakable echo of the neofeminist aversion to Freud. Masson appeals unabashedly to the sentiment that Freud turned his back on the real sufferings of women and children when he deserted the seduction hypothesis. Psychoanalysis, in this view, is fundamentally a male plot, one that aims to perpetuate the physical and emotional victimization of the powerless. Significantly, Masson found his most sympathetic audience among feminists.

My claim that Freud's recent troubles owe something to what I've called a neopositivist backlash will seem less immediately plausible. The most conspicuous and apparently encompassing intellectual phenomenon of the 1980s was the so-called linguistic turn, the effort of philosophers and literary theorists to understand human culture and behavior in terms of the interpretive structures of language—to treat them, in short, as texts. The linguistic turn was hostile to science, or at least to the positivist assumption that human experience could be analyzed in a manner analogous to the scientific study of nature. In general, its adepts regarded Freud—the interpreter of dreams, slips, and symptoms—as an important forerunner of their own point of view. In the writings of Jürgen Habermas and Paul Ricoeur there even emerged a distinctly hermeneutic version of Freud himself, which claimed him as the most significant progenitor of the shift from an objectifying, empiricist understanding of the human realm to one stressing subjectivity and interpretation. The phenomenon is closely related to the contemporaneous embrace of Freud by literary critics and the efflorescence of what is sometimes called "the literary Freud."

The most striking thing about the anti-Freudian writings of the 1980s, and particularly those of Sulloway, Masson, and Grünbaum, is their obliviousness to the linguistic turn in intellectual affairs. One hesitates to speak of an express rejection of the skeptical and relativistic views propounded in advanced intellectual circles, because they give no evidence of even being conscious of the prevailing *Zeitgeist*. To be sure, Adolf Grünbaum spends some time demolishing the hermeneutic interpretations of Freud proposed by Habermas and Ricoeur, but he seems quite unaware of the broader intellectual movement they represent. One would simply never know from reading Sulloway, Masson, and Grünbaum that many of their contemporaries entertained profound doubts about science, objectivity, truth, and the possibility of achieving stable, irrefragable knowledge of the self and society. Perhaps I ought to speak not so much of an intellectual backlash as of the unperturbed adherence to an older habit of thought and a remarkable indifference to what has proved the cutting edge in academic circles.

Unquestionably this imperviousness to the linguistic turn is the most striking common denominator linking the intellectual habits of my three critics. All of them are unreconstructed, indeed unapologetic, positivists. Frank Sulloway's sole concern is to demonstrate that Freud's thinking reflected the methods and views of Darwinian evolution and that he anticipated contemporary sociobiology. Sulloway clearly regards the matter of interpreting Freud as a simple question of reading documents, assembling evidence, and seeing to it that the manifestly correct account displaces the false one (tendentiously constructed by Freud's psychoanalytic biographers). Jeffrey Masson, for his part, talks about documents and facts, truth and lies, proof and disproof, right and wrong with such

breathtaking insouciance as almost to persuade one that
not merely the linguistic turn but the entire twentieth-
century revolt against positivism never took place. Adolf
Grünbaum is more sophisticated than his fellow critics,
and, by comparison, he carries his positivism with greater
awareness. But his tolerance for ambiguity is nonetheless
low, and he gives Freud a hard-nosed empiricist dressing-
down for his evidential shortcomings. I don't necessarily
dislike Sulloway, Masson, and Grünbaum for their unex-
amined positivist ways. On the contrary, I find them attractively innocent of the pretensions afflicting many of
those who have taken the linguistic turn—or perhaps one
should say gone around the linguistic bend. My point,
rather, is to draw attention to the shared assumptions that
unite their otherwise dissimilar views and to suggest that
the anti-Freudian impulse of recent vintage stands at odds
with the most visible intellectual current of the age. Sty-
listically, the opposition to Freud has a decidedly conser-
vative feel about it, lending it a curious resonance with the
politics of the 1980s.

This brings me to my final thought about the significance of Freud's fall from grace. I detect in it an underlying
rejection of the modern, and in particular the modern conception of the self that Freud did so much to create. We
might even characterize the reaction against Freud as postmodern if we agree to use that term analogously to the
way it is used in architecture, where it denotes a rejection
of the modernist aesthetic. In the intellectual and artistic
realms, modernism entailed a loss of confidence in the
stability and transparency of the self. It also entailed the
recognition that all human knowledge is subjective and in-
determinate. Freud's theory of the unconscious, which denies that the self is aware even of its own ideas, was the
most powerful articulation of this modernist sensibility.

If I am not mistaken, the hostility to Freud that emerged so spectacularly in the 1980s was part of a broad-scale revolt against the culture of modernism. It was a revolt against the uncertainties and ambiguities that the modernist legacy burdened us with, above all the sense that the self is unreliable, indeed largely unknowable. The antimodernist persuasion longs for confidence about what can and cannot be known; it wants to believe that the choice between correct and incorrect behavior is unambiguous; it holds that definitive conclusions (about the self, society, the world) can be confidently reached on the basis of unimpeachable evidence. I cannot think it without significance that Freud's recent critics should exhibit precisely such uninflected positivist views. They not only assail Freud, but do so in a manner—at once blithe and apodictic—that implies a rejection of the entire modernist enterprise. The attack on Freud, I am suggesting, ultimately registers a profound discomfort with the fundamental intellectual transformation of the twentieth century.

I

Frank Sulloway:
Freud as Closet Sociobiologist

In its opening sentence, Frank Sulloway's *Freud, Biologist of the Mind* announces itself as "a comprehensive intellectual biography of Sigmund Freud."[1] Sulloway would doubtless protest my calling his book anti-Freudian, because his explicit purpose is not to denigrate Freud but to interpret him aright. The dominant biographical tradition, he insists, has misrepresented Freud. By breaking with that tradition, Sulloway aims to usher in a new understanding of the master: "In this intellectual biography I have aspired to mark a watershed in the history of Freud studies" (xiii). But despite its manifest enthusiasm for Freud's achievement, the book's latent hostility is easily discernible. Appropriately, more resolute anti-Freudians, like Frederick Crews, have been quick to seize on its critical implications. It will be the burden of my argument in this chapter to show that Sulloway's new interpretation, whatever its empirical merits (and I will try to assess them), ultimately serves to diminish Freud. His book is thus legitimately

1. Frank J. Sulloway, *Freud, Biologist of the Mind* (New York, 1979), p. xiii. Hereafter, page references to this work will appear in parentheses in the text.

reckoned among the most important anti-Freudian writings of the recent past. Not only is it one of the earliest documents in a rising tide of hostility to Freud, but it remains in some respects the most impressive.

The school of interpretation Sulloway sets out to discredit he calls "the Freud legend," a legend he sees embodied most perfectly in the three-volume authorized biography by Ernest Jones. But Jones merely heads a long list of psychoanalytic mythologizers of Freud's life. Jones has been aided by Freud himself (whose autobiographical remarks and writings constitute the original version of the legend), as well as by "the Freud family, psychoanalysts-turned-historians, and former patients" (xiii). At the heart of the legend stands the proposition that Freud's science— psychoanalysis—is a "pure psychology": its fundamental concepts are strictly mental, in both derivation and content. Those concepts were developed by Freud only when he gave up his earlier identity as a neurologist and stopped trying to understand mental life in terms of biology and chemistry. Thus the legend recounts Freud's intellectual development in the crucial years of discovery—the 1890s—as a journey from a materialist to a mentalist conception of human psychology. Similarly, credit for that intellectual transformation has been awarded principally to Freud's self-analysis: the painful examination of his interior life, through which Freud discovered the elements of his new psychology, above all infantile sexuality and the unconscious. Psychoanalysis, according to the legend, is not only a pure psychology but one discovered by purely psychological means.

Against the Freud legend Sulloway pits his own conviction that Freud was in fact a "crypto-biologist." In inventing psychoanalysis, Freud did not abandon biological reductionism in favor of an autonomous conception of mind. Rather, psychoanalytic theory was rooted in a set of biological assumptions and modes of reasoning. "It is my contention," Sulloway writes, "that many, if not most, of Freud's fundamental conceptions were biological by inspiration as well as by implication" (5). Subjected to close scrutiny, Freud's ideas reveal "an otherwise hidden rationality" (5) that is essentially evolutionary. This assertion of an underlying evolutionary logic lies at the heart of Sulloway's reinterpretation of Freud's thought, and the persuasiveness of Sulloway's account ultimately stands or falls with his ability to convince us of the determining presence of that logic. If Sulloway is right, Freud's position in the intellectual landscape fundamentally alters. Rather than being the inventor of a new psychology, he finds his place in the tradition of biological theorizing that reaches from Charles Darwin to Edward O. Wilson. Sulloway himself draws just such a historical trajectory: "Freud stands squarely within an intellectual lineage where he is, at once, a principal scientific heir of Charles Darwin and other evolutionary thinkers in the nineteenth century and a major forerunner of the ethologists and sociobiologists of the twentieth century" (5). Hence Sulloway's title: "Biologist of the Mind."

Sulloway's placing of Freud between Darwin and Wilson suggests a more general tactic of his reinterpretation. He is eager to disabuse us of the notion that Freud conceived his ideas in intellectual isolation. The legend, Sulloway contends, has greatly overstated Freud's independence and originality. Not only did Freud enjoy the sustaining inspiration of Darwin, but he also made his critical discoveries within a rich context of contemporary intellectual influences. Wilhelm Fliess, to whose relationship with Freud Sulloway devotes his two central chapters, was only the most prominent among those influences.

Whether by way of personal and professional association (as with Fliess, Jean Martin Charcot, and Josef Breuer) or by way of books and correspondence (as with the sexologists Havelock Ellis and Albert Moll), Freud developed his ideas not through courageous and lonely self-examination but through the familiar vehicle of intellectual dialogue. Sulloway argues, in particular, that the figures who influenced Freud most profoundly shared the evolutionary assumptions and modes of reasoning that constitute the "hidden rationality" of psychoanalysis. Thus Freud becomes merely the most prominent of a generation of intellectuals working within the same scientific paradigm—the representative spokesman of an age devoted to understanding human thought and behavior in evolutionary terms. "His theories—right or wrong—stand as an epitome of the late-nineteenth-century vision of man put forth by so many of his forgotten contemporaries" (497).

Sulloway calls Freud a "crypto-biologist" rather than a biologist *tout court* because his biographers have systematically disguised the evolutionary assumptions and reasoning that lay at the heart of his insights. For this reason, the inner rationality of Freud's thought has remained hidden, waiting for Sulloway to reveal it. Not surprisingly, Sulloway devotes a good deal of energy to explaining just why the Freudian establishment has gone to such lengths to hide Freud's biological legacy. After all, it is hardly scandalous to accuse Freud of being a Darwinian—or even a Lamarckian—especially when the "accusation" assumes the form, as it does here, of celebrating the rigor and imagination with which Freud applied evolutionary concepts to an understanding of mind. It becomes a scandal, in Sulloway's view, only because it diminishes Freud's claim to originality. Sulloway holds that such a claim was essential to Freud's self-image, as well as enormously useful to the psychoanalytic movement. By representing Freud as an original, a loner—the rebellious defender of the purely mental in an age of materialism and biological reductionism—the analytic establishment cultivated a revolutionary combativeness that kept its enemies at bay. The historical reconstruction of Freud as pure psychologist and the repression of his debt to evolutionary biology are thus, in Sulloway's analysis, essentially political acts. The plausibility of his case, he recognizes, depends heavily on whether he can persuade us of the central role this ideological motive has played in fashioning the story of Freud's life. Otherwise, the elaborate biological cover-up makes no sense. Appropriately, Sulloway spends the final two chapters of his intellectual biography attempting to prove the decisiveness of this ideological agenda. As he writes in his preface: "I have dedicated the third and concluding part of this book to elucidating the brilliant political strategy embodied in the Freud legend" (xiii).

■　　■　　■

For a book that presents itself as a comprehensive intellectual biography, *Freud, Biologist of the Mind* is very strangely proportioned. As just noted, a substantial part of it deals not with Freud at all but with the fabrication of his legend. More striking yet, less than one hundred of its five hundred pages of text are devoted to the four decades of Freud's public career, stretching from *The Interpretation of Dreams* in 1900 to *Moses and Monotheism* in 1939. By way of comparison, both the second and third volumes of Ernest Jones's biography deal entirely with the post-1900 years, as do all but the first one hundred pages of Peter Gay's 650-page *Freud: A Life for Our Time*. The great bulk of Sulloway's biography, in sharp contrast, treats the years before the public emergence of psychoanalysis. This shift of attention to the young Freud, the preanalytic Freud, is characteristic of other recent critics as well, in particular Jeffrey Masson, Marianne Krüll, and Marie Balmary, whose studies focus on a few years, even a few months, in the 1890s. An analogous development took place in studies of Marx during the 1920s and 1930s, when attention to his earlier concerns virtually revolutionized our conception of Marx as a thinker, replacing the economic determinist and materialist of the older biographical tradition with a young Hegelian humanist. One might even argue that the Fliess correspondence, which provides a unique window on Freud's intellectual evolution in the 1890s, has served in this process of biographical reconstruction a function similar to that of Marx's *Economic and Philosophical Manuscripts of 1844*—although in Marx's case the reinterpreters (such as Georg Lukács and Erich Fromm) were a good deal more sympathetic to Marx than Masson, Krüll, Balmary, and even Sulloway are to Freud. Just as Marx's new biographers found a strain of youthful philosophical idealism beneath the austerely economic argument of *Das Kapital,* so Sulloway pretends to detect a youthful biologist alive and well beneath the "purely psychological" argument of *Die Traumdeutung.*

Nor does Sulloway's extended treatment of the preanalytic Freud present a chronological narrative of Freud's interests and achievements during the quarter century from his first biological papers of the 1870s through the neurological essays of the 1890s. Indeed, these chapters are organized not around Freud at all, but rather around a series of figures whose relationships with Freud, Sulloway contends, were crucial to his intellectual development. This maneuver is essential to the aim of discrediting the image of Freud as an isolated revolutionary: by consistently

linking Freud with significant others, Sulloway creates an
impression that might be called "diminishment by association." Freud is always seen as one figure in a dyad, or
sometimes—as in the chapter on the turn-of-the-century
sexologists—a group portrait, a device that effectively reduces Freud to the sum of his associations. Not surprisingly, certain of these associations lend themselves more
readily than others to Sulloway's object of identifying the
biological rationale lurking behind Freud's thinking. But
even those that prove recalcitrant in this regard nonetheless
contribute to the subtle process of whittling Freud down
to size. And if their intellectual significance fails to support
Sulloway's evolutionary argument, they often turn out to
be useful in documenting personal failings on Freud's part,
thus casting doubt on his integrity, if not his originality.

Sulloway's book is very much a matter of bits and
pieces. He seeks to make his case through a close examination of individual documents, many of them written by
persons other than Freud. Often his point hangs on an individual word or phrase, just as the spin that he puts on a
given utterance depends on his choice of adjectives or operative verbs. All of this means that one can present his argument—or subject it to criticism—only through equally
intimate attention to specific pieces of evidence and to the
textual strategies Sulloway deploys to interpret them. His
claims may be large, but his method of substantiating them
is pointillistic. His book, in short, demands a close reading.

ERNST BRÜCKE, JEAN MARTIN CHARCOT, AND JOSEF BREUER

One might expect Sulloway to make much of Freud's
years as a student and researcher in the laboratory of Ernst

Brücke's Physiological Institute, where from 1876 to 1882 Freud worked on biological problems set for him by Brücke. During these years Freud not only honed his knowledge of anatomy and physiology but came to identify himself with the ideals of nineteenth-century biological science, as embodied above all in the person of Ernst Brücke himself. For two reasons, however, Sulloway passes briskly over the Brücke period and makes no effort to enlist Freud's biological apprenticeship in the cause of his revisionist thesis. First, Freud's identification with Brücke and his early commitment to a career in biology are already fixed motifs in the received biographical tradition that Sulloway wishes to discredit. In fact, they are the necessary presuppositions of the conversion from biology to psychology that, in the familiar account, constitutes the central event in Freud's intellectual biography. At best, then, Brücke is irrelevant to Sulloway's argument, and he even poses a subtle threat insofar as he sets up the first term of a dichotomy that Sulloway hopes to collapse.

At the same time (and this is the second reason), Brücke stands for a conception of biology very different from the one Sulloway seeks to identify as the hidden rationale of Freud's thought. Brücke, along with Emil du Bois-Reymond, Hermann Helmholtz, and Carl Ludwig, was a leading figure in the nineteenth-century effort to transform biology into a quantitative science by reducing it to the laws of chemistry and physics. As du Bois-Reymond expressed their ideal: "No other forces than the common physical-chemical ones are active within the organism."[2] This scientific philosophy is altogether foreign to the evolutionary vision Sulloway places at the heart of Freud's

2. Quoted by Ernest Jones, *The Life and Work of Sigmund Freud* (New York, 1953–57), I:40.

biologism. Naturally, Sulloway must allow that Freud subscribed to the philosophy for a while, but it is as essential to Sulloway's thesis as it is to the traditional account that Freud be seen as rejecting this hoary brand of positivism. Indeed, Brücke actually figures more prominently in Ernest Jones's version of events than he does in Sulloway's. In sum, Brücke is not a major player in Sulloway's game of diminishment by association.

■   ■   ■

If Brücke is irrelevant to Sulloway's strategy, Jean Martin Charcot is a positive obstacle. In the familiar biographical account, Freud's period of study under the famous French neurologist in 1885–86 marks a turning point in his conversion to psychology. Charcot demonstrated that neurotic symptoms, such as hysterical paralyses, could be artificially induced by hypnosis. That is, individuals could be made to fall ill through purely mental stimuli. This revelation effectively collapsed the materialist assumptions of the medical tradition in which Freud had been trained. The mind, it seemed, could be the source of its own sickness.

Accordingly, the study under Charcot figures as a decisive moment in the canonical interpretation that sees Freud moving inexorably from a materialist to a psychological conception of the self. Sulloway, perforce, must do what he can to diffuse its significance. He adopts a three-pronged strategy. His first—and most disconcerting—procedure is to present a bland and utterly familiar recital of the Charcot experience, while refusing to acknowledge its obvious implications. Thus Sulloway quotes, without comment, Freud's assertion of 1893 that "M. Charcot was the first to teach us that to explain hysterical neurosis we must apply to psychology."[3] Sensing, perhaps, that in so quoting Freud he has granted Charcot too much authority, Sulloway then seeks to play down his significance:

While it is true that Charcot's influence introduced the young Viennese brain anatomist to a number of new and important psychological insights about psychoneurosis, one must be careful not to read more into this influence than was there at the time. . . . It would be fair to say that, while in Paris, Freud found Charcot's ideas on hypnotism and hysteria as fascinating as he did precisely because they appealed to a long-standing personal interest in the subject of psychology. (49)

In other words, Charcot was little more than a diversion, a man who charmed Freud because his ideas happened to correspond to something innocuously referred to as "a long-standing personal interest in the subject of psychology"—the otherwise innocent adjective "personal" implying that psychology was for Freud more a hobby than a serious intellectual concern. This accomplished, Sulloway turns to one final tactic to avoid the traditional reading of the Charcot experience: he insists that it involved not a conversion to pure psychology but a reaffirmation of Freud's sensible philosophical dualism. Charcot simply offered a corrective to the prejudices of Freud's Viennese mentors, thereby confirming Freud's natural inclination toward an evenhanded assessment of the claims of mind and body. "His interest in phenomena like hypnosis and

3. Freud, "Some Points for a Comparative Study of Organic and Hysterical Motor Paralyses," in *The Standard Edition of the Complete Psychological Works of Sigmund Freud,* translated from the German under the general editorship of James Strachey (London, 1953–74), vol. I, p. 171.

hysteria was accompanied from the first by a balanced concern for the intricacies of the age–old mind–body problem" (51). Sulloway's interpretation not only contradicts Freud's own vivid account of the Charcot episode but ascribes to Freud a metaphysical judiciousness altogether foreign to his unphilosophical habit of mind. It reduces what was clearly an exciting and dramatic moment of intellectual transformation to a banal abstraction.

One further symptomatic feature of Sulloway's discussion of the Charcot episode calls for comment, to wit, his treatment of the idea of the unconscious. In the traditional view, Charcot was important for Freud not only because he established the autonomy of the purely mental but also because his experiments showed that the mind was divided into conscious and unconscious parts. Again, Sulloway doesn't deny this. He writes that Charcot's "dramatic demonstrations—particularly those of hypnotism—first revealed to Freud the remarkable circumstance that multiple states of consciousness could simultaneously coexist in one and the same individual without either state apparently having knowledge of the other" (32). But Sulloway attaches no particular importance to this revelation and assigns it no special prominence in his account. On the contrary, it is allowed to sink amid a mass of further particulars, as he moves on to a detailed and not very consequential account of Freud's opinion on the squabble between Charcot and Bernheim over the nature of hypnotic suggestion.

Why this indifference? It is especially striking in view of Sulloway's own statement that Charcot was the *first* to teach Freud of "multiple states of consciousness" unknown to one another. The answer, quite simply, is that in Sulloway's interpretation of Freud the unconscious counts for very little. To be sure, Sulloway mentions it from time to time, but he never acknowledges it as a central and revolutionary idea in Freud's psychoanalytic conception of the self. Perhaps Sulloway thinks that, because the idea had been so richly anticipated by earlier thinkers, it is in no way distinctively Freudian. Or perhaps, himself a product of the late twentieth century, he finds the idea too familiar and obvious to require remark. In any event, the virtual disappearance of the unconscious as a subject in Freud's intellectual history is the most remarkable elision in Sulloway's book. One suspects, moreover, that it has been rendered invisible because Sulloway can find no way to make it fit his hypothesis of a hidden biological rationale. The unconscious, after all, belongs uncompromisingly to the realm of the psychological. Accordingly, it is neglected. I hardly need add that this neglect stands in stark contrast to Freud's own assessment of its significance. The unconscious was for him his single most important contribution, an idea of truly epochal consequence, whose discovery he compared, in a famous passage, to the revolutions in thought brought about by Copernicus and Darwin before him. Just as Copernicus had removed humanity from the center of the universe and Darwin denied it any special place in the hierarchy of nature, so Freud himself, he boasted, had delivered an even more devastating insult to mankind's self-confidence. "Human megalomania will have suffered its third and most wounding blow from the psychological research of the present time which seeks to prove to the ego that it is not even master in its own house, but must content itself with scanty information of what is going on unconsciously in its mind."[4] In Sulloway's interpretation, this "Freudian revolution" effectively collapses.

4. Freud, *Introductory Lectures on Psycho-Analysis, Standard Edition,* vol. XVI, p. 285.

■   ■   ■

In contrast to his treatment of Freud's experiences with Brücke and Charcot, Sulloway subjects his association with Josef Breuer to extensive analysis. In fact, it receives more attention than any of Freud's relationships other than that with Fliess. (By comparison, the Freud-Jung relationship—of such great interest to the traditional biographies—is dispensed with in a brisk four pages.) The reason Breuer figures so prominently in Sulloway's account is not, however, so readily discernible. Unlike Fliess, Breuer cannot be made to contribute to the central effort of identifying a hidden biological theme in Freud's intellectual development. There is not a word here about "cryptobiology." Rather, Breuer serves the more general purpose of revealing, by way of contrast, Freud's distinctive intellectual style. At the same time, the collaboration between the two men follows a familiar pattern in which Freud first uses and then abuses a chosen friend and accomplice. It thus casts usefully invidious light on Freud's character. But just as important, Sulloway finds in the orthodox account of the Breuer-Freud relationship an archetypal instance of the mythmaking propensity of the established biographical tradition. Breuer thus becomes "the first major victim of psychoanalytically reconstructed history" (100).

As in his treatment of Charcot, Sulloway considerably dulls the significance of the collaboration with Breuer for Freud's conversion to an essentially psychological conception of mind. The case histories in their jointly authored *Studies on Hysteria* (1895) were important above all because they allowed Freud and Breuer to conclude that their patients' illnesses derived from memories, which had been repressed at the time of the experience only to return, often years later, in the disguised form of symptoms. The theory, in other words, insists on the etiological power of the purely psychological, and it holds that a significant portion of mental life is unconscious. In this respect it was the logical extension of what Freud had learned about the autonomy of the psychological and the importance of the unconscious in his study of hypnotism under Charcot. In the traditional accounts of Freud's intellectual development, *Studies on Hysteria* accordingly marks a milestone in his gradual abandonment of the materialist prejudices of his earlier mentors and his embrace of psychoanalysis proper. Indeed, it figures as his first truly psychoanalytic writing.

Not surprisingly, in Sulloway's account this story is largely repressed. To speak precisely, it is confined to a single sentence. He quotes the famous conclusion from the book that *"hysterics suffer mainly from reminiscences,"*[5] to which he adds: "This was the fundamental clinical message of Breuer and Freud's joint theory of hysteria" (61). But Sulloway has nothing more to say about the book's central and most novel proposition. Instead, he immediately diverts attention by launching into an intricate discussion of the theory's "psychophysicalist" assumptions concerning the investment and displacement of mental energy. In other words, Sulloway chooses to stress the book's positivist language rather than its psychological substance: *Studies on Hysteria* becomes a book not about the persistence and transformation of recollection but about "a 'short circuit' in the normal flow of electric fluid" (62). The significance of *Studies on Hysteria* for the idea of the unconscious is similarly marginalized. The unconscious is demoted to a mere "aspect" of the theory—in

---

5. Breuer and Freud, *Studies on Hysteria, Standard Edition,* vol. II, p. 7.

fact, the last (and, presumably, least important) aspect. Again, the entire concept is dispensed with in a single sentence: "The last or topographical aspect of the Breuer-Freud theory of hysteria inheres in the hypothesis of an 'unconscious' portion of the mind" (64). Why the quotation marks around "unconscious" if not to cast doubt on its reality? Thus does the Freudian revolution end once more with a whimper.

Perhaps predictably, Sulloway's account focuses as much on the breakup of the Freud–Breuer relationship as on its accomplishments. The dominant biographical tradition, Sulloway argues, has unfairly blamed their ultimate alienation on Breuer's prudery, in particular on Breuer's inability to accept Freud's ideas about the role of sex in the origin of hysteria. Although on the whole Sulloway's construction is defensible, the evidence is less conclusive than he thinks. Breuer, he shows, agreed with Freud that hysterical symptoms sometimes arise from the repression of a sexual trauma. The disagreement, as one might expect, was over just how often this is the case. Without ever actually saying so, Sulloway gives the impression that Breuer considered it a common occurrence: sexuality for Breuer was "one of the most important factors in hysteria" (79). But this formulation commits Breuer to no particular percentage; even as "one of the most important factors," sexuality might still figure in less than the majority of cases. What *is* absolutely certain is that Freud considered sex the essential cause of every hysteria, whereas Breuer found this conclusion unacceptable. The question then becomes, Did Breuer break with Freud because he objected to Freud's unjustified universalism or, as Freud himself came to believe, because of Breuer's own resistance to the emphasis on sex?

There can be no simple answer: as already noted, the evidence calls for interpretation. One can reasonably argue that sexual considerations predominated, or that intellectual ones did, or that the two simply complemented each other. But Sulloway allows for no such interpretive ambiguity. For him the answer is obvious: because Breuer had been willing to acknowledge the sexual factor in *some* cases of hysteria, his real objection to Freud must have been intellectual. "The estrangement between Breuer and Freud was, more than anything else, simply a matter of incompatible scientific styles" (98–99).

Sulloway's treatment of this matter of antithetical styles is revealing. He introduces the distinction as if it were entirely disinterested. Scientists come in two varieties: the circumspect and the bold, neither one more legitimate than the other. Thus, if Freud practiced a "more visionary style" (86) of science than the careful Breuer, this reflects no discredit on Freud. It merely means that he "feared mediocrity . . . more than he feared error" (87).

Examined more closely, however, Sulloway's seemingly neutral distinction turns out to be profoundly invidious. His prose undergoes a rhetorical sea change, by which Breuer's caution comes to appear decidedly more admirable than Freud's vision. The effect resembles the return of the repressed, as Sulloway's latent hostility to Freud eventually overwhelms his manifest (and official) evenhandedness. Thus "the much-misunderstood Josef Breuer" (83) is described as "meticulous" (53), "systematic" (56), "painstaking" and "unassuming" (83), and a physician of "unusual diligence, perspicacity, and extreme patience" (64). Never does Sulloway suggest that Breuer's caution might at times have become plodding unimaginativeness. By contrast, Freud's "visionary style" is quickly deconstructed into a series of much less attractive qualities. Unlike Breuer, Freud suffered from "pent-up frustrations and the associated capacity for fanaticism" (83); he sought "rigid and incontrovertible laws" in keeping with his "more dogmatic and revolutionary" image of himself (99); he indulged in "extremist and speculative" hypotheses (86); and he exhibited a "fanatical propensity for exclusive scientific formulation" (99). Bit by bit, the image of Freud as visionary gives way to repeated assertions of his "growing fanaticism" (89). Sulloway himself may pretend to take no sides in the matter of scientific styles, but his language serves to rehabilitate Breuer and discredit Freud.

The purely intellectual difference between Freud and Breuer is underscored by an even more unflattering personal comparison of the two. Breuer, it turns out, was not only careful but nice. He was "generous and even-tempered" (83) and "widely esteemed as an unusually selfless and warm-hearted individual" (54). He even subsidized Freud. Freud, however, was hard and unforgiving. Rather than accept the legitimacy of Breuer's intellectual reservations, he let his former affection turn to hate:

By 1897, Freud was telling Fliess that the very sight of Breuer would make him want to emigrate, and he even took to avoiding Breuer's neighborhood for fear of having to meet him on the street. Many years later Breuer's daughter recalled just such an accidental meeting between the two men when she and her father, now elderly, were out walking one day. Breuer instinctively threw open his arms, while Freud, head down and doing his best to ignore his old friend, marched briskly by.[6] (99)

6. Here Sulloway has been misled by Ernest Jones's mistranslation (Jones, *Life and Work,* I:255). Freud's actual comment to Fliess in 1897 was: "How fortunate that I no longer see Br[euer]. He would surely

Even allowing for a certain amount of dramatic license on the part of Breuer's daughter, the picture is not an attractive one. We are left with the impression that, characterologically as well as intellectually, it was better to be Josef Breuer than Sigmund Freud.

WILHELM FLIESS

With Wilhelm Fliess we come to the key figure in Sulloway's reinterpretation. Fliess is more important than Brücke, Charcot, or Breuer, first, because he was Freud's closest friend and interlocutor during "the period of Freud's most creative intellectual achievements" (xiv) in the 1890s and, second, because he provided Freud with the specific evolutionary ideas that form the hidden core of psychoanalytic theory:

> The long-misunderstood role of Fliess in Freud's intellectual life reflects, in microcosm, the crypto-biological nature of Freud's entire psychoanalytic legacy to the twentieth century. For it was precisely this new evolutionary vision that . . . exerted the greatest single and most far-reaching theoretical influence upon Freud's conception of human psychosexual development. (237)

Freud's relationship with Fliess thus forms the heart of Sulloway's thesis.

By focusing on Fliess, Sulloway attacks the received biographical tradition at perhaps its most vulnerable point. Ernest Jones, for example, begins his treatment of the

---

have advised me to emigrate" (Freud, *The Complete Letters of Sigmund Freud to Wilhelm Fliess, 1887–1907*, ed. and trans. Jeffrey Moussaieff Masson [Cambridge, Mass., 1985], p. 233).

Fliess episode with the revealing assertion: "We come here to the only really extraordinary experience in Freud's life."[7] Fliess is an embarrassment for Freud's psychoanalytic biographers because his ideas seem so extravagant, yet there can be no denying that Freud valued him immensely and, for many years, professed nothing but the greatest enthusiasm for his strange notions. Fliess thus threatens Freud's intellectual respectability: if Freud could admire such manifestly outrageous notions, does this not imply that his own system was constructed of similarly suspect materials—that psychoanalysis is just as much a pseudoscience as Fliess's outlandish theories about the relation of the nose to sexuality and the pervasive influence of the numbers 23 and 28? The orthodox solution to this predicament has been to stress the obvious madness of Fliess's ideas and then to insist that, precisely because his ideas were so bizarre, they could never have appealed to Freud on purely intellectual grounds. Instead, the relationship can be explained only by way of personal, indeed psychological, considerations. In commonsense terms, this view holds that Fliess offered a much-needed source of encouragement in the years when Freud was making his revolutionary intellectual breakthroughs and felt most isolated from the scientific community. In psychoanalytic terms, the association has been interpreted as a transference relationship, in which Fliess assumed the role of Freud's father. Like any classic Oedipal drama, it entailed a period of uncritical admiration and dependence followed by an inevitable alienation, which began—so the theory goes—when Freud's self-analysis revealed the idea of the Oedipus complex. Only through this insight was Freud finally liberated from Fliess.

7. Jones, *Life and Work*, I:287.

Sulloway seeks to render this line of reasoning super-fluous by arguing that Freud's dependence on Fliess can be explained entirely on rational, intellectual grounds. Sulloway recognizes that his contention requires that he rehabilitate Fliess as a thinker, and he accordingly devotes practically a full chapter of his book to this enterprise. It is in many respects an astonishing display of erudition. Sulloway takes up each of Fliess's supposedly crazy ideas and shows, first, that Fliess was not alone among his contemporaries in championing such notions and, second, that none of the ideas is nearly so outlandish as the orthodox biographers have maintained. Furthermore, Sulloway insists that Fliess's favorite notions were all informed by an evolutionary logic, even if that logic was sometimes strained or has proved faulty in the light of subsequent research. Sulloway's exposition of Fliess's thought thus also contributes to his larger strategy of revealing the hidden biological rationale of psychoanalysis. Sulloway's solicitude for Fliess's reputation and his ingenuity in finding Darwinian excuses for Fliess's theories are so impressive that one almost feels he should have written Fliess's biography rather than Freud's. The ultimate effect of this "rehabilitation," not incidentally, is to bring Freud down to Fliess's level—to obliterate any sense that Freud and Fliess, as thinkers, are categorically distinct.

Like the traditional biographers, Sulloway sees Fliess as preoccupied with three ideas. First, he insists that there is a crucial physiological connection between the nose and the female genitals; in particular, the nose contains "genital zones" linked to sexual and reproductive functions—from which it follows that sexual disorders can be treated by anesthetizing the offending spot in the nose with cocaine. Second, "vital periodicities" govern all physiological processes, such that life can ultimately be explained in terms of two numbers, 23 and 28, the former being the masculine principle and the latter the feminine. Finally, all human beings are bisexual, and thus the periodicities governed by 23 and 28 are observable in both sexes.

Sulloway shows that none of these ideas—not even the numerological fantasy concerning 23 and 28—was unique to Fliess. Take the matter of the nose and sex. Sulloway finds that a perfectly respectable Baltimore laryngologist, John Noland Mackenzie, had already proposed such a connection back in the 1880s. In fact, when Fliess's theory appeared in 1897, Mackenzie greeted it enthusiastically as a confirmation of his own ideas. By the end of the century, "the Mackenzie-Fliess naso-genital theory," according to Sulloway, "had come to be a common topic of discussion among rhinologists" (150) and was embraced by no less an authority than Richard von Krafft-Ebing, as well as by the "ever-cautious" (151) Josef Breuer. Most of the evidence that Fliess, Mackenzie, and others cited in support of the theory was clinical—such as nasal bleeding or swelling during menstruation or during sexual arousal. For purposes of Sulloway's thesis, however, the really important features of the theory were evolutionary, notably the phylogenetic implications of the link between sexuality and the sense of smell in the lower animals. The nose-genital connection begins to take on a kind of Darwinian sense if one views it as a residue in human beings of the olfactory sexuality of our animal ancestors. Sulloway thus emphasizes "the general evolutionary context in which Fliess's theories were discussed" (150), concluding that there was an "important grain of scientific truth in Fliess's now-defunct nasal theories" (152).

The notion of vital periodicities was, if anything, even more popular among turn-of-the-century scientists, and for exactly the same reasons. Fliess's "scientific interests in vital and sexual periodicity were becoming positively fashionable by the mid-1890s" (152–53). Sulloway discusses the work of more than a half-dozen figures—including Havelock Ellis and Krafft-Ebing—who contributed to the idea's prestige. With a view to his larger thesis, Sulloway stresses in particular the attention Charles Darwin bestowed on it. Darwin recognized a wide variety of periodic processes in nature and was especially fascinated by weekly cycles and their multiples, which he found "in virtually all temporal aspects of growth, reproduction, and disease known to life science" (153). Naturally, Darwin sought to interpret these periodic phenomena in evolutionary terms. To be precise, he connected them with the rhythm of the tides, arguing that they were phylogenetic residues from our tidal-dependent marine ancestors.

Even Fliess's chosen numbers, 23 and 28, found other scientific advocates. In the case of the "female" number, 28, this is not especially remarkable. It is based on the menstrual cycle, which in turn is grounded in the 28-day lunar period and thus can be linked to the evolutionary argument about our tidal heritage. But Sulloway's most spectacular find is the Scotsman John Beard, another nineteenth-century scientist, who, independently of Fliess but virtually simultaneously, propounded the existence of a 23-day cycle. The argument here involves a convoluted piece of reasoning concerning patterns of ovulation and gestation. But Sulloway's point is the same: Fliess's idea was not unique and was, moreover, grounded in evolutionary logic, even if Beard's presentation of that logic was more explicit than Fliess's.

Sulloway's discussion of Fliess's third preoccupation, bisexuality, is much briefer. I suspect this is because the notion has never been considered as bizarre as Fliess's other *idées fixes*. On the contrary, among Fliess's many notions, it alone survived to become an important tenet of mature psychoanalytic theory, a debt Freud acknowledges in his *Three Essays on the Theory of Sexuality*. It is thus not a candidate for rehabilitation, unlike the naso-genital theory or the idea of vital periodicity. Still, Sulloway documents its vogue and stresses its grounding in embryology (the sexual organs of both sexes are visible in the early stages of embryonic development) and in evolutionary theory—notably in Darwin's conclusion, in *The Descent of Man,* that a distant ancestor of the vertebrates may have been androgynous.

In short, in Sulloway's view, Fliess was a solid scientific citizen of his age, his ideas resting on widely accepted evolutionary convictions. More than a solid citizen: his work placed him on the cutting edge of contemporary science. "There was," Sulloway concludes,

enough method and consistency to Fliess's madness to convince many—Sigmund Freud included—from a whole generation of scientific contemporaries that he had made a series of profound scientific discoveries. Above all, to those contemporaries who shared Fliess's biological assumptions, his ideas seemed to occupy the visionary forefront, not the lunatic fringe, of "hard" science. (169)

■   ■   ■

Having established to his satisfaction that Fliess was not a crackpot but a reputable scientist—one whose intellectual credentials were fully worthy of Freud's respect—Sulloway turns to the specific evidence of his influence on Freud. He does not belabor Freud's express admiration for Fliess's ideas, because the orthodox biographical tradition has already conceded the point. Nor is his effort primarily directed to arguing that those ideas—other than bisexuality—found a significant place in psychoanalytic theory, because transparently they did not. Rather, Sulloway marshals his forces essentially along two fronts. First, through a close reading of Fliess's 1897 monograph *Die Beziehungen zwischen Nase und weiblichen Geschlectsorganen,* he tries to show that several of Freud's most important psychoanalytic concepts, above all the idea of infantile sexuality, were propounded by Fliess before they were by Freud. Second, through an equally close reading of Freud's letters to Fliess, he claims to discover direct evidence that Freud adopted or modified Fliessian themes into recognizably psychoanalytic form. In both efforts Sulloway stresses that Freud's intellectual affinities with Fliess rested on a shared evolutionary point of view. "As for Fliess's influence upon Freud," Sulloway writes, "it was the physiological and particularly evolutionary framework implicit in Fliess's ideas that led Freud to take him so seriously" (170). This two-pronged tactic—showing how Fliess anticipated Freud and Freud adapted Fliess—stands at the argumentative heart of Sulloway's book. It aims to prove nothing less than that psychoanalysis was, in essence, a "transformation of the Fliessian id" (171).

Let us begin with the matter of Fliess's anticipation of Freud in his monograph of 1897. Before we consider the specific instances of anticipation that Sulloway advances, however, we need to note the dubious logic upon which the entire enterprise rests. Sulloway claims that whenever Fliess's remarks in the monograph express views that later became part of psychoanalytic theory, they illustrate "the impact of Fliess's influence" (173) on Freud. But, of course, this is not necessarily the case. For one thing, even though Freud published a particular idea after Fliess, Freud may well have developed the idea on his own, or have taken it from a source other than Fliess. Equally plausible, Fliess may have heard the idea from Freud in one of their many meetings, or "congresses." Sulloway raises this possibility himself and tries to diffuse it by retreating from his bold claim of influence to the softer notion of collaboration: "Putting aside for the moment the more technical issue of *who* really influenced *whom* (and *how*), it is still true that many of the ideas embodied in Fliess's published discussions of human psychosexual development constitute an important and much-neglected collaborative phase through which Freud's thinking likewise passed" (188–89). But this modulation of his argument has little effect on the way Sulloway presents his case. Throughout the text he speaks as if the presence of "Freudian" themes in Fliess's book offer unambiguous proof of influence and thus justify Sulloway's characterization of psychoanalysis as, at bottom, a transformation of Fliessian sexual biology.

Sulloway's argument, then, fails to do justice to the complexity of the notion of influence or to its evidentiary demands. But leaving this thorny matter aside for the moment, what evidence does he present that Fliess in fact anticipated Freud? I'm afraid the answer is, considerably less than he promises. With a characteristic show of precision Sulloway announces that Fliess's imprint on psychoanalysis can be detected "at five important points" (173). Several of these points, however, turn out to be less impressive than his assertion would lead us to expect. One of the five points, for example, is bisexuality. But, of course, this influence was conceded by Freud himself and has never been denied by his biographers—so while it's true, it's not news. A second point is the "periodic ebb and flow" (179) of libidinal development. As we know, this was certainly a major concern of Fliess's, and in his correspondence with Fliess, Freud sometimes supplied corroboration for Fliess's periodic calculations (as, for example, when Freud sent information about his wife's menstrual pattern and the birth of his daughter Anna). But the fact remains that the idea of periodicity plays no role in Freud's mature thought, and Sulloway can find only the most fugitive allusions to it in the canonical writings. A third point is the notion that childhood masturbation was psychologically harmful. Without question Freud believed this to be true, but it figures only as a residual idea in psychoanalytic theory, namely, in the etiology of the so-called actual neuroses, an increasingly neglected category in Freud's thinking after 1900. The idea, in other words, is hardly a central tenet of the mature Freudian system. More important, it is clearly a Victorian leftover in both Freud and Fliess; Sulloway himself admits that it represents "more a conceptual overlap than an instance . . . of Fliess's direct influence upon Freud" (184).

The five points thus quickly reduce themselves to two, and these two—the ideas of a latency period and of childhood erotogenic zones—are really components of a single theme, infantile sexuality. Here, at last, we have a genuinely Freudian idea, one of absolute centrality to psychoanalytic theory. Indeed, infantile sexuality is, with the unconscious, one of the two intellectual pillars of psychoanalysis. And while we stumble on bits and pieces of the idea in a number of other thinkers (to whom Sulloway turns in his chapter on sexologists), no one gave it the systematic articulation and conceptual prominence that Freud did. If Sulloway can find infantile sexuality, in the Freudian sense, in the pages of Fliess's 1897 monograph, he will have scored an undeniable coup, one that would render at least plausible his thesis about Fliess's role in the emergence of psychoanalytic theory. When I say "in a Freudian sense," I mean not merely the proposition that

children are sexual creatures (that they masturbate, become genitally aroused, and so on), but the more radical
proposition that their pursuit of oral and anal pleasure
must also be regarded as erotic, indeed as significant sexual organizations in a development pattern leading from
polymorphous perversity, through the pregenital stages,
to the supremacy of genital sexuality at puberty. What evidence of a conception of this sort does Sulloway uncover
in Fliess's monograph?

The answer has to be, at most a few scraps. Sulloway
argues, for example, that Fliess's theory of vital periodicity
necessarily committed him to a belief in infantile sexuality, because, according to the theory, both the 23- and 28-
day cycles were present in every individual throughout
life. This may make infantile sexuality a logical necessity
for Fliess, but such a fragile inference can hardly support
so imposing an edifice as Freud's mature conception.
Nor is what Fliess has to say about childhood erections
(whose supposedly periodic occurrences, observed in his
son Robert, figure in his argument) distinctly Freudian.
More to the point are Fliess's remarks about the sexual significance of oral and anal activities. On the oral side,
Sulloway is able to cite one passage that has a distinctly
Freudian ring:

I would just like to point out that the sucking movements that
small children make with their lips and tongue on periodic
days . . . , the so-called *"Ludeln,"* as well as thumb-sucking,
must be considered as an equivalent of masturbation. Such activity likewise brings on anxiety, sometimes combined with
neurasthenia, just as does true masturbation. It comes on impul-
sively and is, on this account, so difficult to wean children
from. . . . The role which the word "sweet" [*süss*] later plays in
the language of love has its initial physiological root here. With

lips and tongue the child first tastes lactose [*Milchzucker*] at his mother's breast, and they provide him with his earliest experience of satisfaction. (173–74)

This may well be an honest anticipation of Freud, but the following caveats need to be entered. First, the observation is an aside, introduced offhandedly with "I would just like to point out" and confined to a footnote in the text. Second, although it makes the essential Freudian link between oral and genital gratification (sucking, Fliess says, is the equivalent of masturbation), so casual an aperçu is, conceptually speaking, light-years removed from the idea of an oral phase of libidinal development, such as Freud was to propose. Finally, here as elsewhere in the monograph, Fliess's real interest is in periodicity, and he latches onto infantile sucking, like infantile masturbation, as one among many phenomena that he believes to be grist for his periodic mill.

After orality, the second great test of a genuinely Freudian conception of infantile sexuality is anality. Sulloway asserts confidently that Fliess was "convinced of a close physiological tie between the *anal* excretory function and the sexual manifestations of children" (174). Unfortunately, the two pieces of evidence Sulloway invokes fail to support this contention. The first is Fliess's "careful documentation of periodic patterns of bowel functioning in childhood" (174–75). True enough, as with anything arguably periodic, Fliess does discuss children's bowel movements. In contrast to his distinctly Freudian comparison of sucking and masturbation, however, nothing in his text identifies bowel movements as sexual—apart, of course, from the generic assumption that anything periodic is in some sense sexual. Second, Sulloway argues that Fliess "stood on Freudian ground when he

drew a connection in his sexual theory between hemor-
rhoids in adults and those 'reflex-neuroses' associated with
the reproductive system" (175). Once again, plausible
enough, but just as there is no mention of sexuality in connection with bowel movements, there is no mention of
childhood here. The telltale Freudian link, in other words,
is missing.

There is perhaps more to Sulloway's contention that
Fliess anticipated Freud's conception of a latency period.
Latency is, essentially, the concept Freud uses to explain
why infantile sexuality undergoes a hiatus between the
fifth year and puberty. This is brought about by two psychic mechanisms: reaction formation, namely, the emergence of shame and disgust, and sublimation, which reflects, as Freud puts it, "the claims of aesthetic and moral
ideals."[8] In the *Three Essays on the Theory of Sexuality*
Freud acknowledges Fliess as the source of the phrase "period of sexual latency."[9] Sulloway, however, argues that
not just the phrase but the idea itself came from Fliess.
Clearly, Fliess's belief that human beings function as a
closed energy system, whose underlying chemical-sexual
stuff is governed by numerical cycles, logically entailed the
idea of sublimation. Moreover, Fliess especially associated
the process with childhood, when the energy that would
later go into sexual life was directed toward growth. But
Fliess's "latency period," unlike Freud's, began not in the
fifth year but at conception. Indeed, Fliess's notion that the
whole of childhood was governed by sublimation not only
differs from Freud's idea of latency but contradicts the very
conception of infantile sexuality, which holds precisely

8. Freud, *Three Essays on the Theory of Sexuality, Standard Edition,*
vol. VII, p. 177.
9. Ibid., p. 178n.

that sublimation is *not* in effect during the earliest years of childhood. Moreover, the general notion of sublimation was hardly unique either to Freud or to Fliess. As Sulloway himself points out—in a footnote—"both the term and the concept were already in common circulation in Freud's day, and they may be traced to Novalis, Schopenhauer, and Nietzsche, among others" (176n).

Sulloway's long discussion of the Freudian ideas supposedly anticipated in Fliess's monograph turns out, then, to be so much sound and fury signifying, if not nothing, then remarkably little. In particular, his claim for Fliess's "systematic and, in many respects, pioneering investigations concerning the existence and the causes of childhood sexuality" (171) is wildly overstated. The very paucity of his evidence makes it seem more likely that, far from being a systematic pioneer, Fliess picked up and repeated these stray notions about sex and childhood from Freud or from other contemporary students of sexuality. Sulloway professes to be shocked "that not a single word has been uttered in the voluminous secondary literature on Freud concerning Fliess's discoveries on this most Freudian of topics" (171). But the silence is hardly surprising. Only desperate ingenuity has enabled Sulloway to fashion his intricate intellectual edifice—a kind of conceptual Rube Goldberg structure—according to which Freud's mature theory can be found, in embryo, in Fliess's monograph. Examined closely, it collapses like the proverbial house of cards.

■　　■　　■

If Fliess was not a Freudian, what about the possibility that Freud was a Fliessian? That is, what of Sulloway's second strategy, his close reading of Freud's correspondence with Fliess, intended to extract evidence of Freud's adapting or "transforming" Fliessian ideas into recognizably psychoanalytic form? The notion of "transformation," like that of "cooperation," serves as a hedge on the more adamantine concept of "influence." It thus introduces a certain elasticity, even slipperiness, into Sulloway's argument. Moreover, the enterprise results in some of the densest, most elusive pages in Sulloway's book. They will require patient scrutiny if we are to judge the merits of his case.

Just as he earlier purported to find five points at which Fliess's 1897 monograph anticipates Freud, Sulloway now asserts that Freud's intellectual transformation of Fliess, as revealed in the letters, involves "three major elements":

(1) Freud's attempts, actively encouraged by Fliess, to use the theories of periodicity and bisexuality to map out various "critical stages" in the development of human psychosexual organization; (2) Freud's speculations on the relationship between "organic" repression, bisexuality, and the sense of smell; and (3) his gradual insight into the phantasy life of neurotics, especially its dynamic psychoanalytic relationship to the developing id. (194)

In order to assess these "elements," we must put two questions to each of them. First, does the particular item represent a psychoanalytic breakthrough—an idea that we encounter in Freud's mature thought, or, if not that, at least a significant step in the direction of such an idea? In other words, is it recognizably Freudian? Second, is the idea clearly inspired by Fliessian considerations (the nose-genital link, the calculus of vital periodicities, or bisexuality), thus qualifying it as a "transformation"? One should also attend to a third consideration, namely, whether the idea is informed by phylogenetic or evolutionary concerns, because this speaks to the larger claim of Sulloway's book regarding the central role of biological reasoning in Freud's thought.

(1) *Mapping out "critical stages" in psychosexual development.* Sulloway's discussion of this first matter is based on Freud's letter of December 6, 1896, a letter, Sulloway says, that "adumbrates a number of Freud's most important insights into human psychosexuality" (196). The "critical stages" in psychosexual development are not, be it noted, the oral, anal, and phallic phases that would later form the core of Freud's theory of infantile sexuality. Rather, Sulloway is referring to a scheme Freud proposed connecting particular neuroses to sexual experiences at specific ages. To be precise, Freud links hysteria to repressed sexual experiences that occurred between the ages of 1½ and 4 years, obsessional neurosis to experiences between the ages of 4 and 8, and paranoia to experiences between the ages of 8 and 14. Can this idea be reckoned a major psychoanalytic breakthrough? Perhaps it can, in the broad structural sense that it posits a developmental pattern organized in terms of stages. But neither the age categories nor their association with particular neuroses would survive into mature psychoanalytic theory. In other words, it has the general form, but not the specific content, of Freud's later conception.

The scheme, then, is arguably proto-Freudian. But is it also Fliessian? Here Sulloway makes what is probably his strongest case. Although Freud most likely arrived at the scheme on the basis of his clinical experiences and hunches, he seeks in the December 6 letter to explain it (or, better, rationalize it) in terms of Fliess's hypothesis of 23- and 28-day cycles—to provide his psychic "superstructure," as Freud puts it, with "organic foundations."[10] In a series of obscure calculations that rival anything in Fliess (and which the original editors of the correspondence chose to suppress), Freud tries to persuade himself that his age

10. Freud, *Complete Letters to Fliess,* p. 210.

categories can indeed be understood as multiples of Fliess's two numbers. His argument is also Fliessian in a second sense: it draws on Fliess's conception of bisexuality, specifically the notion of a 23-day "male substance" and a 28-day "female substance," the former equated by Freud with pleasure, the latter with repression. I would note, however, that these specifically Fliessian notions are used mainly to justify the critical ages in Freud's scheme: 1½, 4, 8, and 14. That is, they are used to support precisely the elements that he would later discard. The conviction that psychic life unfolds by stages clearly preceded these calculations; it was an idea Freud had been moving toward (independently of periodicity and bisexuality) for some time. The December 6 letter, then, doesn't really support Sulloway's conclusion that "the theories of bisexuality and biorhythmic development fruitfully directed Freud's psychoanalytic attention toward possible critical stages in infantile psychosexual development" (198). A more plausible reading would be that the letter shows Freud struggling toward a developmental conception of psychosexual life, making a false landing on this particular scheme, and grasping at Fliess's periodic calculations in an effort to stabilize his somewhat shaky trial balloon.

The December 6 letter offers stronger support for a different contention of Sulloway's. In the letter, Freud seems to use Fliessian reasoning to arrive at the notion that the neuroses are the "negative" of the perversions. Here is an idea that would find a permanent place in psychoanalytic thought. In the *Three Essays*, Freud writes: "Symptoms are formed in part at the cost of *abnormal* sexuality; *neuroses are, so to say, the negative of perversions.*"[11] In other words, Freud believed that when childhood sexual experiences are

11. Freud, *Three Essays*, *SE*, vol. VII, p. 165.

repressed, they return as neurotic symptoms, whereas when they are simply responded to pleasurably and acted upon, the individual escapes illness, so to speak, by becoming a pervert. Needless to say, the theory faces the difficulty of explaining why some early sexual experiences are repressed while others are acted upon. A passage from the December 6 letter, which Sulloway cites, seeks to cast light on this mystery by way of Fliess's notions of bisexuality and of male and female sexual substances:

In order to account for why the outcome [of premature sexual experience] is sometimes perversion and sometimes neurosis, I avail myself of the bisexuality of all human beings. In a purely male being there would be a surplus of male release at the two sexual boundaries [i.e., ages 4 and 8]—that is, pleasure would be generated and consequently perversion; in purely female beings there would be a surplus of unpleasurable substance at these times. In the first phases the releases would be parallel: that is, they would produce a normal surplus of pleasure. This would explain the preference of true females for neuroses of defense.[12]

The reasoning is less than entirely lucid, and it depends on Freud's decision, not further explained, to equate Fliess's male substance with pleasure and his female substance with repression. (A year later, in the letter of November 14, Freud says that he has given up this equation.) But the passage strongly suggests that Fliessian assumptions played a role in Freud's thinking about the perversions. Perhaps this is not so surprising when one recalls that the perversions were always associated in Freud's mind (as in the minds of many contemporary sexologists) with the idea of bisexuality, for which Freud acknowledged his debt to Fliess.

12. Freud, *Complete Letters to Fliess,* p. 212.

(2) *"Organic" repression and the sense of smell.* Sulloway's discussion of this issue turns largely on Freud's letter
of November 14, 1897, which Sulloway calls "fascinating
and, in general, insufficiently appreciated" (203). The key
item in the letter is the idea of "abandoned erotogenic
zones," a notion that was to remain part of psychoanalytic
theory in its mature form. Abandoned erotogenic zones
are areas of the body—Freud mentions the anus, the
mouth, and the throat—that are important sources of sexual gratification in childhood but cease to be such in normal adults. "We must assume," Freud writes, "that in infancy the release of sexuality is not yet so much localized
as it is later, so that the zones which are later abandoned
(and perhaps the whole surface of the body as well) also in-
stigate something that is analogous to the later release of
sexuality."[13] In the November 14 letter Freud has not yet
connected these zones to a specific chronological scheme,
although Sulloway tries to give the impression that he has.
The idea, then, while decidedly psychoanalytic, has not
achieved its classic form.

Sulloway argues that the notion of abandoned erotogenic zones was "Fliessian inspired" (198). He makes this assertion in part because, when Freud first mentions the idea
(in the letter of December 6, 1896), he alludes to Fliess's
"28-day anxiety substance."[14] But, for Sulloway, there is
more important evidence. Freud ties the abandonment of
erotogenic zones after childhood to an evolutionary speculation about the repression of the sense of smell, which
took place when mankind adopted upright posture. The
notion of abandoned sexual zones, Freud hazards paren-
thetically, may be "linked to the changed part played by
sensations of smell: upright walking, nose raised from the

13. Ibid., p. 279.   14. Ibid., p. 212.

ground, at the same time a number of formerly interesting sensations attached to the earth becoming repulsive—by a process still unknown to me."[15] This phylogenetic hypothesis seems to imply that childhood erotogenic zones might be thought of as the residue of our one-time olfactory sexuality, just as the abandoning of these zones as the child grows up recapitulates the process by which the race gave up the nose as an important source of sexual stimulation when it adopted erect posture. The emergence of a sense of shame would thus appear to have an evolutionary basis: repression, in this sense, is at least partly organic.

For Sulloway this line of reasoning is Fliessian—rather than merely evolutionary—because of the role it ascribes to the nose, that quintessentially Fliessian organ. He stresses that Freud's argument "focused upon the nose," which for Fliess was not merely a "sex-linked organ" but "an erotogenic zone par excellence" (198). Yet what is striking about Freud's discussion, one could argue, is that he does *not* mention the nose as an erotogenic zone, abandoned or otherwise, but only the anus, mouth, and throat. Still, I am inclined to agree that Freud's phylogenetic speculation has a decidedly Fliessian ring. The more important question concerns just how central a place one should assign to the idea in Freud's thinking. It surfaces again in the Rat Man case and in *Civilization and Its Discontents,* where Sulloway places it at the very center of Freud's theory of culture. But, as it does in both its later incarnations, the idea appears in the letter of 1897 as an aside, a parenthetical speculation, one that admittedly adds an evolutionary dimension to the argument but hardly establishes itself as a foundational assumption on which the entire Freudian edifice would be built. Thus Sulloway's conclusion that

15. Ibid., p. 279.

Freud "seized upon the sense of smell as a major agent in
the developmental processes of reaction formation and repression" (199) seems exaggerated.

(3) *The fantasy life of neurotics*. This is, for Sulloway,
the least important of the three allegedly Fliessian transformations, and his argument for it is correspondingly
more tentative. What he is concerned with here is Freud's
decision to abandon the seduction theory and replace it
with the idea of children's seduction fantasies. In a very
general sense, he wants to associate the collapse of the seduction theory with Fliess's influence because he views
Fliess as the spokesman for spontaneous infantile sexuality.
Here, however, Sulloway seeks to identify a more specific
derivation, namely, a Fliessian source for the notion that
repressed sexual impulses in childhood can give rise to
neurotic fantasies, including fantasies of seduction. "While
I do not wish to downplay, by any means, the magnitude
of Freud's personal achievement in reaching this last insight,
I am also inclined to count it among the most important of
the post-*Project* derivatives of his scientific relationship
with Fliess" (205). The assertion is appropriately hedged.

The only evidence Sulloway can adduce to support his
idea are two passing allusions to something "chemical" in
Freud's discussion of neurotic fantasies. From a document
labeled "Draft M" by the editors of the *Project* (and dated
May 25, 1897), Sulloway quotes Freud as saying that hysterical fantasies arise "automatically (by a chemical process)" (205). (Freud's actual statement is rather more circumspect: he writes that fantasies "seem to have arisen, as
it were, automatically [by a chemical process].")[16] Sullo-

16. Freud, *The Origins of Psychoanalysis*, ed. Marie Bonaparte, Anna
Freud, and Ernst Kris, trans. Eric Mosbacher and James Strachey (New
York, 1954), p. 205.

way also quotes another sentence from the same draft in which Freud proposes a chemical analogy: "Phantasies are constructed by a process of fusion and distortion analogous to the decomposition of a chemical body which is combined with another one" (205), which prompts the following ejaculation on Sulloway's part: "Not a far distant shade, I submit, of Wilhelm Fliess's two combining bisexual substances!" (205). That's the sum of Sulloway's hard evidence, which amounts only to saying that Freud's analogies perhaps bear a resemblance to Fliess's sexual substances. The proposition—to put the best possible light on it—can only be called shadowy.

·   ·   ·

At what general conclusion, then, can we arrive regarding Sulloway's contention that psychoanalysis is a transformation of the Fliessian id? Clearly, in my view the case is very weak. The assortment of ideas on which Sulloway lavishes such attention—the "critical stages," the perversions as the negative of the neuroses, the repression of the sense of smell, and the chemistry of neurotic fantasies—simply does not add up to "psychoanalysis." Some of the ideas (the critical stages, the chemistry of fantasies) find no place in Freud's later thinking, while others (the perversions as the negative of the neuroses, the repression of the sense of smell) are authentically psychoanalytic but far from central pillars of the doctrine. Moreover, many, indeed most, of the ideas essential to mature psychoanalytic theory are entirely absent from Sulloway's collection. At the same time, Sulloway's effort to give the ideas he does discuss a Fliessian reading is often labored, and hence unpersuasive. A sense of intellectual strain—of looking for a needle in a haystack—is evident throughout. Not surprisingly, his argument is extraordinarily difficult to remember. This is not merely because Sulloway overwhelms the reader with detail but because all that detail finally bears such a tenuous link to his conclusions.

In the end, Sulloway fundamentally misrepresents the relationship between Freud and Fliess when he treats it as a partnership of equals. Freud's letters to Fliess convey the impression of a singularly one-sided conversation—almost a monologue—with Freud showing just enough interest in Fliess's ideas to keep the latter listening. Fliess was essentially a sounding board, a sympathetic ear, who indulged Freud's elaborate, self-absorbed, and often fumbling expositions of his emerging theories (along with the letters, Freud sent Fliess more than a dozen drafts, including the book-length *Project for a Scientific Psychology*). Of course, Fliess's responses, if we had them, would no doubt modify our sense of the degree to which Freud dominated the conversation. But I doubt they would tip the scales altogether. Likewise, I also suspect that the many meetings or "congresses" between Freud and Fliess on the occasion of their summer holidays found Freud doing the lion's share of the talking. Freud, after all, was a genius and a person of boundless self-confidence. Whatever Fliess's intellectual merits, they could hardly overcome the categorical distance separating the two men.

To grant Sulloway his due, he makes a plausible case for Fliess's having exercised a more substantial intellectual (as opposed to psychological) influence on Freud than a devoted psychoanalytic biographer like Ernest Jones would allow. But Jones represents the extreme case. Other psychoanalytic historians, such as Kurt Eissler and Didier Anzieu, while not going so far as Sulloway, have been willing to grant Fliess a role in Freud's intellectual development. Anzieu—the author of an exhaustive study of Freud's self-analysis—calls Jones's contempt for Fliess "distinctly unfair" and concludes boldly: "Had it not been for Fliess, psychoanalysis would probably not have been discovered."[17]

Finally, the significance of Fliess for Sulloway's overarching proposition that psychoanalysis is at bottom an evolutionary science—that Freud was a "biologist of the mind"—remains equivocal. For Sulloway's case to persuade, we must accept not only that Fliess's influence was substantial but that anything Fliessian is fundamentally evolutionary. Because, however, Sulloway succeeds only partially in giving Fliess's ideas an evolutionary reading, the attempt to transform Freud into a psychobiologist by virtue of Fliess is, one might say, doubly derivative. Far easier to regard Freud and Fliess, like most scientists of their day, as equally immersed in a Darwinian intellectual culture. Indeed, Sulloway himself argues as much in the chapter of his book on Freud and Darwin. In other words, one does not need Fliess to explain Freud's interest in evolutionary biology. The sole point at which Fliess's influence may have proved decisive is Freud's phylogenetic speculation, in the letter of November 14, 1897, about the suppression of the sense of smell. But Sulloway's efforts to promote this idea into one of the central precepts of psychoanalysis (rather than merely an *obiter dictum*) seems, at best, idiosyncratic.

▪   ▪   ▪

Sulloway concludes his treatment of Fliess with a long discussion of the alienation that ultimately set in between

17. Didier Anzieu, *Freud's Self-Analysis,* trans. Peter Graham (Madison, Conn., 1986; French original, *L'Auto-analyse: Son Rôle dans la découverte de la psychoanalyse, sa fonction en psychoanalyse* [Paris, 1975]), p. 114.

the two men. In contrast to the standard psychoanalytic
account, he argues that Fliess, rather than Freud, initiated
the break. More important, he rejects the notion that the
end of the friendship can be explained in terms of Freud's
overcoming his Oedipal transference to Fliess or by his
suddenly recognizing the pseudoscientific nature of Fliess's
ideas. Rather, Sulloway says, the real cause of the alienation was Freud's ambition: when Freud gave up the seduction theory and embraced instead the notion of infantile sexuality, he began to fear being swamped by Fliess's
ideas. As long as the seduction theory lasted, Freud could
see himself specializing in the psychological side of things,
while Fliess specialized in the biological. But by rejecting
the seduction theory in favor of infantile sexuality, Freud
was moving deeper into Fliess's biological territory—and
the old division of labor was no longer tolerable. Accordingly, "his previous dependence upon Fliess gradually
turned to rivalry, and he began to see their scientific work
as potentially competing" (219). This bit of psychological
reasoning is, of course, just as speculative as the orthodox
notion of a transference relationship, and Sulloway's presentation of it is, quite appropriately, conducted largely in
hypothetical language. He gives a similarly speculative
analysis of the so-called Weininger-Swoboda affair, a kind
of coda to the Fliess relationship, in which Freud, as even
Ernest Jones admits, dissembled about leaking Fliess's
ideas on bisexuality to one of his students. This too, according to Sulloway, reflected Freud's sense of "growing
ambivalence and intellectual rivalry" (231). Sulloway devotes such substantial space to these issues mainly because,
in his view, they show Freud trying to cover up his biological tracks. They also provide Sulloway with an opportunity to vent his latent hostility to Freud. As in his earlier
treatment of the break with Breuer, Sulloway contrasts a

brutally ambitious Freud with an apparently tractable Fliess, who, to the end of his life, "preserved a considerable interest in psychoanalysis, reading the latest publications by Freud and referring suitable patients to Freud's Berlin followers for psychoanalytic treatment" (233). Sulloway's ostensible enthusiasm for Freud's "creative" transformation of Fliess's ideas gives way to a sustained indictment of Freud's dishonesty, ingratitude, and "obsessional need for intellectual immortality" (217). It is another instance of the return of the repressed.

THE *PROJECT*, THE SEDUCTION THEORY, AND THE SELF-ANALYSIS

Sulloway's promotion of Wilhelm Fliess into a major player in Freud's intellectual biography has a correspondingly profound effect on his interpretation of three landmarks in Freud's odyssey during the 1890s: the *Project for a Scientific Psychology,* the decision to abandon the seduction theory, and, most important, Freud's famous self-analysis, for which the Fliess correspondence has always been the main documentary source. Each of the episodes must now be adjusted to accommodate Fliess's new preeminence and the central role that Sulloway would assign to evolutionary theory.

Ever since its publication in 1950, along with a selection of the Fliess correspondence, in *Aus den Anfängen der Psychoanalyse,* Freud's *Project for a Scientific Psychology* has proved controversial. It consists of two handwritten notebooks that Freud composed in late 1895 and sent to Fliess for examination and criticism. Freud never published the work, and he never asked Fliess to return the notebooks. The *Project* can accurately be described as Freud's most

extravagant attempt to ground psychology in neurology—
a work of speculative physiological reductionism, portraying the mind, in James Strachey's words, as "a piece of
neurological machinery."[18] This point of view is vividly
conveyed by its programmatic opening sentence. "The intention," Freud writes, "is to furnish a psychology that
shall be a natural science: that is, to represent psychical
processes as quantitatively determinate states of specifiable
material particles, thus making those processes perspicu-
ous and free from contradiction."[19] The "specifiable material particles" are the so-called neurones, and Freud seeks
to explain all aspects of psychic life, from perception to
dreaming, in terms of their interaction.

A number of scholars have argued about the cogency of
Freud's ideas in the *Project* and about their relation to his
mature psychoanalytic theory of mind. Sulloway discusses
these controversies at some length, taking, for the most
part, a judicious middle-of-the-road position. But his real
concern is to dispute the way Freud's psychoanalytic biographers have interpreted the document. For the orthodox,
the *Project* represents the dying gasp of Freud's "need to
neurologize" (121), "a last desperate effort," in Ernest
Jones's words, "to cling to the safety of cerebral anatomy."[20] They therefore view Freud's failure to publish it,
or even to ask for its return, as a tacit recognition on his
part that the attempt to understand the mind in reductive
physiological terms—an ideal traceable to Freud's days as
a student under Brücke and redolent of nineteenth-century

18. James Strachey, "Editor's Introduction," in Freud, *The Interpretation of Dreams, Standard Edition*, vol. IV, p. xvii.
19. Freud, *Project for a Scientific Psychology, Standard Edition*, vol. I,
p. 295.
20. Jones, *Life and Work*, I:384.

positivism—had to be abandoned. By virtue of its very excess, the *Project* marks for them the final watershed in Freud's epoch-making movement from neurology to psychology. Now that Freud had finally unburdened himself of his most ambitious neurophysiological speculations, psychoanalysis was free to be born.

Sulloway disagrees. He insists that Freud abandoned the *Project* simply because he was unable to complete the third notebook, dealing with repression, and that this failing in no way implies a repudiation of the reductionist ideal embodied in the first two notebooks. But, in his own way, Sulloway, too, wants to view the abandonment of the *Project* as a watershed. For Sulloway, however, it marks not the end of Freud's commitment to scientific reductionism but his conversion from one form of reductionism to another, namely, from neurophysiological reductionism to organic or evolutionary reductionism. "It is often assumed, erroneously, that there is only one form of reductionism in science—to the laws of physics and chemistry. But in certain sciences, particularly the life sciences, there are two major forms of reductionism—physical-chemical and historical-evolutionary" (131). Sulloway argues, accordingly, that the *Project* shows Freud coming to grief in his efforts to reduce mind to the laws of physics and chemistry, and turning instead to an equally reductive explanation in terms of the laws of evolution. In other words, the relative failure of the *Project* resulted in a shift not from neurophysiology to psychology but from neurophysiology to biology. It thus supports Sulloway's general portrait of Freud as a biologist of the mind. "The *Project*," Sulloway concludes, "contains the (at first) reluctant biogenetic seed of Freud's later and far more enthusiastic endorsement of the *developmental* point of view in psychoanalysis" (131).

As with his interpretation of the Fliess correspondence, the construction Sulloway places on the *Project for a Scientific Psychology* depends on a distinctive reading of a handful of isolated sentences—even phrases—from the text. The *Project* is combed for any remark, no matter how brief, tentative, or hypothetical, that might be construed to support the notion of an evolutionary conversion. Thus, for example, Sulloway transforms what is a manifestly fleeting allusion to a possible "Darwinian line of thought" into a veritable biological epiphany.[21] Not by the farthest, or most charitable, stretch of the imagination do these slender offerings justify the generalization that, "when necessary, Freud was able to renounce in the *Project* the concepts of a reductionist physiologist in favor of concepts proper to an organismic and evolutionary biologist"—"a conceptual step" whose importance "cannot be overestimated" (122). Admittedly, the *Project* is not finally a major building block in Sulloway's interpretation of Freud as a crypto-biologist: his larger argument would scarcely be affected if his whole discussion of the work were excised. But Sulloway's effort to force this reluctant document to fit his thesis is symptomatic of his intellectual manners throughout.

■   ■   ■

During the 1980s the seduction theory would become the most controversial issue in Freud's biography, largely as a result of Jeffrey Masson's book *The Assault on Truth: Freud's Suppression of the Seduction Theory*. In the light of this subsequent development, perhaps the first thing to be said about Sulloway's treatment of the seduction theory is

21. Freud, *Project, SE,* vol. I, p. 303.

that it is in many respects consonant with the view taken by Freud himself and by his major psychoanalytic biographers. That is, for Sulloway the seduction theory was a mistake, and Freud judged correctly when he abandoned the idea. As we will see, Sulloway also accepts most of the usual reasons cited for this decision. But he seeks to give the episode a distinctive gloss, by which it is made to fit into his thesis of Freud's increasing dependence on evolutionary biology, and in particular on Wilhelm Fliess. It would be no exaggeration to say that, for Sulloway, the seduction theory became superfluous precisely because of Fliess's growing intellectual influence over Freud. The vicissitudes of the theory are thus subordinated to his book's larger conceit.

In the traditional account of Freud's intellectual development, the abandonment of the seduction theory and the emergence of the idea of infantile sexuality are intimately linked. When, for a variety of reasons, Freud reluctantly concluded that his patients' stories about childhood seductions—the very experiences he took as the source of their neuroses—did not always prove to have real historical roots, he was forced to recognize that these neuroses were sometimes based on mere fantasies of seduction. But the notion of childhood sexual fantasy makes sense only if one assumes that children have an autonomous and spontaneous sexuality of their own. In other words, the discovery of the role of fantasy in the origins of neurosis caused Freud to abandon the notion of childhood sexual innocence (disturbed traumatically, according to the seduction hypothesis, by the sexual aggressions of adults) in favor of the notion of infantile sexuality.

Inasmuch as Sulloway accepts the general proposition that the idea of infantile sexuality displaced the seduction theory, his view corresponds to the received version of the episode. But he objects to seeing this displacement as a purely intrapsychic event in Freud's mind, just as he objects to tying it to the self-analysis. Freud, Sulloway insists, was moving toward a notion of autonomous infantile sexuality *before* the collapse of the seduction theory, and he was doing so largely under Fliess's influence. Thus, instead of saying that the theory's collapse forced Freud to develop the idea of infantile sexuality, Sulloway prefers to suggest that it simply cleared the way for Freud to embrace an essentially Fliessian conception whose appeal he no longer had reason to resist. This entire line of reasoning depends on our accepting Sulloway's earlier demonstration that Fliess was the source of Freud's ideas about infantile sexuality—a demonstration that, as I've suggested, is far from conclusive. Nevertheless, the abandonment of the seduction theory is for Sulloway a salutary moment, in which Freud wisely discarded his "extreme environmentalism" (377) in favor of a firmly biological (and Fliessian) notion of indigenous childhood sexuality. Interestingly, Sulloway fails to notice that the abandonment of the seduction theory pushed Freud's thinking in an even more radically psychological direction than had his earlier discovery that people can fall ill because of memories. Now, apparently, they could also fall ill because of fantasies, which are, so to speak, twice removed from reality. But to construe the episode in this fashion would undermine Sulloway's aim of rescuing Freud from the grasp of "pure psychology."

· · ·

As one might expect, Sulloway is also eager to diminish the intellectual significance of Freud's self-analysis. He complains that the self-analysis on which Freud embarked in 1897 "has tended to become an overburdened catchall for many developments in his thinking that have hitherto possessed no better historical explanation" (208). Sulloway objects to this emphasis on two grounds. First, it effectively makes Freud's discovery of psychoanalysis the result of a purely psychological episode, which in turn complements (indeed, determines) the equally unacceptable notion that psychoanalysis itself is an essentially psychological theory. Second, it implies that the discovery of psychoanalysis occurred in intellectual isolation: Freud's thinking, it suggests, was so antithetical to the views of his contemporaries that the only way he could achieve his great breakthrough was by lonely self-scrutiny.

Sulloway rejects in particular the notion that the self-analysis played "a crucial role" (18n) in Freud's discovery of infantile sexuality. His dismissal of this idea is not based on any examination of Freud's very substantial account, in the Fliess correspondence, of the insights into childhood sexual life that the self-analysis in fact made possible. Indeed, it is not based on any immediate argument at all. Ultimately, it assumes once again that we are convinced, with Sulloway, that the real author of infantile sexuality was Fliess, who, aided by contemporary sexologists, made the idea available to Freud. Sulloway's treatment of this issue stands in sharp antithesis to Didier Anzieu's magisterial *Freud's Self-Analysis,* a long, patient, and extraordinarily detailed reconstruction of the self-analysis, aimed at assessing its intellectual significance. Anzieu concludes that "the basic corpus of psychoanalytic notions," including of course the theory of infantile sexuality, can be directly attributed to the self-analysis.[22] Sulloway appears to have consulted only the original 1959

22. Anzieu, *Freud's Self-Analysis,* p. 232.

version of Anzieu's book, not the much expanded two-volume edition of 1975. In any event, the empirical richness and logical rigor of Anzieu's case for the self-analysis contrasts markedly with the thinness and sleight-of-hand of Sulloway's counterargument regarding the preeminent role of Fliess. For Sulloway, naturally, Anzieu is just another apologist for the Freud legend.

Sulloway does not utterly dismiss the self-analysis. But his assessment of its "real scientific value" is revealing. Through self-analysis, Sulloway tell us, Freud was able

to confirm from his own experience just how remarkably widespread the opportunities were in every *normal* childhood for both traumatic and spontaneous sexual activity. At the same time, self-analysis enabled Freud to extend significantly his understanding of the various psychological correlates of such early sexual experience. He was able to recall feelings of jealousy and hatred at the birth of a younger male sibling, one year his junior (and who died after only eight months of life). He also recognized love for the mother and jealousy of the father in the early years of his childhood and therefore concluded that such feelings must be a universal concomitant of this period of life. (209)

Surely the most remarkable thing about this passage is its reduction of the Oedipus complex to a mere "psychological correlate"—almost an afterthought, whose discovery Sulloway gladly concedes to the self-analysis. The self-analysis, in other words, revealed only the psychological filigree, not the solid biological foundations, on which Freud's claim to immortality must rest. At such moments, one recognizes that the two opposing views of the self-analysis reflect a more basic disagreement about what Freud actually accomplished when he created psychoanalysis. Behind the discrepancy lies what can best be described as Sulloway's antipsychological prejudice. A psychological discovery, such as the Oedipus complex, is for him inevitably something lesser, something that can never aspire to the dignity of true scientific knowledge. For the same reason, Sulloway cannot allow that an act of pure psychological self-examination could result in a profound intellectual transformation. Freud will be great only if he can be made to resemble Darwin; it will not do to suggest that his achievement was more like that of Augustine or Rousseau.

DARWIN AND THE SEXOLOGISTS

Sulloway devotes an entire chapter of his book to Darwin's influence on Freud. His treatment of Darwin is similar to his treatment of Fliess, although there are important differences as well. For one thing, Darwin is a figure of the first magnitude. Consequently, he doesn't need the sort of intellectual rehabilitation that Sulloway graciously performs for Fliess. Similarly, the orthodox biographical tradition has always recognized Darwin as an important influence—Ernest Jones called Freud the "Darwin of the Mind"[23]—in contrast to its efforts to minimize Fliess's influence. Sulloway nevertheless complains that traditional Freud scholarship has paid only "formal lip service" (xiv) to Darwin and has failed to identify the precise nature of his impact on psychoanalysis.

Sulloway sets out to correct these errors. As he did with Fliess, he argues, first, that Darwin anticipated Freud on a number of issues—that Darwin was a proto-Freudian of sorts—and, second, that certain of Freud's mature psycho-

23. Ernest Jones, *Papers on Psycho-Analysis* (London, 1913), p. xii.

analytic ideas, when examined carefully, turn out to be much more Darwinian than has generally been recognized. In effect, Sulloway tries to bring Darwin and Freud—"two of the most important revolutionaries in the history of scientific thought" (xiv)—into closer intellectual proximity. Whether this tactic results in Freud's subordination to Darwin or his unwarrantable elevation to the status of a scientist of equal genius is a question of perspective. But, for Sulloway, Freud is clearly Darwin's most important intellectual heir.

Sulloway's case for Darwin as a proto-Freudian consists largely in showing, at some length, that Darwin was interested in psychology. The claim that "Darwin undertook to explore a whole medley of later Freudian themes" (241) inspires a litany of supposedly Freudian topics, including dreams, mentioned by Darwin in his M and N notebooks of the 1830s. But Sulloway produces no evidence to justify the assertion that "much in these notebooks sounds remarkably like Freud himself" (242). Sulloway hopes to give Darwin's psychological concerns a Freudian cast by stressing Darwin's interest in the mental life of children. But the mental repertory of Darwin's child is decidedly pre-analytic, indeed Victorian: anger, fear, pleasure, affection, reason, and moral sense. Even Sulloway is forced to admit that the ties between Darwin and Freud on this subject are for the most part distant.

Along with childhood emotions, the other putatively Freudian topic pursued by Darwin was sex. Here Sulloway has in mind Darwin's theory of sexual selection, according to which the existence of physical traits with no clear value for survival can be explained in terms of their differential effect on reproduction. Thus the colorful but apparently useless ornamental plumage of male birds in fact helps them to attract females. Sulloway suggests that

Darwin's theory was responsible for the broad surge of intellectual interest in sex during the late nineteenth century, and, by implication, for Freud's sexual ideas as well. But, of course, Darwin's theory could just as easily reflect that interest; it is not necessarily its source. More important, the theory of sexual selection is in no way distinctively Freudian and plays no role in Freud's sexual doctrines. In the end, Sulloway must content himself with the orotund judgment that Darwin provided a theoretical rationale for the time-honored dictum about love and hunger ruling the world. This, it seems, is the ultimate justification for Sulloway's belief that Darwin "probably did more than any other individual to pave the way for Sigmund Freud and the psychoanalytic revolution" (238).

Sulloway's more intriguing argument holds not that Darwin anticipated Freud but that Darwin's ideas are deeply embedded in some of Freud's most characteristic psychoanalytic concepts. Sulloway mentions several such concepts, including fixation and regression (which he ties to the evolutionary notion of developmental arrests). Once again, however, the centerpiece of his case is Freud's theory of childhood psychosexual stages. Although Sulloway had earlier traced this theory to Fliess, he now proposes that Darwin was the more significant source of Freud's inspiration. Actually, the link with Darwin is not direct, but by way of Ernst Haeckel's famous hypothesis that "ontogeny recapitulates phylogeny"—that is, that an individual's development from conception to adulthood repeats the evolutionary history of the race. "Freud's implicit endorsement of this law," Sulloway writes, "constitutes perhaps the least appreciated source of a priori biological influence in all of psychoanalytic theory" (259).

How, exactly, does the so-called fundamental biogenetic law figure in Freud's theory of infantile sexuality?

According to Sulloway, this recapitulatory hypothesis was the deep source of Freud's surprising conviction that children's oral and anal activities are in reality sexual. The takeoff point for Sulloway's thesis is highly promising. He reminds us that Freud's characterization of infantile sucking and defecating as sexual has always struck outsiders as so very improbable that they wonder how Freud could possibly have been as confident as he was of its accuracy:

Why are oral and anal zones such basic sources of infantile sexual excitation in Freudian theory? Granted that feeding at the mother's breast constitutes a highly pleasurable experience for the hungry infant, how could Freud conceive of this activity as a form of sexual experience? Many non-Freudians have long been amazed by his nonchalant assurance about the answer to this debatable question. (258)

Sulloway responds that Freud's confidence sprang precisely from his belief in the biogenetic law. Freud reasoned, says Sulloway, that "if the developing child recapitulates the history of the race, it must likewise recapitulate the *sexual* history of the race," which meant that the child experiences "all the archaic forms of sexual pleasure that once characterized the mature life stages of our remote ancestors" (259). The most important among such archaic sources of sexual pleasure are the mouth and the anus.

Sulloway cites three passages as evidence that Freud drew on phylogenetic considerations to support his conception of oral and anal stages. Unfortunately, the passages do not in fact prove that the phylogenetic argument was the real source of Freud's conviction. On the contrary, Freud's language points to an altogether different conclusion, to wit, that the phylogenetic argument was for him something of an afterthought, a welcome crutch perhaps, but hardly the clinching evidence or the true basis for his persuasion.

One of these passages comes from a section added to the 1915 edition of the *Three Essays on the Theory of Sexuality*— the most systematic and detailed exposition of his ideas about sexual life, and so presumably the place where Freud could be expected to present the strongest case for his particular conception of infantile sexuality. It reads as follows: "We shall give the name of 'pregenital' to the organizations of sexual life in which the genital zones have not yet taken over their predominant part. We have hitherto identified two such organizations [the oral and the anal], which almost seem as though they were harking back to early animal forms of life."[24] This is a curiously laconic and offhand way to draw attention to what, in Sulloway's estimation, afforded the all-important inspiration for Freud's most controversial claim. The reticence of the passage stands in marked contrast to the vigor and expansiveness of the *clinical* argument for infantile sexuality that Freud mounts in his text. The *Three Essays* conveys the unmistakable impression that the real source of his conviction was not, as Sulloway would have it, the elusive biogenetic law but the observable (contemporary) fact that the mouth and anus persist as organs of sexual gratification among adults, particularly in kissing and anal intercourse. Freud asks, in effect, why these activities play such a significant role in the sexual lives of grown-ups, when they are not essential to intercourse and thus to reproduction. His answer is that the mouth and anus can readily be reinstated as organs of sexual gratification because they have already been such in infancy. Sulloway ignores this line of reasoning, powerfully advanced in the pages of the *Three Essays,*

24. Freud, *Three Essays, SE,* vol. VII, p. 198.

because it renders his hypothesis about a phylogenetic source of Freud's conviction largely superfluous. And if we were inclined to think that Freud has perhaps chosen to suppress the real evolutionary rationale for his belief and to present his clinical argument merely as a camouflage, then one must wonder why he allowed himself even the passing allusion to "early animal forms of life" cited by Sulloway. It makes him a rather poor dissembler.

Ironically, Sulloway's insistence on phylogenetic rather than clinical reasoning causes him to overlook what is probably Freud's most important intellectual debt to Darwin. The truly Darwinian feature of his argument about infantile sexuality in the *Three Essays on the Theory of Sexuality* is not its content but its form. It is largely an inferential argument, whose most obvious model is Darwin's argument for natural selection in *The Origin of Species*. There Darwin concedes that he has no direct empirical evidence of natural selection, only the implicit evidence of fossil remains and the like. But these, Darwin holds, make it legitimate for him to *infer* the action of natural selection in order to account for their existence. Freud's argument for infantile sexuality is structurally identical: he cannot directly demonstrate that the child's oral and anal activities are sexual (as opposed to simply pleasurable), but the inference is nonetheless justified because it explains certain things that we *can* observe, in particular, such adult sexual practices as kissing and anal intercourse. Darwin's primary significance for Freud, in short, was conceptual, not substantive.

Given his interest in portraying Freud as an evolutionary thinker, Sulloway is noticeably quiet about Freud's Lamarckism, which he disposes of in two brief paragraphs. Partly, no doubt, this is because the orthodox biographical tradition has always stressed, indeed lamented,

Freud's partiality to Lamarck. A deeper reason, I suspect, is that to underline Freud's Lamarckism would detract from the Darwinian connection Sulloway is laboring to establish. But the specifically Darwinian contribution to evolutionary theory, natural selection, plays no role in psychoanalysis. Instead, Freud draws repeatedly on the Lamarckian doctrine of the inheritance of acquired characteristics—for example, to explain how the memory of the primal crime has been passed down from generation to generation—a doctrine whose importance Darwin in fact sought to diminish by the theory of natural selection.

If we are forced to conclude that Sulloway's case for Freud as a Darwinian is no more persuasive than his case for Freud as a Fliessian, we should not overlook a useful corrective implicit in his argument. Perhaps the greatest virtue of Sulloway's largely wrongheaded book is to remind us that Freud's strongest allegiance was to science, indeed to science precisely on the model of Darwin. We are in danger of forgetting this profound truth about Freud's intellectual identity because over the past two decades we have grown accustomed to the portrait of Freud as a hermeneutician and philosopher—a figure on the model not of Darwin but of Nietzsche. Paul Ricoeur's *Freud and Philosophy* (1970) is the *locus classicus* of this portrait, which has dominated the largely literary and philosophical representations of Freud in recent scholarship. There is much truth in the hermeneutic Freud, and it is a truth that Sulloway ignores. But he also has the advantage of his myopia. Exactly because his account of Freud is so supremely unfashionable—so innocent of current literary prejudices—it forces us to recall that part of Freud has always strenuously resisted the effort to transform him into a philosopher of language. Lionel Trilling, himself a literary critic, drew attention to this recalcitrance over thirty

years ago in *Freud and the Crisis of Our Culture*. Thus, while
Sulloway may not convince us that psychoanalysis is a
form of Darwinism, he does help us to remember that
Freud thought of himself above all as a scientist.

■   ■   ■

The chapter on Darwin is followed by one on sexology. Sulloway's desire to group Freud among the late-
nineteenth-century sexologists reflects his more general
object of undermining Freud's claim to originality and
the associated image of his intellectual isolation. Yet it
also reflects Sulloway's genuine enthusiasm for psychoanalysis's emphasis on sex. He may be indifferent to the
unconscious, but he has nothing but admiration for
Freud's supposed pansexualism. Sex, after all, is for Sulloway the biological hook in Freud: if anything, Sulloway
wants to make even more of it than do the traditional
biographers.

Sulloway's enchantment with turn-of-the-century sexology leads him to compose a little narrative of its development, and for many pages Freud disappears from view.
The general point he wants to make is that almost every element of Freud's sexual theory can be found in the writings of these contemporaries, the majority of whom published their ideas before the appearance of the *Three Essays
on the Theory of Sexuality* in 1905. Sulloway emphasizes, in
particular, that the sexologists anticipated Freud's thinking
about the perversions and, even more important, about the
sexuality of children and infants. In the latter instance, Sulloway follows in the footsteps of Stephen Kern, who argued, in 1973, that "almost every element of Freud's theory of child sexuality was exactly anticipated, or in some

way implied or suggested, before him."[25] Sulloway hardly seems to notice that, by promoting the influence of Krafft-Ebing, Havelock Ellis, and Albert Moll on Freud's ideas about infantile sexuality, he effectively undermines his earlier case for Fliess as the source of those ideas.

The charge that Freud's sexual ideas were unoriginal, and that he has received undue credit for an intellectual revolution whose real authors have fallen victim to historical amnesia, is not without merit. But it betrays a certain naïveté about the issue of originality. As Sulloway notes, Freud made no secret of his borrowings from other authors. He begins the first of his *Three Essays,* "The Sexual Aberrations," by acknowledging his intellectual debts, and the text is generously footnoted throughout. But there is a more fundamental, and subtle, consideration: the elements of a theory never add up to the theory itself. In judging a theory's originality one must do more than compile a list of those components that can be traced to earlier sources. One must also assess the structural power of the conceptual whole into which the components have been fitted. In this respect, Freud's achievement can be usefully compared to the intellectual syntheses created by Marx or Darwin. Numerous scholars have shown that all the components of Darwin's theory of natural selection and of Marx's theory of historical materialism had been anticipated by earlier thinkers. But Marx and Darwin have been rightly judged great innovators because they were the first to shape those ideas into a rigorous and comprehensive analytic structure. Anyone who has spent much time

25. Stephen Kern, "Freud and the Discovery of Child Sexuality," *History of Childhood Quarterly* 1 (1973), p. 137; quoted by Sulloway, p. 279.

reading the sexual writings of even the best of Freud's contemporaries, such as Havelock Ellis, will have no difficulty
in recognizing that Freud achieved the same sort of quan-
tum leap in the *Three Essays*. The conceptual power and in-
clusiveness of Freud's volume set it categorically apart.
Sulloway's complaint that Freud's name has "become associated with many important ideas about human sexuality that he did not originate" (277) thus misses the point. No
practiced student of the history of ideas expects intellectual revolutions to occur in a vacuum. On the contrary, as
Thomas Kuhn has shown, they are always richly prepared.

By placing his discussion of the sexologists right after
his chapter on Darwin, Sulloway presumably aims to suggest that their influence on Freud be viewed as a kind of
extension of Darwin's own influence. In this fashion, Sulloway hopes to enlist them as accomplices in his broader
enterprise of promoting the importance of evolutionary
theory in the emergence of psychoanalysis. "It was largely
through the sexologists," he asserts, "that Freud was
prompted to substitute an evolutionary and phylogenetic
conception of psychosexuality for the physiochemical one
with which he and Josef Breuer began their pioneering
studies of the neuroses" (xiv). But Sulloway is no more
successful with the sexologists than he was with Fliess (or
with Freud himself, for that matter) in demonstrating that
turn-of-the-century sexology represented "a major conceptual offshoot of the Darwinian Revolution" (318). Like
virtually all scientists of their day, these men were indeed
students of evolution, and their writings hence contain a
smattering of phylogenetic ruminations, which Sulloway
does his best to highlight. But the firm impression remains
that their views were shaped above all by clinical considerations, especially case histories. Evolutionary theory, in
other words, does not seem integral to the sexual ideas

they embraced, and Sulloway's effort to transform the sexologists into Darwinian acolytes is ultimately an exercise in wishful thinking. Thus the sexologists—the last of the "significant others" to whom the bulk of his book is devoted—do very little to advance his evolutionary case.

DREAMS

The period from 1899 to 1905 was undoubtedly the most fecund in Freud's career. During these years his essential psychoanalytic ideas first saw the light of print. Together, the five major writings of the period constitute the intellectual centerpiece of the revolution associated with his name: *The Interpretation of Dreams* (1900), considered by virtually all (including Freud himself) his most important book; *The Psychopathology of Everyday Life* (1901), with its theory of "Freudian" slips; his study of the psychology of humor, *Jokes and Their Relation to the Unconscious* (1905); the first of the great case histories, "Dora" (written in 1901, published in 1905); and the *Three Essays on the Theory of Sexuality* (1905). Sulloway does not dissent from the consensus about the significance of these writings. On the contrary, he is lavish in his praise: "These five works constitute a magnificent achievement, which certainly places Freud among the most creative scientific minds of all time" (358). Yet in Sulloway's intellectual biography of Freud, they receive less than half the attention devoted to Wilhelm Fliess. Too famous to be ignored, but unreceptive to Sulloway's evolutionary thesis, the five seminal texts shrink in stature and come to occupy a kind of conceptual limbo. Even Sulloway's praise sounds hollow.

Sulloway directs most of his attention to the theory of dreams. In many respects his treatment of the theory is unexceptionable. He has no objection to Freud's interpretations of individual dreams; he admires Freud's courage in revealing so much of himself in his book; and he judges its conception of dreams as wish fulfillments not only correct but profound. "Freud's mature theory of dreaming is virtually unparalleled, even today, for the remarkable insight that it brought to bear upon the psychological mechanisms of dreaming" (334). The book, he says, belongs among the "great classics in science" (346). Clearly, Sulloway is far removed from Frederick Crews, for whom *The Interpretation of Dreams* is just so much pretentious nonsense.

On the whole, then, Sulloway's discussion of the dream theory is entirely familiar, indeed dutiful. Sensing perhaps that his revisionist stance requires that he say something provocative about the book, he advances the proposition that it is among the "least understood" (320) of Freud's writings. Yet Sulloway is extraordinarily reticent about specifying exactly how it has been misunderstood. The "foremost" (347) misunderstanding, we learn, has to do not with the book's argument but with its initial reception. Here Sulloway takes issue with the traditional psychoanalytic account, according to which Freud's masterpiece met with "icy silence" and "annihilating criticism" (347). Sulloway sees this characterization as part of the broader strategy to represent Freud as a lonely genius, and he makes a plausible case that the response to the book was, while not enthusiastic, at least respectful, and certainly more generous than Freud allowed. Freud, it seems, was no different from any other author in finding that his reviewers left much to be desired. (One suspects that, given the hostile reception of his own book, Sulloway would now look more sympathetically on Freud's complaints.) But even if Sulloway is correct about the book's reception, this hardly justifies his description of *The Inter-*

pretation of Dreams as Freud's most misunderstood work. Sulloway seems right on the verge of revealing some explosive secret about the book, but none is forthcoming.

Wherein, then, lies the misunderstanding? As he did with the idea of infantile sexuality, Sulloway notes that Freud's theory of dreams "had been anticipated piecemeal in almost every major constituent by prior students of the problem" (322). But he does not try to get much mileage out of this charge, mainly because Freud devotes the first chapter of *The Interpretation of Dreams* to a long and full discussion of his important predecessors. Gradually, however, it becomes apparent that Sulloway wants to disturb our comfortable certainties about the dream theory primarily in order to insinuate his evolutionary thesis concerning Freud's hidden biological agenda. Needless to say, the unrelentingly psychological texture of the book makes this a decidedly uphill interpretive battle.

Sulloway contends that Freud actually had two theories of dreams. The first is contained in the *Project for a Scientific Psychology,* and, not surprisingly, it turns out to be fundamentally mechanistic. Dreams, according to the *Project,* "are simply hallucinations motivated by the small residues of energy that are ordinarily left over in an otherwise sleeping (or energyless) mind" (327). But just as the physiological reductionism of the *Project* was superseded, in Sulloway's view, by the biological reductionism of mature psychoanalytic theory, so the *Project's* mechanistic dream theory gave way, in *The Interpretation of Dreams,* to a theory Sulloway repeatedly characterizes as "genetic" (329) or "dynamic-genetic" (328). In Sulloway's mind, these catchwords obviously conjure up the full panoply of evolutionary speculation that, for him, constitutes the secret rationality of Freud's thought. But one nevertheless wants to know just what in Freud's conception of dreams as wish fulfillments might reasonably be termed "genetic," and hence evolutionary. The theory, after all, seems to be fashioned of the purest psychological stuff.

The answer to this mystery—and the ultimate rationale for Sulloway's evolutionary insinuations—lies in Freud's contention that every dream represents a wish from childhood:

> In contrast [to the theory of the *Project*], Freud's later (1900) conception of dream distortion was based upon a dynamic-genetic model of human psychosexual development. With the discovery of the id, the primary reason for dreaming became genetic rather than economic: that is, we dream because the infantile id clamors for nightly self-expression, rather than because impinging energy residues or unresolved daytime conflicts happen to discharge themselves in the sleeping mind. (328–29)

In effect, Freud's insistence on the childhood origin of dream wishes permits Sulloway to link the dream theory to the notion of infantile psychosexual stages. In his peculiar reading, the psychosexual stages mean the Fliessian confection of phylogenetic ideas to whose elucidation he devoted such solicitude earlier in his book. Sulloway doesn't spell out this connection explicitly, probably because it is so hopelessly strained, but he does cite a passage from a letter to Fliess in which Freud remarks that "biologically dream-life seems to me to proceed directly from the residue of the prehistoric stage of life (one to three years)."[26] Sulloway also asserts that, in the Dora case history, "the theory of dreams blends inextricably into the theory of sexuality and hence into the biological substratum of Freud's thinking" (346). Even when any explicit invocation of

26. Freud, *The Origins of Psychoanalysis*, p. 246.

Fliess is suppressed, one senses him hovering in the wings. The failure to recognize the dream theory's deep evolutionary logic, one concludes, is the ultimate source of Sulloway's brooding allusions to its having been so greatly misunderstood.

THE PRIMAL CRIME AND THE DEATH INSTINCT

One would not expect a book championing Freud's claim to scientific rigor to have much use for *Totem and Taboo* (1912–13) or *Beyond the Pleasure Principle* (1920), two of his most fanciful works, which propound, respectively, the theory of the primal crime and the notion of the death instinct. Even the psychoanalytic establishment has tended to wash its hands of these writings, fearing that they bring disrepute on an intellectual enterprise that pretends to be empirical. But once he has disposed of the greatly misunderstood *Interpretation of Dreams* (and given the other major writings of the 1900–05 period even shorter shrift), Sulloway devotes much of the remainder of his intellectual biography to an elucidation of precisely these two works.

In Sulloway's view, Freud's intellectual development from 1905 until his death in 1939 underwent a gradual "rebiologization." Sulloway grants that the writings from 1900 to 1905 are heavily weighted toward psychology, but thereafter, he insists, Freud reverted to the evolutionary preoccupations of the period of his tutelage under Fliess in the 1890s. "Freud's psychoanalytic theories became *more* biological, not less so, after the crucial years of discovery" (391).

In order to sustain this view, Sulloway subjects Freud's work during the final thirty-four years of his life to a radically selective reading. His first move is to place the cultural works, particularly *Totem and Taboo* and *Civilization and Its Discontents,* at the very center of Freud's concerns. Thus the great bulk of his post-1905 writings—the case histories, the metapsychological treatises (except for *Beyond the Pleasure Principle*), the several volumes of expository writings, the essays of applied psychoanalysis—are largely ignored. Sulloway turns to them only when he can extract the occasional sentence or phrase that might lend support to his evolutionary construction. Likewise, within the cultural works, he limits his attention to those passages in which Freud enters upon phylogenetic speculations. *Totem and Taboo,* with its theory of the primal crime, is thus his favorite text, and the other cultural writings catch his eye mainly when they, too, turn to phylogenetic themes. Within the phylogenetic material itself, Sulloway labors heroically to draw attention to one idea in particular, namely, the hypothesis of "olfactory repression," according to which the link between sexuality and the sense of smell was suppressed when mankind adopted upright posture. Virtually the whole of Freud's mature psychoanalytic thought is made to emanate from this single proposition. In effect, Wilhelm Fliess's infamous "naso-genital" hypothesis resurrects itself as the secret heart of the entire psychoanalytic apparatus. Small wonder that anti-Freudians should find Sulloway's book so congenial.

This brutal reordering of Freud's intellectual priorities demands not only that the vast bulk of what he wrote be neglected but also that the phylogenetic speculations themselves be subjected to major distortion. The primal crime is a case in point. In *Totem and Taboo* Freud advances this "just-so" story in order to explain the origins of morality and religion. The crucial moment in his phylogenetic tale occurs when the brothers, having dispatched their father, suddenly decide to forgo intercourse with their newly liberated mother and sisters. They raise their act of renunciation into a principle, the first moral law (the incest taboo), and they transform the murdered father into a god, thereby establishing religion as well. Freud seeks to explain this extraordinary decision, which marks the birth of civilization, in terms of two considerations, one practical, the other psychological. In practical terms, the incest taboo was necessary to prevent civil war from breaking out among the brothers over the spoils of victory. But more important than this Hobbesian motive was the sons' discovery of their Oedipal ambivalence. After their bloody deed, they recalled that they had also loved their father. The institution of the incest taboo, and, later, of the totem religion with its father god, represented an act of remorse, an attempt by the sons to appease their overwhelming sense of guilt.

When Sulloway recounts the story of the primal crime, however, he effectively strips it of its Oedipal logic. He stresses the brothers' pragmatic wish to avert the outbreak of fraternal strife and drastically mutes the distinctively psychological motif in Freud's hypothesis: the notion that civilization originated in a dramatic acting out of the Oedipal emotions of resentment and guilt. This erasure serves Sulloway's purposes in two ways. First, insofar as it "depsychologizes" the primal crime, it contributes to the general demotion of psychology in Sulloway's reading of Freud. In this sense, it is of a piece with Sulloway's reduction of the Oedipus complex itself to a mere "psychological correlate" of Freud's deeper biological concerns. At the same time, it also obscures the link between Freud's phylogenetic hypothesis and his theory of individual psychological development. For Freud, the primal crime acquires a profound emotional resonance because that same crime is rehearsed in the life of every child as it passes through the psychological vortex of the Oedipus crisis. To be sure, Freud believed that every child is born into the world with a memory of the primal crime as part of the mind's "archaic heritage." But that heritage can exercise its power only because it is revitalized in the concrete family experience of the individual. By ignoring the Oedipal dimension of Freud's argument, Sulloway makes the theory of the primal crime more purely phylogenetic, more committed to a disembodied notion of prehistorical "organic repression," than is in fact the case. Freud's richly nuanced interweaving of historical speculation and clinical observation unravels.

Sulloway must regret that nowhere in *Totem and Taboo*—the most extensive of the phylogenetic writings— does Freud remember to mention the nose and the repression of the sense of smell. Once again, an idea we are asked to consider absolutely central to Freud's thought fails to put in an appearance just where we would most expect to find it. On the few occasions that Freud does mention the repressed sense of smell in his writings, he takes great care to subordinate the idea to other matters, always presenting it in a suitably tentative and hypothetical fashion. In *Civilization and Its Discontents* the subordination is literal: the idea is consigned to two footnotes (where it occupies a position comparable to the notorious footnote in which Freud attributes the conquest of fire to the repression of the competitive homosexual practice of extinguishing fires by urinating on them). Sulloway ignores the obvious implications of this literary gesture. Quite arbitrarily, he promotes the idea from its marginal place in Freud's text (and presumably in his thought) to the status of a central and fundamental concept. Likewise, where Freud's language is hedged and subjunctive, Sulloway's is emphatic and indicative. The evidence of the texts themselves suggests that the phylogenetic hypothesis of upright posture and olfactory repression served Freud as a kind of safety valve or fallback, resorted to when better (namely, clinical) arguments seemed in need of help. Such is its role, for example, in the Rat Man case: having noted that his patient was a *renifleur,* who as a child could recognize people by their smell, Freud observes that an inclination to take pleasure in smell "may play a part in the genesis of neurosis." He then seeks to support his hunch with a brief phylogenetic excursus:

And here I should like to raise the general question whether the atrophy of the sense of smell (which is an inevitable result of man's assumption of an erect posture) and the consequent organic repression of his pleasure in smell may not have had a considerable share in the origin of his susceptibility to nervous disease.[27]

Phylogeny, in effect, is the argument of last resort—not, as Sulloway would have it, of first preference. As Freud wrote in the Wolf Man case: "I regard it as a methodological error to seize on a phylogenetic explanation before the ontogenetic possibilities have been exhausted."[28] No doubt Freud believed in his speculations. But they remain, nonetheless, residues of his nineteenth-century scientific education, relegated to the digressive margins in his new psychological science. Even if we were to accept Sulloway's argument that phylogenetic ideas such as the repressed sense of smell were dearer to Freud than his textual subordination of them implies, we must ask whether

27. Freud, "Notes upon a Case of Obsessional Neurosis," *Standard Edition,* vol. X, pp. 247–48.
28. Freud, "From the History of an Infantile Neurosis," *Standard Edition,* vol. XVII, p. 97.

Freud's claim to greatness could possibly rest on such speculations. Much as Sulloway may revel in them, they are simply not the ideas that transformed intellectual history—that created the modern sense of self and made us all, in effect, Freudians. It is thus dubious praise when Sulloway celebrates Freud's phylogenetic musings—the intellectual counterpart, one might say, of his private collection of archaeological artifacts—as "one of the most sophisticated psychobiological conceptions of mind yet proposed" (392). For, in truth, if Sulloway is right, Freud's intellectual achievement is no more worthy of admiration than Fliess's. Only someone deeply hostile to Freud could urge us to embrace such a trivialization of his thought.

■   ■   ■

Sulloway is the first writer since Herbert Marcuse and Norman O. Brown—two very unlikely bedfellows—to put in a good word for the death instinct. (Interestingly, Marcuse and Brown were also devotees of the primal crime.) Sulloway not only praises the idea of the death instinct but makes its formulation in *Beyond the Pleasure Principle* the subject of the final chapter in his intellectual biography. His enthusiasm is not as surprising as one might think. The death instinct is in some ways rather like Fliess: it has proven to be an embarrassment to Freud's orthodox biographers, who have reacted by invoking Freud's personal psychology. Much as they prefer to view Freud's fascination with Fliess as an instance of transference, these biographers have sought to explain away the notion of the death instinct in terms of Freud's personal preoccupation with death (about which he had been obsessing since the 1890s) or his equally personal responses to the destructiveness of the Great War, in which three of his sons fought, and to the death of his daughter Sophie from influenza in January 1920. Almost on principle, Sulloway objects to such psychologizing. "One must not forget," he writes, "how extremely logical Freud was in his thinking" (395). Sulloway thus tries to show that Freud's embrace of the death instinct, like the friendship with Fliess, was utterly rational, and that it provided the conceptual basis for virtually all the important changes in his thought after 1920.

When Sulloway insists that the death instinct "has a perfectly rational logic" (395), he does not mean that it is supported by clear empirical evidence from which the assumption of a fundamental urge toward self-destruction—or, as Freud preferred to say, toward restoring an earlier state of things—follows according to a rigorous sequence of inferences. Rather, he means that the idea served to resolve a number of inconsistencies—pertaining especially to narcissism, regression, and fixation to traumas—that had developed in Freud's theoretical views during the years from 1910 to 1920. Sulloway's exposition both of those inconsistencies and of their supposed resolution by the new instinctual hypothesis is even more tortuous than Freud's own exposition in *Beyond the Pleasure Principle,* which is arguably the most obscure piece of writing he ever produced. The contention that the death instinct emerged as a solution to certain theoretical difficulties is plausible enough; indeed, it is an explanation offered by the orthodox biographers as well. Whether such an apology is sufficient excuse to call the theory "rational" is another matter.

The real source of Sulloway's enthusiasm for the death instinct is not, of course, that it is rational but that it is biological—for which he seems prepared to forgive any amount of ungrounded speculation. The death instinct may be, as he says, a biological "romance" (393), but he is willing to put up with the romance for the sake of the biology, since it lends weight to his proposition that Freud's mature thought underwent a process of "rebiologization." Undeniably the death instinct is biological, although it is scarcely evolutionary. Sulloway frankly concedes that it has nothing to do with Darwin, indeed that it is anti-Darwinian, because an innate urge to die would hardly give an organism a competitive advantage in the struggle for existence. But neither does Sulloway offer any reason for considering the idea evolutionary in a more general sense. The sort of phylogenetic logic that informs both the theory of the primal crime and the random observations about upright posture and the repression of the sense of smell is nowhere to be found in *Beyond the Pleasure Principle,* whose speculative reasoning works at a much higher level of abstraction.

Finally, Sulloway's effort to explain most of the important changes in Freud's thought after 1920 in terms of the death instinct is unusually feeble. In particular, his argument that such major transformations as the new structural theory of the mind and the revised theory of anxiety derive from the death instinct is cryptic and unpersuasive. No more than the idea of "olfactory repression" will the death instinct support so massive an intellectual burden. There is something attractively quixotic in Sulloway's readiness to go to bat for this much maligned concept, and he is correct to remind us of Freud's biological loyalties. But as a master explanatory hypothesis for the evolution of Freud's thought after 1920 it is woefully inadequate. Freud always insisted on the provisional nature of his notion of life and death instincts, stressing that he was not even convinced of the conception himself, and its traces in his subsequent thinking are much fainter than Sulloway thinks.

PSYCHOANALYTIC POLITICS

Ultimately, Sulloway is obliged to explain why the biological essence of Freud's thought has remained hidden. In my view, of course, the question is entirely gratuitous, because the secret biological rationale Sulloway pretends to find doesn't exist—either that, or it is such a paltry affair that its invisibility hardly needs explaining. But, logically, Sulloway must account for its apparent repression, and the final section of his book is devoted to this undertaking.

His principal explanation is very simple: the portrayal of Freud as a pure psychologist, working in lonely isolation, served the institutional needs of the psychoanalytic movement by providing it with the militant self-image it required to defeat its opponents. But alongside this central motive, Sulloway identifies two lesser political advantages that supposedly accrued from the systematic denial of Freud's debt to biology. First, it helped in characterizing psychoanalysis as an empirical, as opposed to a theoretical, doctrine. Undeniably Freud stressed the experiential basis of his ideas. But why would psychoanalysis have been made to seem unempirical or unscientific by admitting its reliance on biology? After all, if Freud had announced himself as heir to Darwin, he could have appealed to the most pervasive scientific prejudice of his age. If, however, his strategy was to avoid any appearance of indebtedness to theory, one is hard put to explain why he was not more consistently circumspect. Especially imprudent from this perspective was his decision to go public with the primal crime, the death instinct, and Sulloway's beloved hypothesis about the nose and upright posture, all of which trumpet Freud's weakness for speculation. I have no wish to dispute the importance of theory in Freud's intellectual achievement, but in insisting so vehemently on its primacy, Sulloway underestimates the role of empirical influences on Freud's thought, above all the evidence gathered from his clinical practice carried on over so many years. To be sure, Freud's ideas were not derived from this clinical material without the assistance of various assumptions and deductions. But neither does the clinical material count for nothing, as one would gather from reading Sulloway.

The second ancillary political motive for denying Freud's debt to biology, according to Sulloway, was the need to combat various psychoanalytic renegades, notably Alfred Adler and Carl Jung. He argues that Adler and Jung were expelled from the ranks because of their excessive biologizing. Because biology was the ultimate source of the defectors' errors, the argument runs, orthodox Freudians (starting with Freud himself) grew ever more set on exorcising it from psychoanalysis. This hypothesis ignores the fact that the real source of disagreement between Freud and both Adler and Jung was not biology but sex: Adler sought to demote the importance of sex by emphasizing aggression; Jung sought to demote it by emphasizing spirituality. Even more significant, while Adler might be construed as a biological deviationist (though Freud objected most to the superficiality of his psychological ideas), Freud's own views were consistently more biological, not less so, than Jung's. Jung was a rampant psychologizer, ever ready to interpret a biological urge in terms of its deeper "symbolic" meaning. Freud, by contrast, insisted on the claims of the body and refused the easy popularity Jung won for himself with his "sex-isn't-everything" propaganda. Freud in fact abhorred Jung's mystical dematerialization of the libido theory, and he wrote *Totem and Taboo,* his most biological book in Sulloway's opinion, precisely in response to Jung's dabblings in mythology and comparative religion. Far from constituting a reversion to biology, Jung's views, to Freud, represented "a new religio-ethical system." "The truth is," he continued, speaking now of both Jung and Adler, "these people have picked out a few cultural overtones from the symphony of life and have once more failed to hear the mighty and primordial melody of the instincts."[29] Thus to attribute the repression of biology to Freud's squabbles with Jung and Adler entails a peculiarly convoluted piece of reasoning.

But in Sulloway's view, Freud's wish to distance himself from Jung, like the question of his empirical credentials, was a less potent reason for the repression of biology than his need to fabricate an image of himself as a heroic innovator engaged in a lonely struggle against the prevailing ideas of his time. To establish that this self-image was in fact mythical, Sulloway proceeds to rehearse the evidence for Freud's isolation and originality, and once again he finds it wanting. Certain of Freud's autobiographical pronouncements provide Sulloway with targets as broad as a barn. In the *Autobiographical Study* of 1925, for example, Freud complains: "For more than ten years after my separation from Breuer I had no followers. I was completely isolated. In Vienna I was shunned, abroad no notice was taken of me. My *Interpretation of Dreams,* published in 1900, was scarcely reviewed in the technical journals."[30] Drawing on the work of previous scholars, notably Henri Ellenberger and Hannah Decker, Sulloway easily shows that the reception of Freud's work was less hostile than this blanket characterization implies. But

29. Freud, "On the History of the Psycho-Analytic Movement," *Standard Edition,* vol. XIV, p. 62.

30. Freud, *An Autobiographical Study, Standard Edition,* vol. XX, p. 48.

where Sulloway finds praise balanced by legitimate reservations in the reviews, Freud could see only grudging acknowledgment amidst an avalanche of criticism and a thoroughgoing refusal to recognize the significance of his discoveries. Isolation, it seems, is in the mind of the beholder. If the scientific world failed to line up in a unified reactionary chorus to condemn Freud's work, that hardly proves that he didn't feel profoundly alone and embattled. To suggest, as Sulloway does, that Freud's complaints of isolation and rejection were a calculated deception—a conspiracy abetted by his biographers—intended to conceal his intellectual debts, especially his biological ones, bespeaks a remarkably ham-fisted conception of human psychology. The Fliess correspondence, with its constant refrain of bitter loneliness from which his interlocutor's friendship provided the only relief, testifies to the depth of Freud's sense of alienation. He may have overestimated the indifference or opposition of his contemporaries, but the notion that he was engaged in a willful misrepresentation of the facts in order to hide his dark biological secret not only contradicts all the existing evidence about his state of mind but imputes to him a degree of cunning that is scarcely credible.

In much the same way, Sulloway repeatedly disputes Freud's pretensions to originality—the second historical distortion, after his isolation, on which his heroic self-image was supposedly constructed. I've already suggested that Sulloway's treatment of this issue is unsophisticated. In his final chapter he turns to Freud's express preoccupation with questions of priority, especially regarding the discovery of infantile sexuality. Following Robert Merton and Paul Roazen, who drew attention some time ago to Freud's prickliness in this respect, Sulloway has little trouble disproving Ernest Jones's contention that "Freud was

never interested in questions of priority."[31] But Freud's
concern with such questions need not be construed as evidence of a propensity for heroic self-mythologizing. If
anything, it was a normal aspect of scientific etiquette, in
Freud's day no less than ours. Scientists are routinely
given to priority disputes, because reputations so often depend on who proposed an idea first. But Sulloway insists
on a more Machiavellian explanation. "For Freud and his
movement, scientific priority was revolutionary propaganda" (476). Claims to priority contributed to the Freudian myth of heroic originality, whose defense in turn inspired the need to repress the master's debt to biology.
Such claims are thereby implicated in the larger biographical conspiracy that Sulloway aims to expose.

Exaggerated isolation and overstated claims to originality, then, do not necessarily support Sulloway's portrait of
Freud as a self-appointed hero. But Sulloway has no real
need of them. Plenty of evidence exists to show that Freud
did indeed entertain a heroic conception of his intellectual
mission. Nor has anyone ever denied this. Not only is it
prominently displayed in all the psychoanalytic biographies, above all in Jones, but Freud's own remarks in this
regard are unequivocal. Most striking is a famous letter to
his fiancée, Martha Bernays, in April 1885, announcing
that he had destroyed his papers and correspondence:

I have just carried out a resolution which one group of people, as
yet unborn and fated to misfortune, will feel acutely. Since you
can't guess whom I mean I will tell you: they are my biographers. I have destroyed all my diaries of the past fourteen years,
with letters, scientific notes and the manuscripts of my publications. . . . Let the biographers chafe; we won't make it too easy

31. Jones, *Life and Work,* III: 100.

for them. Let each one of them believe he is right in his "Conception of the Development of the Hero": even now I enjoy the thought of how they will all go astray.[32]

It is a statement of peerless self-confidence, if not outright arrogance. Even more stunning than the allusion to "the Development of the Hero" is Freud's certainty, while still less than thirty, that he would have not just one biographer but many. In the same heroic vein is the equally revealing observation, also in a letter to Martha, that "I have often felt as though I had inherited all the defiance and all the passions with which our ancestors defended their temple and could gladly sacrifice my life for one great moment in history."[33] Freud's heroic self-image expressed itself, over the course of his life, through a series of identifications, first with generals and politicians like Hannibal, Cromwell, and Napoleon, then with scientists and intellectuals like Goethe and Darwin, and finally—and most profoundly—with the revolutionary religious figure of Moses. As he told Fliess in 1900, "I am actually not at all a man of science, not an observer, not an experimenter, not a thinker. I am by temperament nothing but a conquistador—an adventurer, if you want it translated—with all the curiosity, daring, and tenacity characteristic of a man of this sort."[34]

By all evidence, then, Freud's heroic self-conception was both pronounced and enduring. Curiously, Sulloway's thesis forces him to imagine, on the contrary, that it was surprisingly fragile, indeed so fragile that it would

32. Freud, quoted in Jones, *Life and Work,* I:xii–xiii.
33. Freud, *The Letters of Sigmund Freud,* ed. Ernst L. Freud, trans. Tania Stern and James Stern (London, 1960), p. 202.
34. Freud, *Complete Letters to Fliess,* p. 398.

have come unstuck had Freud or his biographers failed to conceal his intellectual debt to biology. To admit any common conceptual ground with Fliess, the sexologists, or even Darwin would, in this view, have reduced Freud to a mere intellectual journeyman. "To Freud," Sulloway writes, "the denial of history was a prerequisite part of being and, above all, of *remaining* a full-fledged hero in the eyes of posterity. By destroying his past, he actively sought to cultivate the 'unknowable' about himself and thereby to set himself apart from the more transparent nonheroes of humanity" (479). Even if one grants, for the sake of argument, that his debt to biology was as substantial as Sulloway says, his sense of heroic destiny was surely robust enough to withstand exposure of any hidden biological rationale lurking behind his thought. In fact, I rather imagine that he would have welcomed it as further evidence of his greatness.

Sulloway accuses the psychoanalytic biographers of perpetuating and refining Freud's own mythical representation of his intellectual odyssey, seeking to expunge even those remnants of his biological heritage that Freud was so imprudent as to reveal. To maintain this view, Sulloway must deny that the biographers were in any way motivated by a desire to understand the evolution of Freud's thought correctly. Rather, they were at all times guided by a single-minded consciousness of the political advantages of presenting Freud as a lonely proponent of unpopular ideas. To this end they denied his biological debts, transformed Fliess into a crackpot, promoted the self-analysis beyond all reason, and ignored his intellectual affinities with his contemporaries. Sulloway's conception of the biographers' motives is as unnuanced as his conception of Freud's own motives. He insists on a strictly conspiratorial view of their enterprise.

In the final segment of his book, its emotional bones are fully bared, as Sulloway's supposedly admiring biography climaxes in an orgy of Freudian mendacity and self-promotion. It is the ultimate return of the repressed, and it exposes the depth of Sulloway's hostility. Yet, ironically, he doesn't quite believe the story himself. Such, at least, is the implication of the extraordinary volte-face with which the book ends:

> In more ways than we can acknowledge, myth rules history with an iron grip, dictating the preservation of mythical fact and the destruction of antimyth long before the historian can even begin to reverse this relentless process. Mankind, it would seem, will not tolerate the critical assaults upon its heroes and the charitable reassessments of its villains that mythless history requires.
>
> In many respects, then, Freud will always remain a crypto-biologist, his self-analysis will always be seen as heroic and unprecedented, and his years of discovery will always partake of a "splendid isolation" and an inscrutable genius. After all, Freud really was a hero. The myths are merely his historical due, and they shall continue to live on, protecting his brilliant legacy to mankind, as long as this legacy remains a powerful part of human consciousness. (503)

This is the only passage in Sulloway's long book that might be described as genuinely Freudian, echoing as it does the melancholy resignation and misanthropy of the great cultural essays, above all *Civilization and Its Discontents*. It is also genuinely Freudian in a deeper sense, because it admits a profound truth to whose obfuscation the complex apparatus of Sulloway's argument has been dedicated: Freud was a hero after all, a figure like Augustine, or Luther, or Darwin, or Marx, who changed the way we think.

Perhaps the final irony is that Sulloway's supposedly contextualist revision ignores the two contexts that recent historical studies have identified as especially pertinent to an accurate understanding of Freud's thought. The first of these is fin-de-siècle Vienna, with its peculiar blend of moribund liberalism and burgeoning anti-Semitism—a political and cultural hothouse from which a number of remarkable creations emerged. This perspective on Freud has been advanced by Carl Schorske, William McGrath, Hannah Decker, and Allan Janik and Stephen Toulmin, all of whom link Freud's psychological ideas in interesting ways to the political ambience of his city. But Sulloway makes little of Vienna, and nothing of its politics. Apparently, the city's sole contribution was to have given Freud an exaggerated impression of nineteenth-century prudery. Likewise Sulloway's few remarks about anti-Semitism indicate that he finds its significance negligible. In fact, anti-Semitism appears in Myth 19 of his comprehensive chart cataloguing twenty-six "Major Freud Myths" (489–95).

A second context, identified in a number of scholarly studies but most impressively in H. Stuart Hughes's *Consciousness and Society: The Reorientation of European Social Thought, 1890–1930,* is the broader configuration of European intellectual life at the turn of the century. Unlike Sulloway's book, *Consciousness and Society* is not a study of influences but an attempt to identify the deep affinities that united a generation of European thinkers in a shared enterprise. Hughes places Freud in the company of such contemporaneous figures as Max Weber, Hans Vaihinger, Ernst Mach, Benedetto Croce, and Georges Sorel, who collectively brought about a dramatic shift in European intellectual concerns. Hughes calls that shift "a revolt against positivism," by which he means the effort to liberate thought from its nineteenth-century scientific fetters and promote instead a greater attention to subjectivity.[35] Freud's move from neurology to psychology was paradigmatic of this intellectual reorientation, and he is, along with Weber, a central presence in Hughes's story. A similar perspective is suggested by the substantial scholarship that links Freud with his somewhat younger contemporary Friedrich Nietzsche. But no more than fin-de-siècle Vienna does the revolt against positivism figure in Sulloway's conception of the intellectual milieu in which psychoanalysis was born. His silence is perfectly understandable: Hughes's argument directly contradicts Sulloway's insistence on the enduring influence of one of the archetypal forms of nineteenth-century positivism, Darwinism. But if Hughes is correct, as I think he is, positivism was in retreat in the early twentieth century, as it came under assault, directly or indirectly, from the new philosophers of self-consciousness, Freud chief among them. Sulloway's repeated invocation of the neglected intellectual context of Freud's ideas thus ignores the most widespread and profound intellectual development of the age.

■   ■   ■

In the bibliographical essay appended to *Freud: A Life for Our Time* Peter Gay dismisses Sulloway's book as "presenting itself as a great unmasking document but bringing the essentially old news that Freud's theory had a biological background."[36] The judgment is unfair insofar as the book proposes a radically new conception of Freud's debt to biology. But it accurately reflects Sulloway's failure to

35. H. Stuart Hughes, *Consciousness and Society: The Reorientation of European Social Thought, 1890–1930* (New York, 1958), p. 37.
36. Peter Gay, *Freud: A Life for Our Time* (New York, 1988), p. 750.

make his case, and, more important, it identifies the true role of biology in Freud's intellectual biography. Indeed, the flat, deflating phrase "biological background"—alluding at once to Freud's early career in neurology and to the residual presence of biological habits of thought behind his psychological theory—nicely captures biology's marginal position in the psychoanalytic revolution.

Perhaps the single most important thing to be said about *Freud, Biologist of the Mind* is that, despite its author's extraordinary efforts, it cannot persuade us to adopt its conception of Freud's intellectual achievement. It cannot move the periphery to the center. In this respect it resembles David Bakan's *Freud and the Jewish Mystical Tradition,* which seeks to derive all of psychoanalysis from cabalistic teachings, creating an image of Freud as a crypto-Jewish-mystic. Sulloway's book thus leaves the traditional portrait of Freud as a psychological innovator with a biological background largely undisturbed. Appropriately, his book has not marked the watershed in Freud studies that he hoped and, I think, expected it would. Its central argument has been ignored not only by Freud's partisans but by his enemies as well. Some part of the book's failure must be attributed to its ambivalence toward its subject. Ostensibly, it presents Freud as an even larger figure than the person we meet in the traditional biographies—a giant whose true intellectual accomplishment has yet to be recognized. In reality, however, it belittles Freud, not merely because of its repeated charges of ruthless ambition and dishonesty, but, more important, because it diminishes the very ideas that have made him one of the most influential thinkers of the century. The Freud it pretends to unveil and celebrate is simply not the Freud of history.

At times, Sulloway seems at least dimly aware of his book's hostile undertow. He notes that "there are many individuals sharing . . . a negative persuasion about psychoanalysis who might easily seize upon the substance of this book in order to bolster their arguments about the folly of Freud's theories" (499). Sulloway assures us that his intent is just the opposite—that he ranks Freud alongside Darwin and Aristotle among the greatest figures in the life sciences. But in truth his book deserves an honored place in the anti-Freudian canon. It may not have inaugurated the scholarly transformation that Sulloway thought it would, but, in hindsight, it can be seen as the opening salvo in the campaign against Freud's reputation that would escalate into war during the succeeding decade. The more consistently anti-Freudian writings of Jeffrey Masson are its natural successor.

II

Jeffrey Masson:
Freud, Seduction,
and the New Puritanism

The intellectual and emotional distance separating Frank Sulloway's *Freud, Biologist of the Mind* (1979) from Jeffrey Masson's *The Assault on Truth: Freud's Suppression of the Seduction Theory* (1984) is substantial. In Masson's book the ambivalence and muteness of Sulloway's anti-Freudianism give way to consistent and strident hostility. Where Sulloway's Freud is an example of hidden greatness marred by ambition, Masson's Freud is one of failed greatness ruined by cowardice. Clearly, by the mid-1980s the anti-Freudian mood was growing more aggressive, and Jeffrey Masson had become its foremost spokesman.

Sulloway's and Masson's books also differ in scope. As we have seen, Sulloway aimed to write a full intellectual biography that would displace the traditional account of Freud's development as a thinker. Masson's ambition initially seems much more modest: he focuses on a single incident in Freud's career, the abandonment of the seduction theory in September 1897. But, for Masson, the whole of Freud's intellectual achievement was at stake in this decision. Indeed, Masson believes that the history not merely of psychoanalysis but of twentieth-century humanity was profoundly altered as a result of Freud's change of heart. Thus the narrowing of focus as one moves from Sulloway to Masson is more apparent than real, especially when one bears in mind that Sulloway's interpretation of Freud is itself limited to identifying the hidden Darwinian rationale of psychoanalysis. One could very well argue that both interpreters are guilty of subordinating Freud's life work to a single preoccupation—in Masson's case the seduction theory, in Sulloway's the repressed sense of smell.

But there is a more important difference between the two. Masson's attack came from within the psychoanalytic establishment and has resulted in a bruising battle of personalities, while Sulloway has remained very much the outsider whose book created nothing like the storm of controversy attending Masson's apostasy. In the 1970s Masson, then a loyal Freudian, insinuated himself into the psychoanalytic hierarchy, befriending some of its most powerful figures and ultimately winning the sponsorship of Kurt Eissler, the director of the Freud Archives, the collection of materials on the history of psychoanalysis now housed in the Library of Congress. So impressed was Eissler with Masson that he chose him to be his successor and installed him in the provisional job of projects director, where Masson was put in charge of the publication of a complete edition of Freud's correspondence with Fliess. But at a meeting of the Western New England Psychoanalytic Society in June of 1981, Masson revealed surprisingly iconoclastic ideas about the seduction theory. *The New York Times* printed two articles reporting on that meeting, as well as a subsequent interview with Masson, after which Eissler felt compelled to fire him. Then, even before the appearance of *The Assault on Truth,* Masson was catapulted to a new level of notoriety by Janet Malcolm's two long articles about him in *The New Yorker,* which appeared in 1983 and were later issued in book form as *In the Freud Archives*. Virtually everybody who read the Malcolm articles remembers them less for their careful account of Masson's views on the seduction theory than for their portrait of an intellectual opportunist and philanderer, who boasted of having slept with nearly a thousand women. Masson sued Malcolm, and the case eventually made its way to the Supreme Court, suggesting that Jeffrey Masson may well be remembered more as a figure in the history of American libel law than as a critic of psychoanalysis. In *Final Analysis: The Making and Unmaking of a Psychoanalyst* (1990) he has written his own version of his rude expulsion from the Freudian empyrean—an account that sheds interesting light on the view of Freud he expounds in *The Assault on Truth*. Meanwhile, Frank Sulloway spent the tumultuous years in which Masson was becoming a celebrity and the subject of much psychoanalytic tooth-gnashing rather quietly as a historian of science (he is now a visiting scholar at MIT) and as the dignified recipient of a MacArthur grant.

This contrast between the contentious, highly visible Masson and the retiring, academic Sulloway is aptly reflected in the tone of their respective books. Actually, by ordinary standards, Sulloway himself is anything but modest. *Freud, Biologist of the Mind* is shamelessly self-regarding, both in its inflated intellectual claims and in the solipsism of its prose. But set beside the slash-and-burn, scorched-earth manner of Masson, Sulloway sounds decidedly pedantic. His sentences are overburdened and ornate, while Masson's are direct, simple, and breezy. Above all, Masson writes in the charged language of moral indignation, his discussion of historical questions giving way easily and often to personal judgment and ad

hominem attack. His idiosyncrasies notwithstanding, with
Sulloway one never doubts that the real issue is one of intellectual history—of getting Freud's story properly told.
With Masson, by way of contrast, the reader is aware that
just beneath the surface of historical debate lies a bitter and
ongoing controversy within the psychoanalytic profession.
Masson's subject may be Freud himself, but the true object
of his enmity is psychoanalysis in the 1980s. He attacks the
root in order to kill the tree.

THE ABANDONED SEDUCTION THEORY

To appreciate the impact of *The Assault on Truth,* one must
begin with a firm understanding of the place of the seduction theory in the history of Freud's thought. More precisely, one must begin with an understanding of the place
the seduction theory has come to occupy in the traditional
story of Freud's intellectual development. Without exaggeration, the abandonment of the seduction hypothesis
figures as the central event in the discovery of psychoanalysis, both in Freud's own account and in that of his biographers. Thus, in championing the seduction theory and
questioning the validity of Freud's reasons for rejecting it,
Masson's book undermines the received conception of
Freud's intellectual achievement, just as it casts doubt on
his integrity.

For approximately four years during the mid-1890s,
Freud believed that certain forms of mental illness, notably hysteria, originated in premature sexual traumas. His
hysterical patients, he became convinced, had been subjected to sexual abuse—seduction—before puberty, and
the repressed memory of those assaults was the cause of
their illness. Typically (although not exclusively) Freud
identified a parent, usually the father, as the author of

these childhood assaults, just as a daughter was the characteristic victim. Freud first mentioned the seduction hypothesis in a letter to Fliess of May 30, 1893, and one can trace Freud's rising confidence in the theory through the correspondence of the following years. On April 21, 1896, he presented his theory to the public in the form of a lecture, "The Aetiology of Hysteria," given before the Society for Psychiatry and Neurology in Vienna. He published the lecture the following month. The theory was also articulated in two other scientific papers of 1896, "Heredity and the Aetiology of the Neuroses" and "Further Remarks on the Neuro-Psychoses of Defence."

But little more than a year later, on September 21, 1897, Freud wrote Fliess what has come to be regarded as the most important letter in the history of psychoanalysis. In it Freud announced that he had lost faith in his seduction hypothesis. As he put the matter himself, "I no longer believe in my *neurotica*"—his theory of the neuroses.[1] Freud gave four reasons for his disbelief, of which the second was doubtless the weightiest:

The surprise that in all cases, the *father,* not excluding my own, had to be accused of being perverse—the realization of the unexpected frequency of hysteria, with precisely the same conditions prevailing in each, whereas surely such widespread perversions against children are not very probable. The [incidence of] perversion would have to be immeasurably more frequent than the [resulting] hysteria because the illness, after all, occurs only where there has been an accumulation of events and there is a contributory factor that weakens the defense.[2]

1. Freud, *The Complete Letters of Sigmund Freud to Wilhelm Fliess, 1887–1907,* ed. and trans. Jeffrey Moussaieff Masson (Cambridge, Mass., 1985), p. 264.
2. Ibid.

Freud didn't confess his change of mind in print until eight years later, in the *Three Essays on the Theory of Sexuality,* and then only in language that is surprisingly evasive. He eventually came to think that his patients' accounts of seduction most often originated in fantasies, and that their root lay not in the perverse actions of adults but in the spontaneous sexual desires of children. In this fashion, the abandonment of the seduction theory promoted the emergence of the idea of infantile sexuality, and in particular the notion of the Oedipus complex—first mentioned in a letter to Fliess of October 15, 1897, less than a month after Freud announced his rejection of the seduction hypothesis. At the same time, the new role assigned to fantasy considerably enhanced the importance of the unconscious in Freud's conception of psychic life. In other words, the two pillars of mature psychoanalytic theory—infantile sexuality and the unconscious—were, one might say, the intellectual beneficiaries of the change of view Freud announced in his September letter. Indeed, in later accounts of his intellectual development, Freud and his biographers were to maintain that if the error of the seduction theory had not been recognized, psychoanalysis would never have been born. Instead, Freud would have remained stuck in a mistaken environmental interpretation of psychological development and would have failed to grasp the role of indigenous desire and the unconscious in mental life.

In *The Assault on Truth,* however, Masson contends that Freud's original view was correct and his abandonment of the seduction theory in error. How Masson knows this is far from clear. The most striking feature of his book is precisely the arguments he does *not* mount. Masson is much given to talking about documents, brandishing an unreconstructed positivism in an age when the linguistic turn has made such passions seem unfashionable, if not entirely without charm. But in fact he has uncovered no documentary evidence that would enable him to settle the empirical question. He does not, for example, have access to information about the cases of hysteria—"The Aetiology of Hysteria" mentions eighteen of them—that first formed the basis of Freud's conviction and later became the source of his doubt. No clinical records or case notes have turned up. Moreover, even if such documents existed, one would be unable to penetrate beyond Freud's conviction, at the time, that the stories he elicited from his patients were true, just as one cannot penetrate beyond his later conviction that many of them were false. The question, after all, is one of interpretation. Ultimately, Masson's blithe assurance that the traumatic narratives are accurate depends on their inaccessibility: because they can never be shown to be false, Masson is free to assert their trustworthiness. Nor can he cite later studies establishing the correctness of Freud's belief that hysteria is always caused by sexual abuse in childhood, because there are no such studies. The best he can do is invoke the opinions of Sandor Ferenczi (in 1932) and Robert Fliess (in 1974), who argued that childhood sexual traumas are more often a cause of mental illness than psychoanalysts have cared to recognize.

The real source of Masson's persuasion lies in the political culture of the past decade, with its rising awareness of the abuse of children. Because we have grown increasingly conscious of sexual violence against children, Freud's belief that his patients suffered such abuse, and that it dramatically shaped their lives, strikes Masson as entirely plausible. One senses that he would prefer to deflect attention from the specific etiological claim Freud advanced—that sexual seduction in childhood is the invariable cause of one particular form of mental illness, hysteria—to a more general assertion that childhood sexual abuse is both common and the source of emotional damage. At the same time, he perhaps feared that this more general proposition would have been easily absorbed by the psychoanalytic community, since, far from clinging obdurately to fantasy as the sole explanation for tales of seduction, any number of analysts have recently put greater emphasis on childhood sexual traumas and their psychic consequences. Masson's hostility to psychoanalysis thus required a more decisive, a more dramatic, gesture. Hence his unqualified assertion that the seduction theory was absolutely correct and Freud's abandonment of it utterly mistaken.

Yet even this assertion—although it might have elicited objections of the sort I have suggested about the lack of historical or clinical evidence—would never have resulted in the major controversy that *The Assault on Truth* unleashed. Credit for the book's explosive impact goes not to the issue of seduction itself but rather to Masson's contention about what motivated Freud to change his mind. Masson argues that Freud abandoned the seduction theory because he was a liar and a coward. Freud was a liar, according to Masson, because, even when he wrote the September 21 letter, at some level he still believed that his patients' stories were true. He was a coward because the only consideration leading him to abandon the theory was his inability to bear the opposition it had provoked among his scientific contemporaries. Here we have a proposition perfectly calculated to cause scandal, especially when it is combined with repeated assertions that Freud's spineless retreat from reality—his blaming of the child for the vices of the parent—established the pattern of psychoanalytic thought and practice right down to the present day.

Not surprisingly, Masson devotes much of his attention in *The Assault on Truth* to arguing the case for this spectacularly irreverent explanation of Freud's change of heart.

Yet even here one is immediately struck by what he does *not* do. In particular, he pays only passing attention to the reasons Freud gives in his September 21 letter for no longer believing the theory. Masson has just one thing to say about these reasons: they cannot be taken seriously because Freud had already raised, and rebutted, the same objections in his articles of 1896. Masson does not bother to demonstrate the identity of these two sets of objections, although such a demonstration would seem to be a minimum requirement for dismissing them as irrelevant. Nor does he seek to answer them. Most striking of all, he gives no ground for thinking that Freud himself did not really find these reasons persuasive. One would especially like to hear why we should not credit the genuineness of Freud's conviction that, in view of the prevalence of hysteria, the traumatic etiology made sexual assaults on children much more common than seemed probable. The issue, be it noted, is not whether this reservation was justified, but whether Freud might legitimately have come to feel its weight. In effect, Masson implies that there could never be intellectually persuasive grounds for altering one's opinion about childhood seduction. Because Freud had once believed his patients' accounts, he must have been lying when he claimed to have changed his mind.

There is merit in Masson's suggestion that the September 21, 1897, letter did not mark the end of Freud's hopes for the seduction theory. In this regard Masson draws attention to two passages from subsequent letters to Fliess. Almost two months later, on December 12, 1897, Freud reported on a patient treated by Emma Eckstein. Eckstein had evidently obtained an account of a childhood seduction by the patient's father: "My confidence in paternal etiology has risen greatly," Freud writes. "Eckstein deliberately treated her patient in such a manner as not to give her

the slightest hint of what would emerge from the unconscious and in the process obtained from her, among other
things, the identical scenes with the father."[3] The phrase
"paternal etiology" is Freud's shorthand for his seduction
hypothesis; the same locution occurs in a letter of April 28,
1897, where its meaning is unambiguous. In the present
comment on Eckstein's patient, Freud seems to be arguing
against an imputation that the seduction stories were elicited by the analyst's suggestion. Nonetheless, the statement that his "confidence" in the seduction theory has
"risen greatly" shows that the renunciation letter of September 21, despite its categorical language ("I no longer
believe in my *neurotica*"), did not mark a clean break with
the hypothesis. But Masson overinterprets Freud's briefly
resurgent expectations, writing that "it was as though
Freud were telling Fliess: I was too hasty, I believe I was
right to think that seductions occur and can be remembered in analysis."[4]

In his next letter, dated December 22, 1897, Freud
recounts another case in which a real childhood trauma
occurs:

The intrinsic authenticity of infantile trauma is borne out by the
following little incident which the patient claims to have observed as a three-year-old child. She goes into a dark room
where her mother is carrying on and eavesdrops. She has good
reason for identifying herself with this mother. The father belongs to the category of *men who stab women,* for whom bloody
injuries are an erotic need. When she was two years old, he bru-

3. Ibid., p. 286.
4. Jeffrey Moussaieff Masson, *The Assault on Truth: Freud's Suppression of the Seduction Theory* (New York, 1984), p. 115. Hereafter, page
references to this work will appear in parentheses in the text.

tally deflowered her and infected her with his gonorrhea, as a consequence of which she became ill and her life was endangered by the loss of blood and vaginitis.[5]

In contrast to his remark on Eckstein's patient, Freud here makes no reference to the import of this case for his conviction about the "paternal etiology." Moreover, even late in his career Freud continued to believe that a significant proportion of his patients' accounts of childhood sexual abuse were genuine. Still, the proximity of this narrative to the Eckstein case mentioned some ten days earlier probably justifies seeing in it revived enthusiasm for the seduction hypothesis. Both passages imply a certain volatility in Freud's thinking on the subject late in 1897. But they do not support the more radical proposition that he was dissembling when, in the famous renunciation letter of September 21, 1897, he told Fliess he no longer believed in the theory. We should hardly be surprised that Freud was reluctant to part with an idea from which, as he confessed, he had expected to win "eternal fame . . . , certain wealth, complete independence, travels, and lifting the children above the severe worries that robbed me of my youth."[6]

Like his contention that Freud's patients were telling the truth about their childhood seductions, Masson's accusation that Freud changed his mind because he couldn't bear the disapproval of his medical colleagues floats in a kind of epistemological void. Masson can assert it without ever fearing that it might be disproved. After all, it alludes to an intrapsychic event—something invisible—against which countervailing evidence isn't even imaginable. Instead, in order to lend the accusation an aura of plausibility,

5. Freud, *Complete Letters to Fliess*, p. 288.
6. Ibid., p. 266.

Masson attempts to clear a kind of historical space for it. In particular he draws attention to the hostile reception that greeted Freud's lecture on "The Aetiology of Hysteria." Writing to Fliess five days afterward, Freud reported:

A lecture on the etiology of hysteria at the psychiatric society was given an icy reception by the asses and a strange evaluation by Krafft-Ebing: "It sounds like a scientific fairy tale." And this, after one has demonstrated to them the solution of a more-than-thousand-year-old problem, a *caput Nili* [source of the Nile]! They can go to hell, euphemistically expressed.[7]

Masson's conclusion that the hostility evoked by the lecture broke Freud's spirit rests, above all, on a complaint registered in the next letter to Fliess: "I am as isolated as you would wish me to be. Word was given out to abandon me, for a void is forming all around me."[8] The presentation of the seduction hypothesis, in other words, resulted in Freud's professional isolation, which he ultimately found unbearable and from which he sought to escape by sacrificing the theory. At the opposite end of the evidential tunnel, Masson notes that only after he had published his recantation (in the *Three Essays on the Theory of Sexuality*) was Freud able to gather about him a group of disciples and thus bring his intolerable isolation to an end.

What most astonishes in Masson's presentation of this hypothesis is his failure to address the obvious objections. Perhaps first is the simple fact that less than two weeks after giving the lecture on "The Aetiology of Hysteria," and after bemoaning his isolation, Freud resolved to publish the essay, almost as if to prove that he was not so easily cowed: "In defiance of my colleagues I wrote down in full

7. Ibid., p. 184.   8. Ibid., p. 185.

for Paschkis [editor of the *Wiener klinische Rundschau*] my lecture on the etiology of hysteria. The first installment appears today."[9] This response is in keeping with everything we know about Freud's character, as attested to by friend and foe alike: he positively reveled in opposition, and his mental toughness and tolerance for conflict were seemingly boundless. Opponents of psychoanalysis have often complained that he was immune to criticism, no matter how just. Masson's image of him caving in to peer pressure on an issue where he felt truth was on his side makes no characterological sense.

The hypothesis is also beset by chronological problems, above all by the fact that Freud's feeling of isolation predates the lecture of April 21, 1896. The Fliess correspondence and even the earlier letters to his wife give the impression that for years Freud positively cultivated his loneliness. In a typical complaint of March 16, 1896, he writes: "I am satisfied with my progress, but am contending with hostility and live in such isolation that one might imagine I had discovered the greatest truths."[10] In editing the Fliess correspondence, Masson tries to shape the evidence to fit his hypothesis by grouping the letters after the April 21, 1896, lecture under the rubric "Isolation from the Scientific Community."[11] But the abandonment of the seduction theory announced on September 21, 1897, cannot be meaningfully correlated with Freud's feelings of isolation, which, while they may have reached a high point in the wake of his April 1896 lecture, pervaded the 1890s.

Masson's own book supplies evidence that scholarly research on childhood sexual abuse did not necessarily

---

9. Ibid., p. 190.   10. Ibid., p. 179.
11. Ibid., p. 183.

constitute a bar to professional recognition in the nineteenth century. His second chapter argues that Freud may
have been introduced to the seduction issue during his visit
to Paris in 1885–86. There, Masson suggests, Freud probably became familiar with the views on child abuse of
Ambroise Tardieu (1818–1879), Paul Bernard (1828–1886),
and Paul Brouardel (1837–1906), all of whom wrote about
sexual assaults on children. Freud attended Brouardel's
lectures at the Paris Morgue—Masson speculates that he
may have observed Brouardel conduct autopsies on victims of child abuse—and he had the relevant publications
of all three authorities in his library (although one cannot
determine when he obtained them or, for that matter,
whether he had read them, since none of them is anno-
tated). If, as Masson argues, Freud was familiar with the
work of these figures, he must also have known that their
exploration of child abuse brought them not ignominy but
renown. Masson himself notes that Tardieu was professor
of legal medicine at the University of Paris, dean of the
Faculty of Medicine, president of the Academy of Medicine in Paris, and, in the words of the *Dictionnaire encyclo-
pédique des sciences médicales* of 1885, "the most eminent
representative of French legal medicine" (15). Bernard was
professor of criminal law on the Faculty of Law in Lyon,
while Brouardel succeeded to Tardieu's chair in Paris and
was known as the "Pontifex Maximus" (30) of French
medicine. These rather inconvenient facts force Masson
into arguing that Freud's isolation was a strictly Viennese
affair and, by implication, that he threw over the seduction
theory to win back the good opinion of his local colleagues. It is a kind of perverse variation on the "Viennese" Freud that both Carl Schorske and William Mc-
Grath champion with such sophistication and delicacy. A
more plausible reading would suggest that the opposition

to the seduction theory, as registered by Freud's colleagues in April of 1896, rested not, as Masson would have it, on some visceral inability to accept the reality of childhood sexual abuse but on a rational skepticism about the sweeping etiological generalization Freud had proposed, namely, that such abuse was the necessary and invariable cause of hysteria.

Surely, however, the most powerful objection to Masson's thesis of moral cowardice is that Freud abandoned the seduction theory only to embrace an idea that was even more offensive to the prejudices of his culture, the theory of infantile sexuality. The new doctrine, far from being a gesture of reconciliation, transgressed the most cherished belief of nineteenth-century sexual ideology, the innocence of childhood. If Freud's decision to abandon the seduction theory was guided by a wish to ingratiate himself once again with Vienna's medical authorities, he chose a most unlikely way to achieve that end.

.   .   .

The extravagance, both intellectual and rhetorical, of Masson's thesis invites reflection. What is the meaning of this interpretation, at once so irreverent, poorly supported, and improbable? Given all the possible ways to account for Freud's decision to abandon the seduction theory, why has Masson gone out of his way to construct a hypothesis that reflects so adversely on Freud's character? The obvious temptation is to believe that Masson wishes to discredit Freud and through him the entire psychoanalytic enterprise. This suspicion finds support in Masson's own unhappy experience with analysis, recounted in *Final Analysis*. Moreover, as I have already suggested, *The Assault on Truth* doubtless mirrors the broadly felt hostility to

Freud that has emerged in the past decade; it testifies to the sensibility of our time.

But more than simple anti-Freudianism is involved. Freud's betrayal of the seduction theory exasperates Masson because it places Freud (and the profession he founded) on the wrong side of what has recently become a major issue in sexual politics: the abuse of women and children. Freud, Masson suggests, was ahead of his time: he had the insight to recognize a profound truth, as it were, prematurely. But he ruined his achievement because he lacked the fortitude to stick by his discovery when the rest of the world opposed it. Worse than this simple failure of nerve, Freud constructed an intellectual system that actually lent new and sophisticated support to the very abuses he had earlier denounced. The theory of infantile sexuality and the notion of unconscious fantasy did not simply divert attention from sexual abuse; they made children themselves responsible for the passions that the seduction theory had correctly located in adults. Thus, rather than alleviating mental illness, psychoanalysis has in fact contributed to the suffering of its patients by denying the reality of the terrible things that had been done to them and insisting that neurotics were ultimately to blame for their own unhappiness. Masson never tires of issuing this indictment, which seems to represent the ultimate source of his antipathy to Freud. He extracts a measure of revenge for Freud's betrayal by attributing his action to the basest of motives.

Beneath the simple hostility to Freud and the indignation about sexual abuse, however, the intellectual historian is inclined to detect an even deeper current of dissatisfaction, one pertaining to the modern conception of the self. When Freud gave up the seduction theory and articulated his ideas about infantile sexuality and the unconscious, he made himself the foremost spokesman for a new way of thinking about the subject. He insisted that the self cannot be imagined as a passive seat of consciousness upon which the external world leaves its impressions. Rather, the self is implicated in its own destiny; it carries within itself secret desires and unknown capacities that profoundly affect its history. Above all, the modern self is a site of internal tension and conflict. This new conception made Freud the central figure in the emergence of the modernist sensibility in the early twentieth century. It is a conception that resonates widely and deeply in the work of his most important contemporaries, whether social theorists, imaginative writers, or artists.

Masson appears to be caught up in a kind of postmodern rejection of this modern self. Repeatedly, he urges us to a return to a conception of human relations in which children are both innocent and inert—never subjects, but always objects. Initiative and aggression are, for Masson, the exclusive property of adults, especially adult males. He seems not at all mystified by the question of how these passive children eventually become dangerously active grown-ups—precisely the mystery that Freud sought to explain with his ideas of infantile sexuality and unconscious motivation. Rather, Masson accepts this dichotomy as part of the order of things. Presumably because they are sexually mature (and physically powerful), adults are the natural repositories of all sexual action. Children figure in the psychosexual economy only as victims. Masson's conception of the self is profoundly nostalgic. He seeks to return us to a sentimental intellectual dispensation that Freud did more than anyone else to undermine.

There is a similarity here between Masson and Sulloway, whose views of Freud are otherwise so unlike. Sulloway, too, sets little store by the intellectual accomplishment that actually accounts for Freud's stature. Sulloway shunts the core psychoanalytic ideas to the margins in order to identify a secret Darwinian teaching as the authentic source of Freud's greatness. For Masson those core psychoanalytic ideas are not inconsequential but malevolent, because they came between Freud and the discovery on which his greatness should have been founded. As Masson is wont to say, they mark not the birth of psychoanalysis but its death.

Masson's resistance to Freud's actual historical achievement—to his stature as the premier modernist—is expressed by way of a political fantasy. Masson constructs an imaginary scenario of what psychoanalysis might have become had Freud remained loyal to the seduction theory. Not surprisingly, this counterfactual history derives from the politics of the 1980s. In *Final Analysis* Masson writes:

I knew what I *imagined* psychoanalysis stood for: the breaking of taboos; fearless invasion into enemy territory, the enemy being ignorance; "speaking truth to power" as we had said in the sixties; abolition of denial; compassion for the suffering of others, especially for those who suffered in childhood; an uncompromising search for historical truth, no matter where this led; finding the hidden injuries of class, sexism, racism. Such was my understanding of the thrust behind Freud's creation of a new discipline, a truth-seeking instrument.[12]

In effect, Masson pictures Freud launching a political rather than an intellectual revolution—becoming the founding father not of modernism, with its richly ambivalent conception of the self, but of a crusade to abolish injustice, in particular to stamp out child abuse. In the in-

12. Jeffrey Moussaieff Masson, *Final Analysis: The Making and Unmaking of a Psychoanalyst* (New York, 1990), pp. 186–87.

troduction to *A Dark Science,* his collection of nineteenth-century psychiatric texts on female sexuality, Masson comments: "The changes that psychoanalysis introduced into society in general were far less fundamental than they would have been had Freud stood by his initial heretical and revolutionary hypothesis."[13] One might object that even during the years when he believed in the seduction theory, Freud showed no inclination to transform himself into a political activist; his hostility to the misbehavior of adults never threatened to explode the individual therapeutic framework within which he tried to undo the damage. But the point of a fantasy is to imagine the historically unimaginable. Thus Masson envisions Freud carrying out the agenda of the 1980s at the end of the nineteenth century, thereby saving humanity decades of needless misery. That modernism would have been sacrificed to this cause is a triviality, of concern only to intellectual historians.

EMMA ECKSTEIN

We have already met Emma Eckstein briefly in her role as the therapist who, in December 1897, revived Freud's hopes for the "paternal etiology" by eliciting a story of childhood seduction from one of her patients. But Emma Eckstein has a much larger part to play in *The Assault on Truth.* More than a quarter of Masson's text is devoted to Eckstein's own experiences as a patient in the mid-1890s, and it would not be inaccurate to call her the book's heroine. In this capacity she is assigned two closely related functions. First, in Freud's response to Eckstein, Masson

13. Jeffrey Moussaieff Masson, ed., *A Dark Science: Women, Sexuality, and Psychiatry in the Nineteenth Century* (New York, 1986), p. 4.

finds an exact structural parallel to the abandonment of the seduction theory, a kind of model for his fateful change of view. To be precise, Freud's treatment of Eckstein exemplifies the same disgraceful pattern whereby fantasy displaced reality in his thinking. Second, Eckstein is herself made the victim of a childhood sexual assault, the reality of which Masson uses to rebuke Freud once again for his intellectual retreat. These two functions are permitted to intermingle, because Masson wishes to keep the seduction hypothesis in the reader's mind even when the events he describes (as in the case of his structural parallel) appear to have nothing to do with seduction.

The saga of Emma Eckstein, as revealed in the Fliess correspondence, is spectacularly interesting. References to her were excised from the original edition of the letters, but Freud's physician, Max Schur, was given access to the originals when he was preparing his biography of Freud, and in 1966 Schur published the deleted passages in an article. They tell a remarkable story of medical malfeasance on the part of Fliess, abetted by Freud, whose reaction to Eckstein's misfortune is the main source of Masson's structural parallel.

Emma Eckstein was one of Freud's early analytic patients. Her exact problem cannot be determined, but she seems to have suffered from painful or irregular menstruation. In accordance with Fliess's naso–genital theory, Freud and Fliess decided she needed an operation on her nose, and in February 1895 Fliess came from Berlin to Vienna to perform the surgery, removing her turbinate bone. Following the operation, however, Eckstein did not heal. Instead, she experienced "persistent swelling," "purulent secretion," and finally "a massive hemorrhage."[14] When

14. Freud, *Complete Letters to Fliess,* p. 113.

her suffering continued, other doctors were summoned. Freud's account (in a letter to Fliess dated March 8, 1895) of what then transpired makes for gripping reading:

I wrote you that the swelling and the hemorrhages would not stop, and that suddenly a fetid odor set in, and that there was an obstacle upon irrigation. . . . I arranged for Gersuny to be called in; he inserted a drainage tube, hoping that things would work out once discharge was reestablished; but otherwise he was rather reserved. Two days later I was awakened in the morning—profuse bleeding had started again, pain, and so on. Gersuny replied on the phone that he was unavailable till evening; so I asked Rosanes to meet me. He did so at noon. There still was moderate bleeding from the nose and mouth; the fetid odor was very bad. Rosanes cleaned the area surrounding the opening, removed some sticky blood clots, and suddenly pulled at something like a thread, kept on pulling. Before either of us had time to think, at least half a meter of gauze had been removed from the cavity. The next moment came a flood of blood. The patient turned white, her eyes bulged, and she had no pulse. Immediately thereafter, however, he again packed the cavity with fresh iodoform gauze and the hemorrhage stopped. It lasted about half a minute, but this was enough to make the poor creature, whom by then we had lying flat, unrecognizable. In the meantime— that is, afterward—something else happened. At the moment the foreign body came out and everything became clear to me— and I immediately afterward was confronted by the sight of the patient—I felt sick. After she had been packed, I fled to the next room, drank a bottle of water, and felt miserable. The brave Frau Doktor then brought me a small glass of cognac and I became myself again.

. . . She had not lost consciousness during the massive hemorrhage; when I returned to the room somewhat shaky, she greeted me with the condescending remark, "So this is the strong sex."

I do not believe it was the blood that overwhelmed me—at that moment strong emotions were welling up in me. So we had done her an unjustice; she was not at all abnormal; rather, a piece of iodoform gauze had gotten torn off as you were removing it and stayed in for fourteen days, preventing healing; at the end it tore off and provoked the bleeding. That this mishap should have happened to you; how you will react to it when you hear about it; what others could make of it; how wrong I was to urge you to operate in a foreign city where you could not follow through on the case; how my intention to do my best for this poor girl was insidiously thwarted and resulted in endangering her life—all this came over me simultaneously.[15]

Despite the removal of the gauze that was the immediate cause of the hemorrhages, Eckstein suffered three more episodes of nasal bleeding over the course of the next month. A year later, in April and May of 1896, Freud developed a psychological explanation for Eckstein's persistent hemorrhaging. He concluded that it was hysterical in origin, "occasioned by *longing*," in particular, longing for Freud himself.[16] He gives the fullest version of his hypothesis in a letter of May 4, 1896:

As for Eckstein—I am taking notes on her history so that I can send it to you—so far I know only that she bled out of *longing*. She has always been a bleeder, when cutting herself and in similar circumstances; as a child she suffered from severe nosebleeds; during the years when she was not yet menstruating, she had headaches which were interpreted to her as malingering and which in truth had been generated by suggestion; for this reason she joyously welcomed her severe menstrual bleeding as proof that her illness was genuine, a proof that was also recognized as such by others. She described a scene from the age of fifteen, in

15. Ibid., pp. 116–17.   16. Ibid., p. 183.

which she suddenly began to bleed from the nose when she had the wish to be treated by a certain young doctor who was present (and who also appeared in the dream). When she saw how affected I was by her first hemorrhage while she was in the hands of Rosanes, she experienced this as the realization of an old wish to be loved in her illness, and in spite of the danger during the succeeding hours she felt happy as never before. Then, in the sanatorium, she became restless during the night because of an unconscious wish to entice me to go there; since I did not come during the night, she renewed the bleedings, as an unfailing means of rearousing my affection. She bled spontaneously three times and each bleeding lasted for four days, which must have some significance. She still owes me details and specific dates.[17]

Max Schur interprets this entire episode in terms of the pathology of Freud's relationship with Fliess. It reveals, according to Schur, the depth of Freud's neurotic dependence on Fliess and his consequent need to go to any length to exonerate his friend. But, unlike Schur and Freud's other biographers, Masson is not interested in Freud's peculiar emotional ties to Fliess. Nor is he interested in Fliess's intellectual influence on Freud, as is Sulloway. Masson chooses instead to construct a reading of the Eckstein episode in which every element is equated with a corresponding moment in the history of the seduction theory. Although the parallel between Eckstein's story and the fate of the seduction theory is not always made explicit, there can be no doubt that it is the underlying source of Masson's interest in her. The Eckstein case, Masson suggests, established an unhappy pattern in Freud's intellectual history.

17. Ibid., p. 186.

In this structural parallel, Fliess's original operation assumes the position of a childhood seduction. It is, above all, a real event, an actual trauma, just as the seductions were real. What's more, like a childhood seduction, it is an abnormal or perverse event, its perversity residing not in the victim but in the authority figures (the counterparts of the parents), Freud and Fliess. Indeed, it is doubly perverse: first, because it was undertaken on the basis of Fliess's crackpot ideas, and second, because Fliess blundered by leaving half a meter of gauze in the wound.

Eckstein's hemorrhaging in turn corresponds to the neurotic illness that, according to the seduction theory, results from childhood sexual abuse. The important thing about the hemorrhaging, given Masson's parallel, is that it was actually caused by the operation, just as hysteria is caused by the real sexual abuse inflicted on children. This is true, Masson firmly implies, not merely of the bleeding that occurred in the immediate wake of Fliess's operation and again when Rosanes removed the gauze, but also of the three hemorrhages during the following month.

Freud's hypothesis, developed a year later, that Eckstein's bleeding was hysterical—the result of an erotic attachment to Freud—corresponds to the abandonment of the seduction theory and the substitution of infantile sexual desire and fantasy as the sources of neurosis. Now Freud says that the patient's illness originated in her own imagination—which, significantly, is erotically charged—rather than in a real traumatic event suffered at the hands of others. The patient/child's fantasy has, in effect, replaced the doctors/parents' perverse actions as the causal agent. To make the analogy perfect, however, Freud would have had to believe that not merely the three final hemorrhages but also the earlier ones (right after Fliess's operation and at the time the gauze was removed) were products of unconscious desire. In this way, Eckstein's original trauma could be made to disappear entirely, as did the childhood sexual assaults when Freud gave up the seduction theory. But Freud's statement, in the May 4 letter, that "she bled spontaneously three times" clearly alludes only to the later episodes. Hence Masson must be satisfied with a weaker version of his parallel: the original operation has not been utterly abolished into fantasy, as were the childhood seductions, but it has "receded far into the background" (102) and "seems to have been completely forgotten" (103).

To round out the analogy, Masson assigns Fliess a role in the episode roughly akin to that of Freud's Viennese colleagues, whom Freud supposedly tried to appease by relinquishing the seduction theory. Granted, Masson does not draw this parallel expressly, but its presence is strongly felt. In this view, Fliess becomes a powerful medical authority whose disapproval Freud could not tolerate and for whose sake Freud was prepared to deny the significance of real abuse—the bungled operation—in favor of a theory of imaginary erotic desires. This explains Masson's lack of interest in the specific psychopathology of Freud's emotional bond to Fliess and his tendency to see Fliess simply as a doctor, another of those colleagues whose ideas and judgment Freud overvalued. In other words, Masson stresses the symptomatic character of Freud's deference to Fliess: the incident shows Freud spinelessly retreating from reality in order to ingratiate himself with a presumed medical expert.

No matter how one construes it, the Emma Eckstein episode makes Freud look bad. Indeed, one suspects that Masson dwells on it at such length at least in part because he is eager to display Freud's shortcomings. But Masson's explicit purpose remains to enlist the episode as evidence for his explanation of the decision to abandon the seduction theory. Unfortunately, the episode can provide only an analogy, and an imperfect one at that. While analogies may lend plausibility to an idea, their authority is always less than decisive. Masson seeks to give his analogy greater weight by introducing evidence concerning Emma Eckstein's own childhood seduction. Freud, Masson argues, must have believed that Eckstein herself was a victim of childhood sexual abuse, because he diagnosed her as a hysteric at a time when he still subscribed to the seduction theory and hence believed that *all* cases of hysteria originated in childhood assaults. Beyond this purely inferential reason, Masson bases his claim on direct evidence of an actual assault in Eckstein's childhood, though not the original (presumably parental) assault that he considers the ultimate source of her illness. This evidence comes from the 1895 *Project for a Scientific Psychology,* which contains an account of a patient called "Emma" whom Masson says, plausibly, is none other than Emma Eckstein. The Emma of the *Project* suffers from a neurotic aversion to entering shops, which Freud traces to an early sexual experience:

Emma is subject at the present time to a compulsion of not being able to go into shops *alone.* As a reason for this, [she produced] a memory from the time when she was twelve years old (shortly after puberty). She went into a shop to buy something, saw the two shop-assistants (one of whom she can remember) laughing together, and ran away in some kind of *affect of fright.* In connection with this, she was led to recall that the two of them were laughing at her clothes and that one of them had pleased her sexually. . . .

Further investigation now revealed a second memory, which she denies having had in mind at the moment of Scene I. . . . On two occasions when she was a child of eight she had gone into a small shop to buy some sweets, and the shopkeeper had grabbed at her genitals through her clothes. In spite of the first experience she had gone there a second time; after the second time she stopped away. She now reproached herself for having gone there the second time, as though she had wanted in that way to provoke the assault. In fact a state of "oppressive bad conscience" is to be traced back to this experience.[18]

In interpreting this account, Masson emphasizes that Freud considered Emma's memory entirely reliable: it accurately recaptured a little girl's abuse by an older man, an experience that subsequently gave rise to her neurotic symptom. Of course, the fact that Freud would attribute Emma's compulsion about entering shops to a real childhood experience is neither surprising nor significant. After all, the *Project for a Scientific Psychology* was written in 1895: the seduction hypothesis was in the ascendant, and the Emma of the *Project* is just one of many hysterical patients whose analysis seemed to support Freud's hypothesis. But Masson conveniently ignores the characteristic way in which Freud's narrative implicates the patient in the origins of her own illness. In terms of the emergence of psychoanalysis, what is in fact most striking about the passage is not Freud's view of the abuse itself but his focus on Emma's return to the scene of the crime, as well as her sexual attraction to one of the shop assistants in the later episode. In other words, where Masson wants to find guilty adult males, Freud presents the much more ambivalent picture of a girl whose desires play into the hands of her abusers.

18. Freud, *Project for a Scientific Psychology*, in *The Standard Edition of the Complete Psychological Works of Sigmund Freud*, translated from the German under the general editorship of James Strachey (London, 1953–74), vol. I, pp. 353–54.

What difference does it make that the Emma whom the shopkeeper abused was apparently the same Emma whose surgical mistreatment by Fliess Freud sought to excuse with his diagnosis of hysterical longing? Logically speaking, there is no connection between the two. But Masson labors mightily to juxtapose them in such a fashion that they might lend substance to his thesis about the abandonment of the seduction theory. He tries to connect the two by arguing that once Freud had explained away Fliess's bungled operation in terms of Emma's hysterical longing, Freud was liberated to think that her story of childhood seduction was also imaginary: "If Emma Eckstein's problems (her bleeding) had nothing to do with the real world (Fliess's operation), then her earlier accounts of seduction could well be fantasies too" (99). This reasoning, however, appears more forcible than it actually is. It rests on the assumption that Freud's conviction about the reality or unreality of Eckstein's childhood seduction was uniquely decisive for the fate of the seduction theory—more decisive, that is, than his conviction about the seduction stories told to him by his many other patients. But there is no reason to think this was the case. The accident of Emma Eckstein being the subject of both stories creates the impression of a meaningful connection when in fact none exists. Recognizing perhaps that he has been unable to forge a persuasive link between the two Emma stories, or to use either one to prove that Freud gave up the seduction theory out of moral cowardice, Masson falls back in the end on a categorical assertion:

From 1894 through 1897, no subjects so preoccupied Freud as the reality of seduction and the fate of Emma Eckstein. The two topics seemed bound together. It is, in my opinion, no coincidence that once Freud had determined that Emma Eckstein's hemorrhages were hysterical, the result of sexual fantasies, he was free to abandon the seduction hypothesis. (107)

Even if we grant Masson's dubious promotion of Emma Eckstein into a major preoccupation, the case for her central role in the abandonment of the seduction theory is hopelessly contrived—an unstable compound of inference, hypothesis, analogy, and not a little sleight-of-hand. Ultimately, as far as the seduction theory is concerned, Eckstein is a red herring. She tells us a good deal about Freud's unhealthy attachment to Fliess and his weakness for psychological speculation (and, as Max Schur has shown, she is also an important source for Freud's famous specimen dream of Irma's injection, the theme of which is medical incompetence). But, when it comes to understanding why, in 1897, Freud ceased to believe in his *neurotica,* Emma Eckstein is no more relevant than Freud's other patients. The fact that Masson lavishes so much attention on her, expending such energy constructing what is finally a ramshackle argument for her significance, again makes one wonder about his motives. Above all, Emma Eckstein is for him a woman whom Freud and Fliess abused. She is thus the prototypical psychoanalytic victim. Through Masson's reconstruction she is empowered to give voice to the mute sufferings of generations of women at the hands of men, notably male analysts. This symbolic function, rather than her putative role in the abandonment of the seduction theory, explains her dominant place in *The Assault on Truth.*

SANDOR FERENCZI

If Emma Eckstein is the heroine of Masson's book (and Freud its villain), then Sandor Ferenczi is its hero. *The*

Assault on Truth ends with a long chapter on what Masson calls "The Strange Case of Ferenczi's Last Paper." Like the chapter on Eckstein, it attempts to lend credibility to Masson's thesis about the seduction theory by way of an argument that is again entirely inferential. At the same time, Ferenczi becomes for Masson the central figure in his imaginary counterhistory of psychoanalysis, whose vicissitudes he traces from Freud in 1896, through Ferenczi in 1932, to his own presentation to the Western New England Psychoanalytic Society in 1981. Ferenczi's paper, delivered at the Wiesbaden Congress of the International Psychoanalytic Association, suggests what psychoanalysis might have become had it remained faithful to Freud's original seduction theory.

The paper, "Confusion of Tongues between Adults and the Child," argues that real childhood seductions are more often the cause of neurosis than psychoanalysts were inclined to acknowledge. Naturally, Masson thinks Ferenczi was right in his judgment, not to mention brave in contesting the orthodox emphasis on fantasy. Masson's subject, however, is not Ferenczi's paper itself but Freud's reaction to it. Masson tries to read in that reaction evidence that, even in 1932, Freud still felt ashamed about his craven abandonment of a theory he knew in his heart was correct. Ferenczi's revival of the seduction hypothesis so threatened Freud, Masson argues, that Freud was driven to terminate their friendship. "Ferenczi's tenacious insistence on the truth of what his patients told him would cost him the friendship of Freud and almost all of his colleagues and leave him in an isolation from which he never would emerge" (148). Only Freud's guilty inability to accept the reality of seduction explains Freud's "otherwise mysterious turning away from Ferenczi" (xviii).

As Peter Gay has observed, the contention that Ferenczi's revival of the seduction theory cost him Freud's friendship is "contradicted by the facts."[19] Throughout the final months of his life, as Ferenczi collapsed both mentally and physically (he died May 22, 1933), Freud continued to correspond with him and his wife, and the letters display great affection as well as distress at Ferenczi's suffering. Whatever tension the Wiesbaden paper may have introduced into the relationship, it did not cause Freud to sever his ties with the man who for many years had been his favorite disciple.

Masson, then, exaggerates when he says that Freud punished Ferenczi for reviving the seduction theory by terminating their friendship. But perhaps his hypothesis can survive without this inflated claim. Freud certainly disapproved of Ferenczi's paper, and Ferenczi's final years did witness an undeniable alienation between the two men, if nothing so extreme as Masson suggests. But is there anything in Freud's response to the paper to indicate that he actually felt threatened by it—that it touched a sore spot in his conscience?

The best evidence of Freud's reaction comes from a letter written to his daughter Anna on September 3, 1932. Four days earlier, on August 30, Ferenzci had visited Freud, who, because of his cancer, did not attend the Wiesbaden congress. Freud appears to have been more startled by Ferenczi's manner than by what he had to say: without so much as a greeting, Ferenczi began, "I want to read you my paper," which he proceeded to do.[20] In his letter to Anna, Freud says that he found the

19. Peter Gay, *Freud: A Life for Our Time* (New York, 1988), p. 775.
20. Quoted by Gay, *Freud*, p. 583.

presentation "confused, obscure, artificial," but he seems mainly concerned that the paper would harm Ferenczi's reputation.[21] The letter, in other words, suggests that Freud felt not threatened but saddened and somewhat embarrassed for Ferenczi. Masson does not cite this letter and appears to be unaware of it, but it can be squared with his interpretation only by arguing that, even in a private communication to his daughter, Freud hypocritically misrepresented his true feelings. This verges dangerously on making Freud's guilt a matter of raw assertion, against which no evidence can prevail. Like his cowardly collapse before his Viennese colleagues more than three decades earlier, it becomes an invisible, intrapsychic event, to which Masson alone has access. In reality, Freud's disapproval of Ferenczi's paper is easily explained by the simple fact that Freud considered it mistaken. The idea that he not only disliked it but also "feared" (153) it is purely suppositional.

Likewise, Masson's characterization of Freud's "turning away" from Ferenczi as "otherwise mysterious" is unjustified. The tension between Freud and Ferenczi had important sources beyond the matter of seduction. Freud was much troubled by Ferenczi's deviations from classical analytic technique and his introduction of a more active form of therapy. In an effort to break with what he considered the ineffective and authoritarian conventions of traditional analysis, Ferenczi had ventured on what, to Freud, was a dangerous experiment in intimacy. Freud wrote him in late 1931: "You have not made a secret of the fact that you kiss your patients and let them kiss you." More ambitious therapists, Freud warned, would feel invited to proceed even further:

21. Ibid., p. 584.

Picture what will be the result of publishing your technique. There is no revolutionary who is not driven out of the field by a still more radical one. A number of independent thinkers in matters of technique will say to themselves: why stop at a kiss? Certainly one gets further when one adopts "pawing" as well, which after all doesn't make a baby. And then bolder ones will come along who will go further to peeping and showing—and soon we shall have accepted in the technique of analysis the whole repertoire of demiviergerie and petting parties, resulting in an enormous increase of interest in psychoanalysis among both analysts and patients. The new adherent, however, will easily claim too much of this interest for himself, the younger of our colleagues will find it hard to stop at the point they originally intended, and God the Father Ferenczi gazing at the lively scene he has created will perhaps say to himself: maybe after all I should have halted in my technique of motherly affection *before* the kiss.[22]

Behind the issue of the kiss stands the fact that Freud and Ferenczi had come to occupy opposite ends of the therapeutic spectrum within psychoanalysis. Freud's expectations for therapy were always modest. At best, he said, analysis aimed at "transforming . . . hysterical misery into common unhappiness."[23] Ferenczi permitted himself to hope for more. "The need to cure and to help had become paramount in him," Freud wrote in his obituary notice for Ferenczi; "he had probably set himself aims which, with our therapeutic means, are altogether out of reach to-day."[24] Such passages afford strong reason to believe that Freud's concern over Ferenczi's approach to ther-

22. Quoted by Ernest Jones, *The Life and Work of Sigmund Freud* (New York, 1953–57), III:163–64.
23. Freud, *Studies on Hysteria, Standard Edition,* vol. II, p. 305.
24. Freud, "Sandor Ferenczi," *Standard Edition,* vol. XXII, p. 229.

apy and its implications for Ferenczi's state of mind was a paramount factor in Freud's withdrawal from his beloved associate. At the very least, the existence of this ongoing therapeutic disagreement considerably weakens Masson's claim that the tension between Freud and Ferenczi derived wholly, or even largely, from the seduction issue.

Because Masson's attempt to use Ferenczi to substantiate Freud's dishonorable motives in giving up the seduction theory is such a lame affair—feebler even than his earlier effort to enlist Emma Eckstein in the cause—one again suspects that Masson's real interest in Ferenczi lies elsewhere. Ferenczi, I would suggest, occupies a significant place in Masson's fantasy about what should have become of psychoanalysis. Contemplating Ferenczi delivering his paper in Wiesbaden, Masson slips easily into the "as-if" language of the imaginary:

Perhaps never before had anyone spoken for the abused child with such sympathy and eloquence. The ideas Freud had propounded to a skeptical medical world in his 1896 papers were here repeated, but expanded through the knowledge gained by analysis in the years after 1896. It is as if Ferenczi were demonstrating to the analytic world how psychoanalysis could have developed had Freud not abandoned the seduction hypothesis. (150)

In effect, Masson pictures Ferenczi's paper as a kind of re-enactment of Freud's own paper on "The Aetiology of Hysteria." This time, however, Ferenczi corrects Freud's error by steadfastly refusing to capitulate before a hostile audience:

It was as if Ferenczi were telling Freud: "You lacked the courage to stay with the truth and defend it. The movement that grew up around you is a product of this cowardice. I will not be a part of it. I will not break faith with what I know to be true." And that is what happened; Ferenczi died, but he did not recant. (186)

Had psychoanalysis followed Ferenczi's lead in 1932, the result, Masson believes, would have been a therapeutic revolution: analysts would have stopped denying their patients' sufferings and confirmed the reality of the abuse to which those patients had been subjected. Sympathy, belief, and affection would have replaced the constipated insistence on emotional restraint and skepticism. Analytic therapy would have developed something of the loving, democratic character (although not the sexual intimacy) of Ferenczi's "mutual analysis," whose attractions Masson was to celebrate later in *Against Therapy* (1988).

But beyond this therapeutic transformation Masson also imagines Ferenczi inspiring a renaissance of the political campaign against sexual abuse that Masson so wanted Freud to launch at the end of the nineteenth century. Revealingly, Masson's fateful presentation of his ideas about the seduction theory before a group of critical analysts in New Haven in 1981 again reenacts the original scenario. Masson was then the same age as Freud was when he gave his paper on "The Aetiology of Hysteria" to the Viennese Society for Psychiatry and Neurology. Masson's account, in *Final Analysis,* of his own reception by those in attendance strongly echoes his account, in *The Assault on Truth,* of Freud's brutal treatment at the hands of his Viennese medical colleagues in 1896. As he did with Freud, Masson stresses the "deathly silence" that followed his talk, as well as his sense of being "completely isolated" afterward.[25] (Masson also portrayed Ferenczi, we will

25. Masson, *Final Analysis,* pp. 190, 192.

recall, as condemned to "an isolation from which he never would emerge.") Like Ferenczi in 1932, Masson in 1981 both repeats and corrects Freud's original gesture: he tells his colleagues the truth about childhood sexual abuse, and he refuses to recant. Moreover, in contrast to the ailing Ferenczi, Masson lives on to repudiate psychoanalysis entirely and become the public crusader against child abuse that Freud should have (and Ferenczi might have) been. In effect, Masson constructs an imaginary political narrative for Freud and then seeks to realize it in his own life. The sequence of embattled lecturers—1896, 1932, 1981—suggests a profound identification not only with Ferenczi but, surprisingly, with Freud himself. Thus, like Emma Eckstein, Ferenczi is first and foremost a symbolic figure for Masson: just as Eckstein is the prototypical psychoanalytic victim, so Ferenczi embodies the liberating ideological promise of Freud's original insight. This explains his place of honor at the end of Masson's book.

AGAINST THERAPY

Masson published *Against Therapy* in 1988, four years after *The Assault on Truth*. In the later book, which is decidedly more radical than its predecessor, the target of Masson's criticism broadens from Freud and psychoanalysis to the entire psychiatric profession. The book consists of a series of case studies, all of which, Masson argues, reveal the fundamental abusiveness of psychotherapy. His examples range from Ludwig Binswanger's Sanitarium Bellevue at the end of the nineteenth century to the American therapist John Rosen, who was forced to surrender his medical license in 1983 after patients accused him of kidnapping and torturing them. Many of Masson's cases offer extreme instances of violence committed by doctors against their patients, and he confidently states that such abuse is not unusual. But his more important point is that grossly abusive therapies are structurally identical to seemingly humane ones and thus ought not to be considered anomalous. They simply make more palpably horrifying what goes on in every therapeutic situation.

Once Masson had come to grief in the psychoanalytic community by publishing his heretical views on the seduction theory, he seems to have felt liberated to embrace a position fully consistent with the implications of his critique of Freud. In *Against Therapy* he argues that *any* kind of psychotherapy, no matter how apparently enlightened or sophisticated, is indefensible. Psychotherapy, Masson charges, claims to help people when its real purpose is to make them conform; it is a vehicle of social control. At the same time Masson criticizes psychotherapy on what might be called epistemological grounds: it rests on an illegitimate pretension to psychological expertise—on a false belief that the so-called professionals have a better understanding of the "patient" than does the individual seeking treatment. Masson's own experience as an analyst, he says, persuaded him that the therapist has no such superior insight, any more than he enjoys superior psychic health:

Many times I sat behind a patient in analysis and became acutely and painfully aware of my inability to help. Many times, indeed, I did feel compassion. But at times I also felt bored, uninterested, irritated, helpless, confused, ignorant, and lost. At times I could offer no genuine assistance, yet rarely did I acknowledge this to the patient. My life was in no better shape than that of my patients. Any advice I might have had to offer would be no better than that of a well-informed friend (and considerably more expensive).[26]

Over and over again Masson returns to the impossibility of knowing a person better than the person knows himself. The individual is always the best judge of his own reality. Psychotherapists falsely pretend to a degree of intellectual intimacy that cannot be achieved even by friends or lovers.

With complete consistency, Masson asserts that the supposed object of psychotherapy—the ailment that justifies its existence—doesn't properly exist. "There is no such medical entity as mental illness," he writes.[27] He does not deny that people experience great suffering and emotional pain, but he argues repeatedly that mental illness is simply a label those in power attach to unpopular opinions or unconventional ways of living. It represents an illegitimate translation into psychological terms of what is at bottom a political matter. Society finds various ideas and actions threatening, and it seeks to repress them by calling them insane. "Mental illness" is thus an ideologically loaded label for a difference in worldview. In the end, psychotherapy amounts to nothing more than the attempt to break a person's will.

With these opinions Masson joins the ranks of a well-established antipsychiatric tradition, whose foremost representatives are Thomas Szasz, R. D. Laing, and Michel Foucault. Masson acknowledges his affinities with Szasz and Laing, and Foucault's *Histoire de la folie à l'âge classique* (which analyzes the asylum as a mechanism of social control) appears in his bibliography, although not in his text.

26. Jeffrey Moussaieff Masson, *Against Therapy: Emotional Tyranny and the Myth of Psychological Healing* (New York, 1988), p. 253.

27. Ibid., p. 1.

But while recognizing that his ideas are not unprecedented, Masson insists that he alone has pursued the antitherapeutic point of view to its logical conclusion: his predecessors hoped only to replace existing forms of therapy with better ones, while he regards the very idea of psychotherapy as misguided.

Seen from the perspective of *The Assault on Truth*, the most striking thing about *Against Therapy* is that it completes the earlier book's implicit move from psychology to politics. In *The Assault on Truth* Masson constructed a fantasy of Freud's evolution into a political activist and the transformation of psychoanalysis into a revolutionary movement. Now he openly attacks the political quietism of all forms of psychotherapy and their corrupt implication in the existing order. The immediate goal of Masson's own politics is to abolish the profession of psychotherapy, which, he writes, "can and should be replaced by open and searching criticisms of the very foundations of our society."[28] And he readily identifies his campaign against psychotherapy with such other recent political causes as Andrea Dworkin's and Catherine MacKinnon's efforts to outlaw pornography and the ban on electroshock passed by Berkeley voters in 1982—despite the failure, Masson notes scornfully, of the local therapeutic community to support it publicly. Masson's turn from psychology to politics brings to mind the analogous development among the neo-Freudians, who, in the 1930s and 1940s, criticized the perceived neglect of social factors in orthodox psychoanalysis. As was the case with the neo-Freudians, Masson's progressive political views have been purchased at the cost of Freud's grim psychological insights. Herbert Marcuse showed in his famous critique of neo-

28. Ibid., p. 250.

Freudianism in *Eros and Civilization* that Freud's unsentimental insistence on the burdens of sexuality and aggression is, in the end, both more radical and more humane than the facile call for social reform.

Masson's unqualified attack on psychotherapy takes him well beyond the bounds of my present concern with recent critics of psychoanalysis. For my purposes, the main interest of *Against Therapy* lies in its implication for Masson's view of Freud and his thesis about the abandonment of the seduction theory. Most immediately, Masson's denial of the reality of mental illness might seem to undermine his contention, in *The Assault on Truth,* that Freud's seduction theory was correct. The whole point of the seduction theory, after all, was that childhood sexual abuse gave rise to neuroses. Indeed, Masson praised Freud as the first thinker in history to have recognized the profound psychological consequences of child abuse. But if hysteria, like all psychiatric diagnoses, is a fiction—a clinical label for ideas or behavior that society disapproves of rather than a genuine illness—then the seduction hypothesis no longer makes any sense. By the logic of *Against Therapy,* Masson himself would seem to have abandoned it.

Masson nowhere admits that he has become ensnarled in contradiction. I suspect his silence is less a matter of bad faith than evidence that, from the start, he understood the seduction theory very differently from Freud. When he wrote *The Assault on Truth,* he still spoke of Freud's patients as hysterics, and he accepted Freud's judgment that they were genuinely sick. But Masson was never especially interested in the specific etiolological proposition Freud advanced, namely, that childhood seductions resulted in one particular neurotic disorder, hysteria. Rather, he sought always to conflate this formulation with the more general idea that childhood sexual abuse had severe and deleterious psychological consequences. Four years later, in *Against Therapy,* Masson refuses to speak of sickness, and he blames Freud for so labeling his patients. But he still believes that childhood seductions cause great suffering, especially if therapists deny their reality. Apparently, when we say that something causes suffering or mental pain, we are not, in Masson's view, pronouncing the sort of intrusive and presumptuous judgment on another person's experience that he so objects to in psychotherapy. But the difference between these two exercises—the one authentic, legitimate, and humane; the other bogus, illicit, and repressive—needs to be more fully explained. Otherwise, the impression persists that Masson's extreme antipsychiatric views in *Against Therapy* contradict his earlier defense of the seduction theory.

Only one chapter of *Against Therapy* deals with Freud. It presents a critical examination of the Dora analysis, which Masson considers the single most influential case in the history of psychiatry—and one that dramatically illustrates the wrongs of psychotherapy. For Freud Dora was a hysteric; he originally titled her case "Dream and Hysteria" ("Traum und Hysterie"). Masson, however, denies that Dora was actually ill. He ignores the various "presenting symptoms"—including a persistent cough, hoarseness, and loss of voice without organic cause—that Freud considered the evidence of her hysteria. Instead, Masson insists, Dora offers a clear-cut example of perfectly reasonable behavior that, because of his intellectual (and ultimately political) prejudices, Freud arbitrarily chose to call pathological.

In 1898, when she was fifteen, Dora was brought to Freud by her father. Alongside her physical symptoms and general sullenness, she had developed, according to her father, an irrational belief that his close friend Herr K. had made sexual advances toward her. Freud's initial response to Dora was not at all what her father expected: Freud concluded that her account of Herr K.'s behavior was accurate, and he agreed with her that her father had in effect handed her over to Herr K. as the price for his own affair with Herr K.'s wife. Freud's response to Dora also seems to surprise Masson, who, in *The Assault on Truth,* alleged that, having abandoned the seduction theory, Freud routinely attributed his patients' stories to fantasy, thereby excusing the abusive actions of adults. In this instance, however, Freud initially took the side of reality against fantasy, and of the child against the parent.

But, Masson complains, Freud's loyalty to Dora was short-lived, his original alliance with her soon giving way to opposition. Instead of accepting that she simply found Herr K.'s attentions unwelcome and was understandably angered by her father's self-interested betrayal, Freud insisted that Dora's hostility to Herr K. was unreasonable and her anger against her father excessive. Indeed, Freud regarded both her intense aversion and her anger as manifestations of her hysteria. After all, Freud reasoned, Herr K. was a prepossessing man still in his thirties: Dora should have been aroused, not disgusted, when he embraced and kissed her (at age fourteen), just as she should have been flattered by his serious romantic interest in her. Freud even suggested that the whole matter could have been satisfactorily resolved had Dora married Herr K., which would of course have freed Frau K. to marry Dora's father.

Masson is far from being the only reader to find Freud's response to Dora lacking in sensitivity—to put it mildly. Peter Gay, for example, is no less appalled by Freud's interpretive aggression and self-righteousness: Gay considers it astonishing that Freud ever published the case. Masson thus easily gets a good deal of legitimate mileage out of Freud's manifestly retrograde views on women and on the proper relations between the sexes. What Freud calls hysteria—namely, Dora's failure to respond to Herr K. and, especially, her anger at her father—is, Masson insists, simply a pejorative label for attitudes and behavior that Freud disapproved of. It is a classic example of the way psychotherapy invidiously uses psychological categories to mask political prejudices.

I am not, of course, eager to defend Freud's treatment of Dora, least of all his blithe recommendation of Herr K.'s attractions. The important feature of Freud's analysis, however—and the point at which Masson's disagreement with Freud is most intriguing—does not lie in Freud's ideologically loaded disregard for Dora's legitimate interests. Much more significant is Freud's belief that her behavior cannot satisfactorily be explained solely by an appeal to her conscious perceptions and intentions. Characteristically, he insists on deeper, unconscious sources for her actions. Freud suggests, in particular, that Dora was unconsciously in love with Herr K. and very much desired a romantic relationship with him. Her unconscious attraction explains why she reacted so violently both to Herr K.'s sexual advances and to her father's contention that she had merely fantasized them. There was in fact an element of fantasy involved in her situation: the advances were real enough, but they were not entirely unwelcome. Dora's extreme disgust disguised feelings of self-reproach. She had, in effect, gotten what she could not admit she wanted.

Here we have the essential point of opposition between Freud and Masson. Once again, as with the seduction theory, it comes down to a disagreement about the self and what can be known about it. Freud articulates a modern conception of the self: it is divided, at odds with itself,

ambivalent. It houses desires that are not always compatible with its conscious convictions, and Freud regards its
self-representations with suspicion. For Masson, on the
other hand, the self is fundamentally unified and reliable.
There are no secret corners, no hidden recesses unavailable
to consciousness, that might stand at odds with explicit
ideas or beliefs. Thus, when Dora says she was disgusted
by Herr K., that settles the matter. Likewise, when Dora
insists she was angry with her father because he questioned
her trustworthiness, no more needs to be said. Only outrageous presumption allows Freud to pretend to know
something about Dora's inner life that she herself denies.
Masson's Dora is a little *philosophe,* driven by a passion for
the truth—just as Masson himself, so he tells us, was
driven by his passion to discover the truth about the seduction theory. Dora is thus allowed none of the psychological
ambiguity that Freud, as a modernist, imputes to her.
Jacques Lacan has identified Dora's unmodern sense of innocence with Hegel's notion of the "beautiful soul." Dora
articulates the beautiful soul's naive protest against what
the world has done to it. But Freud responds: "Look
at your own involvement in the disorder which you
bemoan."[29] The modern self, in other words, is complicit
in its own disarray, whereas Masson's Dora, like the hysterical patients of the seduction theory, is an innocent.

Already in *The Assault on Truth* Masson showed little
sympathy for the idea of the unconscious. He did not explicitly dismiss it, but he objected to Freud's invoking unconscious fantasies to explain what were, in Masson's
view, perfectly straightforward recollections of past mis-

29. Jacques Lacan, "Intervention on Transference," in *In Dora's
Case,* ed. Charles Bernheimer and Claire Kahane (New York, 1985),
p. 96.

treatment. At the very least, the unconscious, like infantile sexuality, had grown superfluous to Masson's understanding of human behavior. In *Against Therapy,* especially in his analysis of the Dora case, his rejection of the unconscious becomes fully transparent. Even if one were to grant that a person might be unaware of certain impulses, those impulses, Masson argues, would be even less accessible to the therapist than they are to the patient. For all practical purposes, therefore, the unconscious simply doesn't exist. Dora's experience in analysis shows that the appeal to the unconscious is gratuitous as well as repressive: when she identified the conspiracy between Herr K. and her father, a conspiracy that Freud, as one of the boys, sought to abet, she had successfully got to the bottom of the problem. Everything else—all of Freud's supposedly expert opinions—was mere presumption. Far from easing his patient's misery, Freud added to it.

What Freud should have done, according to Masson, is not analyzed Dora—which was unnecessary and abusive—but taken her side in the controversy. Because the issue was essentially political, it called for a political response: a denunciation of male sexual exploitation and hypocrisy. But the burden of the correct political response had, in the end, to be borne by Dora alone. When Freud continued to insist that she was unconsciously in love with Herr K., she walked out on Freud. She later confronted Herr K. and his wife and obtained confessions from them, an action that Masson applauds as "a political statement of remarkable maturity."[30] Dora, in his view, was not a hysteric but an emerging feminist.

Masson makes no effort to bring the Dora case into line with the seduction hypothesis. In *The Assault on Truth*

30. Masson, *Against Therapy,* p. 74.

Masson assumed, in keeping with the seduction theory, that whenever Freud identified a patient as a hysteric, the patient had been sexually abused as a child. But Masson advances no such claim about Dora. On the contrary, he suggests that, by finally publishing her case (in 1905), Freud intended to send a muted signal to his professional colleagues that he had given up his heretical views about seduction. Nor does Masson try to establish a structural parallel between the Dora case and the seduction model, as he did with Emma Eckstein's operation and Freud's diagnosis of hysterical longing—presumably because Freud's acknowledgment that Dora was the object of a genuine seduction by Herr K. effectively rules out any such structural argument. But, more fundamentally, Masson's newly acquired antitherapeutic bias and his denial of the reality of mental illness seem to have dimmed his enthusiasm for what was, after all, essentially a diagnostic theory linking childhood abuse with adult neurosis. Like it or not, the seduction theory belongs to the old psychiatric order, which Masson is out to discredit in *Against Therapy*. Thus, without explicitly rejecting the theory, he consigns it to a conceptual limbo.

MARIANNE KRÜLL AND MARIE BALMARY

In 1979, five years before the appearance of *The Assault on Truth* and two years before Masson's address to the Western New England Psychoanalytic Society, two European scholars, working independently of one another, published books on Freud's abandonment of the seduction theory. The coincidence is in itself striking. But Marianne Krüll's *Freud und sein Vater* and Marie Balmary's *L'Homme aux statues: Freud et la faute cachée du père* share a good deal more than their interest in the fate of the seduction hypothesis. In particular, Krüll and Balmary agree with Masson that Freud's decision to abandon the seduction theory in favor of the idea of infantile sexuality was a mistake, and one with grave consequences for the history of psychoanalysis at that. Like Masson, they see the decision as marking a retreat from reality to fantasy—from a view of human development in which experiences with other people, above all family members, are the chief influences on a child to one in which the self is a creation strictly of internal needs and desires. Both lament Freud's selective reading of the Oedipus legend, from which he suppressed the origins of the tragedy in the sins of Oedipus's father, Laius—notably Laius's attempt to murder his son—in order to focus on the purely intrapsychic drama, Oedipus's love of his mother and hatred of his father. The Oedipus complex, they protest, made the child the source of its own misery, thereby exonerating the parents.

Krüll and Balmary, again like Masson, aim above all to provide an explanation for Freud's fateful decision to give up the seduction hypothesis. In contrast to Masson, however, they look for that explanation not in Freud's professional concerns of the 1890s but in his personal life, especially his relationship with his father. In this respect their studies are profoundly Freudian. Both adhere to the psychoanalytic doctrine that the crucial developments of adult life are shaped in childhood, and both reconstruct Freud's childhood experiences by means of a psychoanalytic interpretation of his dreams, associations, remarks, and quirks of character. This shared commitment to the intellectual methods of psychoanalysis sharply distinguishes them from Masson. Their criticisms of Freud are pointed and often irreverent, but they nonetheless write from the perspective of the loyal opposition. Krüll in particular takes a dim view of Masson's work. In the foreword to the American edition of *Freud and His Father,* published in 1986, she writes: "Since Masson knew my book, I find it surprising that he neglected to mention alternative explanations for Freud's abandonment of the seduction theory, no doubt the better to press his—to my mind—quite absurd idea that Freud was little more than a liar craving fame."[31] In effect, Krüll's and Balmary's books show that one can disagree with Freud on the issue of seduction without throwing over the whole of his intellectual system.

Given the speculative nature of their reconstructions, it is not surprising that Krüll and Balmary come up with very different versions of Freud's childhood and equally different accounts of the psychodynamic factors at work in his change of heart about seduction. Krüll bases her argument on a close analysis of the reasons Freud gives for abandoning the seduction theory in his letter to Fliess of September 21, 1897. Only one of those reasons, she says, is persuasive, and it is entirely personal, as opposed to clinical or logical. This is Freud's conclusion that if the seduction theory were correct, then "in all cases, the *father,* not excluding my own, had to be accused of being perverse."[32] Had he retained the theory, Krüll argues, "Freud would have had to assume that even his own father was a seducer and so 'perverse.'"[33] Unable to face such an unsavory prospect, Freud developed the Oedipus theory—in which all "perversions" become autonomous creations of the infantile imagination—to avoid confronting his father's misdeeds. According to Krüll, Freud's reluctance to accuse his

31. Marianne Krüll, *Freud and His Father,* trans. Arnold J. Pomerans (New York, 1986; German original, Munich, 1979), p. xvi.

32. Freud, *Complete Letters to Fliess,* p. 264.

33. Krüll, *Freud and His Father,* p. 56.

father stemmed less from filial piety than from an unspoken taboo, passed on to him in early childhood, that forbade him from delving into Jacob Freud's past. She deduces the existence of this taboo from a dream Freud had on the night of his father's funeral, October 25, 1896. In it Freud saw a sign reading, "You are requested to close the eyes," which Freud himself interpreted as a reproach for having economized on funeral expenses and for arriving late at the ceremonies, but which Krüll believes alludes to a childhood injunction that Freud "avert his eyes" from his father's sins. The bulk of her book consists of an effort to establish just what those sins were and how they influenced Sigmund Freud's development.

The reader of Krüll's book fully expects her historical reconstruction to culminate in the revelation that Jacob Freud had seduced his own children. After all, it was the intolerable prospect of his father's guilt in this regard, according to Krüll's hypothesis, that had caused Freud to give up the seduction theory in September 1897: the theory, if true, incriminated "the *father*, not excluding my own." The expectation is heightened by evidence from the Fliess letters that Freud himself had entertained this very possibility. On February 11, 1897, he wrote Fliess: "Unfortunately, my own father was one of these perverts and is responsible for the hysteria of my brother (all of whose symptoms are identifications) and those of several younger sisters."[34] Krüll published her book before the appearance of the complete Fliess correspondence, and thus she knew this remarkable passage only in the bowdlerized version of Ernest Jones, who summarizes: "[Freud] inferred, from the existence of some hysterical symptoms in his brother and several sisters (not himself: *nota bene*), that even his

34. Freud, *Complete Letters to Fliess,* pp. 230–31.

own father had to be thus incriminated."[35] Krüll, in other words, was unaware that Freud had actually called his father a pervert, the same label he used in the crucial passage about fathers (including his own) in the famous renunciation letter of September 21, 1897. Still, one is surprised that she makes so little of Freud's express indictment of his father (she cites the sentence from Jones, but without comment), because the passage seems almost tailor-made for her thesis. But while she accuses Jacob Freud of many failings, large and small, she never says that he abused his children sexually. Of course, Freud's seemingly dispassionate contemplation of his father's misbehavior—in a letter written not all that long after Jacob Freud's death and the dream enjoining Freud to avert his eyes—undermines Krüll's conclusion that, seven months later, Freud gave up the seduction theory precisely in order to *protect* his father from the charge of being a seducer and a pervert.

If Jacob Freud was not guilty of actual seduction, what, then, were the paternal misdeeds from which Sigmund Freud was to avert his eyes? Most of them, it seems, had to do with masturbation. Krüll concludes, not unreasonably, that Jacob Freud threatened young Sigmund with castration for masturbating. More spectacularly, she surmises that at age three, when the family moved from Freiberg in Moravia to Leipzig, Freud may actually have seen his father masturbating during the train journey. She also believes that Jacob Freud committed adultery (he was, after all, a traveling salesman) and that he bore a burden of guilt for abandoning the orthodox Judaism of his family. Taken together, these trespasses constitute the paternal heritage that Freud was prohibited from exploring, a prohibition he honored when he gave up the seduction theory and

35. Jones, *Life and Work,* I:322.

ceased attributing the unhappiness of children to the misbehavior of adults.

In Krüll's analysis, the paternal taboo is extended from the sins of Freud's father to include those of other "primary caretakers" and significant figures in young Sigmund's world. Long stretches of her book are given over to equally speculative constructions of the various misdeeds of Freud's half brother Philipp, his nephew John, and his nursemaid, Resi Wittek. In effect, she overloads Freud's childhood with catastrophes, thereby diffusing the notion that a single traumatic event, like a parental seduction, might have dramatically shaped his character. In Krüll's hands the seduction theory becomes a kind of intellectual catchall for a wide range of childhood experiences in which parents or other members of the household exert some significant influence on a child's development. In Freud's own case, most of those experiences had a sexual cast, but none of them even remotely resembled the sort of abusive assault that Freud seems to have had in mind when he formulated his theory. In fact, Krüll's main objection to the seduction theory is its exclusively sexual focus. Accordingly, she suggests that instead of abandoning the theory, Freud should have broadened and desexualized it to incorporate the full spectrum of acts through which parents deceive and misguide their children:

In my view, Freud had developed a true psychoanalytical theory with his seduction theory—all that he needed to do was to rid it of its extreme fixation on *sexual* seduction. Freud could easily have expanded his seduction theory into a "misguidance" theory: the child is misguided by his or her parents or primary caretakers and hence develops neurotic aberrations.[36]

36. Krüll, *Freud and His Father*, pp. 69–70.

Krüll's reading of the seduction theory thus has an ideological valence radically different from Masson's. Masson of course stresses precisely the opposite—the sexual content of the theory—as it becomes for him an early manifesto in the campaign against the sexual abuse of children. Perhaps because she was writing in the 1970s, Krüll seems largely unconcerned with this issue, and her book is innocent of the feminist ethos that informs Masson's *Assault on Truth*. Instead, as a professional sociologist, she champions the seduction theory because it properly acknowledges the influence of the family on the developing child, an influence that psychoanalysis has neglected in its preoccupation with the child's own desires and imaginings. Krüll agrees with Masson only in regretting that Freud relinquished the actual world of interpersonal relations in favor of a purely psychological conception of the child's reality.

■   ■   ■

The argument of Marie Balmary's *Psychoanalyzing Psychoanalysis: Freud and the Hidden Fault of the Father* is structurally identical to that of Krüll's *Freud and His Father*. According to Balmary, when Freud rejected the seduction theory in favor of the Oedipus theory, he mistakenly substituted a purely intrapsychic phantasm (derived from his self-analysis) for the real experiences that his patients had revealed in their accounts of seduction. Moreover, he abandoned the seduction theory and developed his truncated conception of the Oedipus complex, in which the crimes of Laius are expunged, in order to hide the transgressions of his own father. Balmary conducts her argument in a manner best described as an exaggerated variation on Krüll's psychoanalytic method. She takes even greater interpretive license with Freud's dreams and personal manias in constructing a version of his childhood adequate to explain why he felt compelled to deny his father's misdeeds. Balmary is a student of Jacques Lacan's, and her work has been influenced as well by Gilles Deleuze and Felix Gauttari's *Anti-Oedipus,* which also sees psychoanalysis going astray with the "discovery" of the Oedipus complex. Her book is written in the gnomic style favored by Lacan and other recent French philosophers and literary theorists. It is something of a *jeu d'esprit,* and its allusive manner contrasts strikingly with the Teutonic thoroughness of Krüll's book.

Where Krüll focuses on masturbation—both Freud's own and his father's—Balmary invents a decidedly more shocking story. She argues that Jacob Freud's hidden fault was to have driven his second wife, Rebekka, to commit suicide, perhaps by jumping from a train. Jacob murdered Rebekka because he had fallen in love with Freud's mother, Amalie Nathansohn, who, Balmary surmises, was already pregnant with young Sigmund when the couple married on July 29, 1855 (a hypothesis based on the dubious assumption that Freud's birthdate was March 6 rather than May 6, 1856). In effect, Jacob's fault consisted of a typically Freudian confection of sex and violence, but located now in the real world of adult relationships, rather than in the overwrought imagination of the child. Balmary's construction rather resembles Freud's own notion of the primal crime, in which the passions of the Oedipus complex are acted out in a highly dramatic fashion by sons who actually murder their father in order to take possession of their mother and sisters.

Balmary faces an uphill battle. Her problems begin with the embarrassment that absolutely nothing is known about Rebekka, who may in fact never have existed. Neither Freud nor any members of the family ever mention her.

The supposition of her marriage to Jacob Freud rests on fragile documentary evidence: a contradictory reference in a register of Jews living in Freiberg and a deleted listing in a passport register, which Marianne Krüll argues should lead one to speak more accurately of an "alleged" marriage.[37] But Balmary is nothing if not resourceful. She gathers an eclectic garland of Freud's idiosyncrasies, which, when subjected to her fierce analytic scrutiny, reveal his unconscious knowledge of Rebekka's fate. Those idiosyncrasies range from his partiality for Mozart's *Don Giovanni* and Michelangelo's *Moses,* to his appetite for mushrooms, which he hunted with his children during summer holidays, to his collection of antiquities, from which he sometimes brought newly acquired statues to the dinner table. In each of these preoccupations Balmary finds evidence that Freud identified his father with Don Juan, a seducer and a murderer. Thus, for example, Freud's statues were in reality symbols of the Stone Guest—the murdered Commander—whom Don Juan invites to dinner and who ultimately wreaks vengeance on him. Freud collected the statues (and "invited" them to dinner) because he unconsciously feared that the same fate awaited his Don Juan father. Michelangelo's *Moses* likewise embodies the Don's avenger, and Freud's obsession with this statue (which he visited repeatedly in the Roman church of San Pietro in Vincoli) again points to his unconscious fixation on the murdered Rebekka. Similarly, his beloved mushrooms, as analyzed by Balmary, turn out to be little statues produced by nature, and thus Freud's otherwise inexplicable devotion to them yields up its hidden biographical meaning. Even more so than Krüll, Balmary displays the indulgent intellectual habits of the psychoanalytic

37. Ibid., p. 96.

style—what Frederick Crews disapprovingly calls "the Freudian way of knowledge."[38]

The link between Freud's unconscious awareness of his father's crime and the abandonment of the seduction theory is, by comparison, fairly straightforward. The seduction theory pinned the blame on fathers—Balmary calls it "the theory of the father's fault"[39]—and, in replacing it with the Oedipus theory, Freud sought to expiate his father's sin by taking the burden of guilt on himself. The new theory denied the criminality of fathers, locating both illicit desire and murder in the imagination of the child. Thus Freud's abandonment of the seduction hypothesis becomes an act of filial piety. Balmary finds textual evidence for this biographical interpretation in an anecdote included in Freud's famous letter of September 21, 1897, announcing his abandonment of the seduction theory. There he identifies himself with the disappointed heroine of a Jewish joke, significantly named Rebecca: "A little story from my collection occurs to me: 'Rebecca, take off your gown; you are no longer a bride.' "[40] Freud's sense of intellectual deflation apparently reminded him of a bride left standing at the altar. He had to take off the gown of "eternal fame, . . . certain wealth, [and] complete independence" that he had anticipated donning as a reward for his great discovery.[41] For Balmary, however, the appearance of this mysterious Rebecca in Freud's letter of renunciation points unmistakably to an unconscious tie between the abandoned seduction theory and Jacob's murdered

38. Frederick Crews, *Skeptical Engagements* (New York, 1986), p. 43.

39. Marie Balmary, *Psychoanalyzing Psychoanalysis: Freud and the Hidden Fault of the Father,* trans. Ned Lukacher (Baltimore, 1982; French original, Paris, 1979), p. 37.

40. Freud, *Complete Letters to Fliess,* p. 266.

41. Ibid.

second wife, another Rebecca whose marriage had come to grief. "If Freud really knew nothing about Rebecca," Balmary concludes, "we would think that her name would not appear as it does, through an association of ideas, at the very moment that Freud renounces revealing the fault of the fathers."[42]

Like Krüll, Balmary wants psychoanalysis to return to its original understanding of mental illness as a product of "the perverse conduct" of adults.[43] Also like Krüll (and in contrast to Masson), she would modify the seduction hypothesis to remove its exclusive focus on sexual abuse. "The origin of neurosis is not sexual desire alone nor even sexual trauma alone, but all the faults committed by the very people who present the law to the child."[44] In Balmary's analysis, we recall, Jacob's sexual misconduct (his impregnation of Amalie) is subordinated to his murderous treatment of Rebekka. Balmary does not even insist that the essential crimes of parents be committed against children: Jacob's victim, after all, was herself an adult. The father's fault, in other words, may be an act to which the child is simply witness.

■   ■   ■

In light of the remarkable similarities between Krüll's and Balmary's views of the seduction theory and Masson's argument in *The Assault on Truth,* one might wonder why Masson nowhere acknowledges either as a significant predecessor. Possibly he did not want to diminish his claim to originality. Or perhaps he was reluctant to associate himself with the extravagant psychoanalytic apparatus they both employ. But the deepest reason, I suspect, lies in the

42. Balmary, *Psychoanalyzing Psychoanalysis,* p. 65.
43. Ibid., p. 154.   44. Ibid., p. 164.

ideological gulf separating him from Krüll and Balmary. Both Europeans write from within an essentially patriarchal framework. The paradigmatic relationship of their analyses, as of Freud's own, remains the male dyad of father and son. Masson, on the other hand, wishes to emphasize the potential feminist logic of the seduction theory, transforming it into a story in which fathers characteristically abuse their daughters. Thus, from Masson's perspective, Krüll's and Balmary's stress on the troubled relationship between Freud and his father must seem a reactionary diversion, serving only to deflect attention from the revolutionary implications of Freud's original discovery.

THE SEDUCTION THEORY AS HISTORICAL CONSTRUCT

The nearly simultaneous appearance of the books written by Masson, Krüll, and Balmary, with their common defense of the seduction hypothesis and their severe criticism of Freud for abandoning it, seems—to use one of Freud's favorite terms—uncanny. It testifies to a renewed appreciation, over the past two decades, of the reality of child abuse and expresses exasperation that psychoanalysis has often functioned to deny that reality. Psychoanalysts, moreover, would appear to be increasingly receptive to the complaint that they have wrongly minimized the incidence and the psychological importance of childhood trauma. The analyst Leonard Shengold's recent book, *Soul Murder: The Effects of Childhood Abuse and Deprivation,* is a case in point. Ironically, Jeffrey Masson—very much *persona non grata* in the psychoanalytic world—may have played a role in bringing about this transformation.

My concern here is not, however, with contemporary psychoanalysis but with Freud. I have tried to show that Masson's, Krüll's, and Balmary's explanations of his decision to abandon the seduction theory are all deeply flawed. But beyond the shortcomings of their individual arguments lurks a more general problem with the story of the seduction theory. This problem is exaggerated in their critical interpretations, but it also afflicts the traditional accounts of the theory and its abandonment, whether in Ernest Jones or in Freud's own autobiographical pronouncements. Neither the critics nor the defenders acknowledge the extent to which the story of the seduction theory is a convenient historical construct—a kind of intellectual shorthand—used to describe developments that in reality were far messier, far less sharply etched, than the story makes them appear. As such a piece of shorthand, it is no more inaccurate than most historical narratives. Nevertheless, we need to recognize in the story of the seduction theory what Stephen Gill, in another context, calls a "retrospective patterning,"[45] one that is altogether too confident and that stands in need of deconstruction. In the following, I hope to draw attention to the many ways in which Freud's thinking about the neuroses in the 1890s corresponded only approximately to the conceptual straitjacket imposed by the seduction story.

To begin with, the seduction theory, especially as explicated by Masson, considerably simplifies Freud's overall view of mental illness during those years. Contrary to what accounts of the theory often imply, Freud never believed that every neurosis originated in a childhood sexual trauma. Rather, he held that the neuroses fell into two broad categories, the psychoneuroses and the actual neuroses, and of these only the former could trace their source to seductions. The actual neuroses ("actual" in the French or German sense of "present-day") were caused by a recent

45. Stephen Gill, *William Wordsworth: A Life* (Oxford, 1990), p. 102.

sexual disturbance, such as *coitus interruptus* or, more fundamentally, masturbation. Thus the seduction theory had to compete for Freud's intellectual allegiance with what might be called the "masturbation theory." Throughout the mid-1890s he was convinced that masturbation and its various derivatives were as important a cause of mental illness as was childhood sexual abuse. Interestingly, the masturbation theory also suffered eclipse in Freud's later thinking, although it was never explicitly repudiated. Indeed, Freud might be accused of having suppressed the masturbation theory, just as he suppressed the seduction theory. If moralists of the 1980s had become as exercised about masturbation as they did about childhood sexual assault, one can even imagine his being attacked for abandoning his original insight into the consequences of self-abuse.

Only the psychoneuroses, then, originated in seductions. Moreover, Freud divided the psychoneuroses themselves into two principal groups, hysteria and obsessional neurosis, which in turn stood in a very different relation to their presumed source in childhood trauma. Hysteria alone fit the seduction model exactly: it was caused by a seduction that the child experienced as a "shock."[46] Obsessional neurosis, by contrast, was caused by a seduction that the child found not shocking but pleasurable. In fact, the obsessional symptom was a reflection of the self-reproach later felt by the patient precisely because the seduction had been enjoyed when it occurred. Freud's image of childhood seduction was thus more complicated than Masson and others imply. Seduction was sometimes a purely negative experience, accompanied, Freud said, by "revulsion

---

46. Freud, *Complete Letters to Fliess*, p. 144.

and fright."[47] In this case it resulted in hysteria. But it could also be gratifying, in which case it gave rise, under later moral pressure, to feelings of guilt that led ultimately to obsessional neurosis.

A second distortion pertains to Freud's model of the seductions responsible for hysteria. As the seduction theory hardened into a historical construct, the victim of abuse was nearly always pictured as a daughter and the perpetrator as a father. Freud himself was increasingly inclined to speak as if he considered the father the archetypal seducer: apart from his two references to the "paternal etiology," we have his conclusion, in the renunciation letter of September 21, 1897, that "in all cases, the *father,* not excluding my own, had to be accused of being perverse." But Freud's actual picture of childhood trauma was decidedly more complex. In "The Aetiology of Hysteria" he writes that six of his eighteen victims were boys—clearly not daughters. Moreover, the Fliess correspondence refers to a number of individual male victims, including, we will recall, Freud's own brother. Freud classified his eighteen cases in terms of three kinds of childhood sexual stimulation. The first group involved "single, or at any rate isolated, instances of abuse, mostly practised on female children, by adults who were strangers."[48] The second, and more numerous, group involved cases "in which some adult looking after the child—a nursery maid or governess or tutor, or, unhappily all too often, a close relative—has initiated the child into sexual intercourse and has maintained a regular love relationship with it."[49] To be sure,

47. Ibid., p. 141.
48. Freud, "The Aetiology of Hysteria," *Standard Edition,* vol. III, p. 208.
49. Ibid.

Freud here disguised his conviction that the "close relative" was often the father, and he later rebuked himself for substituting an uncle for the father in two cases mentioned in *Studies on Hysteria*. But he nonetheless thought that seductions were also carried out by adults other than the father. For example, Freud believed he had himself been seduced by his nursemaid. "The old man plays no active part in my case," he wrote Fliess; rather, his " 'prime originator' was an ugly, elderly, but clever woman" whom his mother remembered as his nurse.[50] Finally, in a significant portion of childhood seductions adults had no direct role at all. The third category of cases discussed in "The Aetiology of Hysteria" involved "child-relationships proper—sexual relations between two children of different sexes, mostly a brother and sister, which are often prolonged beyond puberty and which have the most far-reaching consequences for the pair."[51] (In his two other papers on the seduction theory, "Heredity and the Aetiology of the Neuroses" and "Further Remarks on the Neuro-Psychoses of Defence," Freud mentions "blameless children" as the "assailants" in more than half the cases.)[52] True, Freud believed that the boys who initiated their sisters had themselves been seduced by adult females; hysteria was thus ultimately traceable to the actions of grown-ups. But the crucial point is that his image of childhood seduction never conformed neatly to a model in which daughters are the victims and fathers the villains. Instead, it incorporated a wide spectrum of relationships, with children and seducers belonging to both sexes and with the active part taken

50. Freud, *Complete Letters to Fliess*, p. 268.
51. Freud, "The Aetiology of Hysteria," *SE*, vol. III, p. 208.
52. Freud, "Heredity and the Aetiology of the Neuroses" and "Further Remarks on the Neuro-Psychoses of Defence," *Standard Edition*, vol. III, pp. 152, 164.

not just by fathers but by other relatives, servants, or even
children themselves. In Masson's version of the seduction
theory, both the theory's gender construction and its gen-
erational pattern have been streamlined to suit an ideological agenda.

A similar streamlining can be observed in the treatment
of Freud's thinking about the role of fantasy in the origin
of the neuroses. The usual accounts of the seduction theory
and its abandonment create a false dichotomy between real
experiences on the one hand and purely imagined ones on
the other. Thus, during the years in which he held to the
seduction theory, Freud is said to have located the origin of
hysteria in actual historical incidents of abuse; after he
abandoned the theory the same conditions were attributed
entirely to fantasy. But fantasy actually played a significant part in the seduction theory itself, and although its
importance was certainly enhanced when Freud gave up
the theory, it was never negligible. In particular, Freud believed that the child rarely had direct access to memory of
the seduction. Rather, the experience was mediated in the
imagination by sexual stories the child had heard and sexual activities it had observed. The whole process, Freud
suggested, was analogous to the formation of dreams, in
that the original scene was fragmented, distorted, and
mixed with elements from other sources. In other words,
the formative power of fantasy was not suddenly and mys-
teriously revealed to Freud in the wake of the seduction
theory. Similarly, the traditional narrative of the seduction
hypothesis and its abandonment overdraws the opposition
between reality and imagination.

■   ■   ■

As a historical construct, in sum, the story of the seduction theory considerably distorts Freud's actual opinions,

during the 1890s, about the causes of mental illness. It also misrepresents the character of his conviction. The construct drastically oversimplifies a complex psychological reality when it presents Freud as warmly embracing the seduction hypothesis between 1893 and 1897 and then coldly rejecting it in September 1897. Instead, one ought to speak of his rising and falling confidence in the theory. Just as Freud never believed in it with absolute certainty, so he never gave it up as completely as "abandonment" would imply. The letter of September 21, 1897, definitely marked an intellectual turning point, but it was not the 180° reversal that the familiar account suggests. We need to attend to the doubts Freud entertained about the theory during the mid-1890s, as well as to the remarkable ambiguities that accompanied his retreat from it after 1897.

Freud's confidence in the seduction theory was always fragile. Reading him, one often gets the impression of a man trying to talk himself into believing something, with doubts constantly emerging and having to be overcome. In a case mentioned in the letter to Fliess of November 2, 1895, Freud almost seems to be willing the theory into existence. When the patient produces the "expected" story, Freud's "confidence" in his idea is increased: "Today I am able to add that one of the cases gave me what I expected (sexual shock—that is, infantile abuse in male hysteria!) and that at the same time a working through of the disputed material strengthened my confidence in the validity of my psychological constructions."[53] Doubts become more frequent and agonizing in the spring and summer of 1897. Thus, in the letter of February 11, 1897—in which Freud accuses his own father of seducing his brother and several younger sisters—he concludes, fretfully: "The frequency of this circumstance often makes me wonder." In

53. Freud, *Complete Letters to Fliess*, p. 149.

April we find him confiding that "I myself am still in doubt about matters concerning fathers." In late May he had his "Hella" dream, in which he experienced "over-affectionate feelings" for his daughter Mathilde, and he frankly interprets this seduction dream as revealing a desire to assuage his misgivings about the "paternal etiology": "The dream of course shows the fulfillment of my wish to catch a *Pater* as the originator of neurosis and thus puts an end to my ever-recurring doubts." Later in the summer his tone becomes more abject. He is, he tells Fliess, "tormented by grave doubts about my theory of the neuroses."[54]

Freud's doubts, in short, had richly prepared the ground for the seeming change of heart announced in the letter of September 21, 1897. Masson may even be right that the hostile response of Freud's Viennese medical colleagues to his presentation of "The Aetiology of Hysteria" before the Society for Psychiatry and Neurology contributed to those doubts—not in the facile and crude sense that Freud succumbed to "peer pressure" but in the perfectly reasonably sense that people who were in the best position to have an informed view of the matter (namely, his fellow physicians) found his theory unpersuasive. Freud's immediate reaction, as we have seen, was to write up the paper and publish it. But there may have been an element of bluster in this act of defiance, as is suggested by the intemperate language with which he ends his account of the society's meeting: "They can go to hell."[55]

In addition to the doubts Freud openly expressed, we ought to consider those he may have felt because of his fear that his patients' stories were being suggested by the analyst. I have already noted the presence of this anxiety in Freud's pointed insistence that suggestion played no role

54. Ibid., pp. 231, 237, 249, 261.   55. Ibid., p. 184.

in the seduction narrative produced by Emma Eckstein's patient: "Eckstein deliberately treated her patient in such a manner as not to give her the slightest hint of what would emerge from the unconscious and in the process obtained from her, among other things, the identical scenes with the father."[56] Even so, the sense of the doctor urging the wanted memory on a reluctant patient is often strongly felt. Freud complains of one neurotic, a banker who fled analysis just at the point where he was about to produce the expected narrative: "My banker, who was furthest along in his analysis, took off at a critical point, just before he was to bring me the last scenes."[57] Ironically, the possibility of suggestion is most evident when, in his published papers on the seduction theory, Freud tries to counter doubts about the genuineness of his patients' stories. In "The Aetiology of Hysteria" he writes: "Before they come for analysis the patients know nothing about these scenes. They are indignant as a rule if we warn them that such scenes are going to emerge. Only the strongest compulsion of the treatment can induce them to embark on a reproduction of them."[58] In "Heredity and the Aetiology of the Neuroses" the feeling of analytic pressure is even more palpable:

The fact is that these patients never repeat these stories spontaneously, nor do they ever in the course of treatment suddenly

56. Ibid., p. 286.
57. Ibid., p. 243. Marianne Krüll makes the plausible suggestion that this uncooperative banker was on Freud's mind when, in his renunciation letter, Freud mentioned as the first reason for no longer believing in his *neurotica* "the running away of people who for a period of time had been most gripped [by analysis]." Krüll, p. 55; *Complete Letters to Fliess*, p. 264.
58. Freud, "The Aetiology of Hysteria," *SE,* vol. III, p. 204.

present the physician with the complete recollection of a scene of this kind. One only succeeds in awakening the psychical trace of a precocious sexual event under the most energetic pressure of the analytic procedure, and against an enormous resistance. Moreover, the memory must be extracted from them piece by piece.[59]

We might legitimately conclude that if Freud was not worried about the possible contamination of the seduction stories by suggestion, he certainly should have been. Perhaps the Viennese doctors who assembled to hear "The Aetiology of Hysteria" raised just this spectre. In view of the doubts Freud actually expressed in his letters to Fliess and the additional doubts that he had good reason to entertain, the failure of confidence announced on September 21, 1897, seems less a sudden volte-face than the long-developing and inevitable collapse of a hypothesis that was the product as much of will as of conviction.

The misgivings that precede the September letter are exactly balanced by the lingering hopes that follow it. Jeffrey Masson's one valuable contribution to Freud studies is to have drawn attention to the two letters of late 1897 in which Freud's belief in the seduction hypothesis enjoys a brief revival. These letters show that the history of Freud's opinions about seduction is not adequately encompassed by the familiar image of an intellectual U-turn. The same conclusion is suggested by Freud's long delay in publicly announcing his change of view and by the ambiguity of his language when, in the *Three Essays on the Theory of Sexuality*, he finally addresses the issue. His supposed retraction

59. Freud, "Heredity and the Aetiology of the Neuroses," *SE*, vol. III, p. 153.

is so tortuously phrased that it sounds more like a reasser-
tion of the theory's correctness than a confession of error:

> The reappearance of sexual activity [in about the fourth year of
> life] is determined by internal causes and external contingencies,
> both of which can be guessed in cases of neurotic illness from
> the form taken by their symptoms and can be discovered with
> certainty by psycho-analytic investigation. I shall have to speak
> presently of the internal causes; great and lasting importance at-
> taches at this period to accidental *external* contingencies. In the
> foreground we find the effects of seduction, which treats a child
> as a sexual object prematurely and teaches him, in highly emo-
> tional circumstances, how to obtain satisfaction from his genital
> zones, a satisfaction which he is then usually obliged to repeat
> again by masturbation. An influence of this kind may originate
> either from adults or from other children. I cannot admit that in
> my paper on "The Aetiology of Hysteria" I exaggerated the fre-
> quency or importance of that influence, though I did not then
> know that persons who remain normal may have had the same
> experiences in their childhood, and though I consequently over-
> rated the importance of seduction in comparison with the factors
> of sexual constitution and development.[60]

This is the language not of abandonment but of reluctant
retreat. The fuller account of Freud's change of opinion
given the following year in "My Views on the Part Played
by Sexuality in the Aetiology of the Neuroses" is hardly
less ambiguous. Once again, there is an awkward to-ing
and fro-ing, in which admissions of the "insufficiencies,"
"displacements," and "misunderstandings" attending his
earlier views jostle uncomfortably with reassertions of their

60. Freud, *Three Essays on the Theory of Sexuality, Standard Edition*,
vol. VII, p. 190.

fundamental accuracy.[61] The avowal of error is anything but full-throated, and the untutored reader could well emerge from Freud's syntactical jungle convinced that he still attributed mental illness to childhood seductions.

As, in an important sense, he still did. Freud never gave up the belief that at least some neuroses originated in real experiences of seduction during childhood. The seduction hypothesis, in other words, was not abandoned but diminished. In the *Introductory Lectures* of 1916–17, Freud tells his audience, "You must not suppose . . . that sexual abuse of a child by its nearest male relatives belongs entirely to the realm of phantasy. Most analysts will have treated cases in which such events were real and could be unimpeachably established."[62] In the Wolf Man case, written in 1914 and published in 1918, he concludes that his patient's seduction at a tender age by his sister was not a fantasy but "an indisputable reality."[63] Similarly, in 1924 Freud added a footnote to the case of Katharina in *Studies on Hysteria* reporting that Katharina had fallen ill "as a result of sexual attempts on the part of her own father."[64] *An Autobiographical Study* of 1925 still finds him affirming that "seduction during childhood retained a certain share, though a humbler one, in the etiology of the neuroses."[65] As late as 1931, in his essay "Female Sexuality," Freud discusses fantasies of seduction by the mother or a nurse, to which he adds:

61. Freud, "My Views on the Part Played by Sexuality in the Aetiology of the Neuroses," *Standard Edition*, vol. VII, p. 274.

62. Freud, *Introductory Lectures on Psycho-Analysis, Standard Edition*, vol. XVI, p. 370.

63. Freud, "From the History of an Infantile Neurosis," *Standard Edition*, vol. XVII, p. 97.

64. Freud, *Studies on Hysteria, SE*, vol. II, p. 134n.

65. Freud, *An Autobiographical Study, Standard Edition*, vol. XX, pp. 34–35.

Actual seduction, too, is common enough; it is initiated either by other children or by someone in charge of the child who wants to soothe it, or send it to sleep or make it dependent on them. Where seduction intervenes it invariably disturbs the natural course of the developmental processes, and it often leaves behind extensive and lasting consequences.[66]

Even the posthumously published *Outline of Psycho-Analysis,* written the year before his death, reaffirms that "the sexual abuse of children by adults" is "common enough" and often results in neurosis.[67] The historical trajectory of Freud's thinking about seduction resembles, if anything, a bell curve. It is not so much a mechanistic narrative of antithesis and displacement as an organic one of growth and decline.

■ ■ ■

The real importance of the story of the seduction theory and its abandonment lies in its role as a myth of origins. In the traditional account of Freud's intellectual development, psychoanalysis is born out of the rubble of the seduction hypothesis. The theory was the crippling error whose repudiation was the sine qua non of Freud's intellectual breakthrough to infantile sexuality and the Oedipus complex, and thus to the foundation of his new science. Ernest Jones calls the abandonment of the seduction theory "one of the great dividing lines in the story" of psychoanalysis.[68] The notion that the seduction theory had to be

66. Freud, "Female Sexuality," *Standard Edition,* vol. XXI, p. 232.
67. Freud, *An Outline of Psycho-Analysis, Standard Edition,* vol. XXIII, p. 187.
68. Jones, *Life and Work,* I:265.

shed in order for psychoanalysis to emerge is indeed the most potent and enduring component of the entire historical construct. It gains its plausibility largely from the circumstance that Freud first mentions the Oedipus complex in letters written in October 1897, less than a month after the famous renunciation of September 21, 1897. But I would suggest that we ought to be suspicious of this excessively mechanical and overneat conception, according to which the new (and historically important) idea automatically occupies the intellectual space vacated by its discredited predecessor. In view of Freud's revived hopes for the seduction theory after September 21, 1897, his long delay in confessing his departures from it, and his continuing belief, to the end of his life, that childhood seductions were real and consequential, we would be better advised to speak of a tension, rather than a categorical opposition, between the seduction theory and the Oedipus theory. The decline of Freud's confidence in the seduction etiology after September 1897 may have sped up the emergence of the Oedipus complex and infantile sexuality. But the proposition that he would never have developed these ideas without abandoning the seduction theory is far from self-evident. Significantly, in a draft sent to Fliess in May 1897—that is, four months before he supposedly jettisoned the seduction hypothesis—Freud had already anticipated an important component of the Oedipus complex. He there observes that neurotics entertain "hostile impulses against parents," and, further, that "this death wish is directed in sons against their fathers and in daughters against their mothers."[69]

The notion that the repudiation of the old theory was a necessary precondition for the rise of the new one did not

---

69. Freud, *Complete Letters to Fliess*, p. 250.

occur to Freud until years later. Nowhere in the Fliess correspondence or in the classic psychoanalytic texts of the first decade of the twentieth century do we find Freud writing that he had to surmount his traumatic theory of hysteria in order to recognize the autonomous sources of infantile sexuality or the preeminent role of fantasy or the existence of Oedipal desires. Apparently he had not yet arrived at this historical construction. Instead, it makes its appearance, appropriately enough, in his earliest sustained attempt to produce an intellectual autobiography, the 1914 essay "On the History of the Psycho-Analytic Movement." Here for the first time we get the story of the seduction theory as a kind of *felix culpa*. Before he could formulate "the hypothesis of infantile sexuality," Freud writes, "a mistaken idea had to be overcome which might have been almost fatal to the young science."[70] The "might have been" and the "almost" somewhat soften the impression of an irreconcilable antithesis between the seduction theory and the theory of infantile sexuality. Nonetheless, the succeeding account of his fortunate escape from the nearly fatal error betrays the sharply dichotomous structure—reality pitted against fantasy—that will distinguish all subsequent accounts of the seduction theory and its abandonment:

Influenced by Charcot's view of the traumatic origin of hysteria, one was readily inclined to accept as true and aetiologically significant the statements made by patients in which they ascribed their symptoms to passive sexual experiences in the first years of childhood—to put it bluntly, to seduction. When this aetiology broke down under the weight of its own improbability and contradiction in definitely ascertainable circumstances, the result at

70. Freud, "On the History of the Psycho-Analytic Movement," *Standard Edition*, vol. XIV, p. 17.

first was helpless bewilderment. Analysis had led back to these infantile sexual traumas by the right path, and yet they were not true. The firm ground of reality was gone. At that time I would gladly have given up the whole work, just as my esteemed predecessor, Breuer, had done when he made his unwelcome discovery. Perhaps I persevered only because I no longer had any choice and could not then begin again at anything else. At last came the reflection that, after all, one had no right to despair because one has been deceived in one's expectations; one must revise those expectations. If hysterical subjects trace back their symptoms to traumas that are fictitious, then the new fact which emerges is precisely that they create such scenes in *phantasy,* and this psychical reality requires to be taken into account alongside practical reality. This reflection was soon followed by the discovery that these phantasies were intended to cover up the autoerotic activity of the first years of childhood, to embellish it and raise it to a higher plane. And now, from behind the phantasies, the whole range of a child's sexual life came to light.[71]

The version of this same historical sequence written a decade later in the *Autobiographical Study*—Freud's most ambitious effort to fashion a coherent narrative of his intellectual development—begins with a slightly stronger assertion of irreconcilable opposition between the two theories. Here Freud refers to the seduction hypothesis as "an error into which I fell for a while and which might well have had fatal consequences for the whole of my work."[72] The antithesis between reality and fantasy is drawn even more extremely than it was in "On the History of the Psycho-Analytic Movement"—to the point that Freud overstates his actual opinion at the time, speaking of the seduction stories as invariably false. Likewise,

71. Ibid., pp. 17–18.
72. Freud, *An Autobiographical Study, SE,* vol. XX, p. 33.

fathers have become the archetypal seducers and daughters the archetypal victims. In effect, the dichotomous historical construct, with its familiar dramatis personae, has hardened into its definitive form:

Under the influence of the technical procedure which I used at that time, the majority of my patients reproduced from their childhood scenes in which they were sexually seduced by some grown-up person. With female patients the part of seducer was almost always assigned to their father. I believed these stories, and consequently supposed that I had discovered the roots of the subsequent neurosis in these experiences of sexual seduction in childhood. My confidence was strengthened by a few cases in which relations of this kind with a father, uncle, or elder brother had continued up to an age at which memory was to be trusted. If the reader feels inclined to shake his head at my credulity, I cannot altogether blame him; though I may plead that this was at a time when I was intentionally keeping my critical faculty in abeyance so as to preserve an unprejudiced and receptive attitude towards the many novelties which were coming to my notice every day. When, however, I was at last obliged to recognize that these scenes of seduction had never taken place, and that they were only phantasies which my patients had made up or which I myself had perhaps forced on them, I was for some time completely at a loss. My confidence alike in my technique and in its results suffered a severe blow; it could not be disputed that I had arrived at these scenes by a technical method which I considered correct, and their subject-matter was unquestionably related to the symptoms from which my investigation had started. When I had pulled myself together, I was able to draw the right conclusions from my discovery: namely, that the neurotic symptoms were not related directly to actual events but to wishful phantasies, and that as far as the neurosis was concerned psychical reality was of more importance than material reality. I do not believe even now that I forced the seduction-phantasies on my patients, that I "suggested" them. I had in fact stumbled for the first time upon the *Oedipus complex,* which was later to assume such an overwhelming importance, but which I did not recognize as yet in its disguise of phantasy.[73]

This account, even more than its predecessor of 1914, has all the earmarks of a well-made play. The narrative is altogether too shapely: its protagonist enters boldly upon his intellectual quest, suffers a crisis of faith, but emerges in the end all the more gloriously for having triumphed over his error. It brings to mind Wordsworth's artful construction of his life as a "crisis-autobiography" in *The Prelude,*[74] where the poet's illusory hopes for the French Revolution play a role analogous to Freud's mistaken belief in the seduction hypothesis. As Freud himself, following Kipling, might have said, it is a "just-so" story, an intellectual romance, written, significantly, long after the events it purports to chronicle. It exhibits exactly the sort of fierce "retrospective patterning" that ought to arouse our suspicions. The actual history of the seduction theory is more prosaic, ragged, and inconclusive.

THE NEW PURITANISM

If I were to speculate about the cultural significance of Jeffrey Masson's attack on Freud for his suppression of the seduction theory, I would be inclined to view it as one manifestation of the sexual counterrevolution that took place in

73. Ibid., pp. 33–34. The passage confirms my suspicion that Freud had been worried about the influence of suggestion on his patients' stories.

74. M. H. Abrams, *Natural Supernaturalism* (New York, 1971), p. 71.

the 1980s. That is, Masson's Freud seems to me a product of the new puritanism of the past decade, in much the way that Sulloway's Freud was a product of the rise of sociobiology in the 1970s. In the realm of sexual thought and behavior—as in politics and economics—the 1980s witnessed a massive reversal of the liberalizing ethos of the 1960s and 1970s. This counterrevolution was adumbrated as early as 1970 in the writings of feminists like Germaine Greer and Kate Millett. In particular, Millett's *Sexual Politics,* whose villains were Freud himself and such prophets of sexual release as Henry Miller and Norman Mailer, had the effect of an intellectual cold shower on the erotic enthusiasms of the previous decade. Later, the antipornography wing of the women's movement, as represented by Andrea Dworkin and Catherine MacKinnon, drew the full repressive implications of Millett's attack. The new puritanism also found powerful advocates on the old political (and sexual) right, among them Allan Bloom, Roger Scruton, and William Bennett, all of whom railed against the promiscuity of the 1960s. Nature itself conspired to provide the counterrevolution with a grim material foundation in the form of the AIDS epidemic. In short, sex had fallen on hard times. We were made intensely conscious of its liabilities—including the threat it could pose to our lives—and we were correspondingly disinclined to celebrate its raptures.

The most striking feature of the treatment of sex in *The Assault on Truth* is precisely its joyless puritanism. Masson has only one register for its discussion. Sex boils down to aggression. It is a source of pain and unhappiness. Masson's book is untouched by any sense of its ecstatic promise, even less by the idea, embraced by such earlier thinkers as Wilhelm Reich and Herbert Marcuse, that sex holds the key to human liberation. Not surprisingly, Masson's profoundly antisexual rhetoric is indistinguishable from that of the burgeoning contemporaneous literature on incest and child abuse. Appropriately, his book received its warmest reception in just those quarters. It is, in sum, very much a product of its time.

That Masson's sensibility is of a piece with the sexual counterrevolution is confirmed by the autobiographical revelations he offers in *Final Analysis*. Nothing obsesses Masson more than his former promiscuity. He originally entered psychoanalytic treatment, he says, in hopes of curbing the compulsive womanizing that was making him so unhappy. Indeed, his promiscuity became the central subject of his training analysis at the Toronto Psychoanalytic Institute. Repeatedly in *Final Analysis* Masson grows indignant over what he now considers the smutty minds of his analytic acquaintances. Whether intentionally or not, Janet Malcolm thus created a misleading impression of Masson when, in her *New Yorker* articles, she portrayed him as a libertine. Masson's suit against Malcolm focuses, revealingly, on the fact that Malcolm presented as direct quotations two phrases that conjure up just this image: his supposed reference to himself as "an intellectual gigolo" and his claim that he intended to transform the Freud Museum into "a place of sex, women, fun."[75] Whatever the truth of the matter, one has to feel a certain sympathy for him. In Masson's imagination, sex has very little to do with fun. It is, rather, a miserable burden and a means of torture.

Freud, ironically, became a ready victim of the counterrevolution because his sexual views were so richly ambivalent, poised as they were between repression and libera-

75. Janet Malcolm, *In the Freud Archives* (New York, 1984), pp. 33, 38.

tion, between Victorianism and modernism. On the one hand, there was the Freud who, in "'Civilized' Sexual Morality and Modern Nervous Illness," lambasted bourgeois repressiveness and who, in 1915, wrote that "sexual morality—as society, in its most extreme form, the American, defines it—seems to me very contemptible. I advocate an incomparably freer sexual life."[76] On the other hand, there was the Freud who recognized that sex is not an unmixed blessing, that it brings its own inherent agonies, and that one person's pleasure is often purchased with another's suffering. Nowhere in his writings did Freud take a more astringent view of sex than in his account of the sexual abuse of children in "The Aetiology of Hysteria," the paper that stands at the heart of Jeffrey Masson's case.

From the perspective of Masson's new puritanism, however, Freud was not a figure who explored the complexity of human sexual life—its promise of fulfillment and its no less significant potential for pain and exploitation. Rather, he was someone who, despite having seen the true ugliness of sex, lacked the courage to stand by his insight when it proved unpopular. Psychoanalysis thus failed to develop, as Masson feels it should have, into a movement against the sexual debasement of women and children. Instead, it became virtually the opposite: a doctrine that excused the sexual transgressions of adults, especially men, by assigning blame to the imagination of children, and that, more generally, advocated the liberalization of sexual values and even (in the minds of certain of its radical

76. *James Jackson Putnam and Psychoanalysis: Letters between Putnam and Sigmund Freud, Ernest Jones, William James, Sandor Ferenczi, and Morton Prince, 1877–1917*, ed. Nathan G. Hale, Jr. (Cambridge, Mass., 1971), p. 376.

adepts) invited sexual revolution. It is, I suppose, testimony to the protean richness of Freud's thought that it could inspire both Masson's fantasied campaign of sexual retrenchment and the utopian anticipations of erotic release imagined by Reich and Marcuse. But Freud's own distinctive ambiguity is sacrificed just as brutally on the new altar as it was on the old. He is, if anything, an even less reliable friend of chastity than of liberation. Ultimately, the opposing visions of him conjured up by the sexual left and the sexual right tell us more about their authors' prejudices and the intellectual climate in which they wrote than about Freud himself.

III

Adolf Grünbaum:
The Philosophical
Critique of Freud

Frank Sulloway and Jeffrey Masson address themselves to questions of Freud's intellectual biography. The target of their criticism is the received account of how Freud's psychoanalytic ideas originated in the crucial decade of the 1890s. Adolf Grünbaum's critique of psychoanalysis takes a very different form. It is above all an evaluation of the evidence and arguments that Freud used to justify his ideas. Grünbaum asks, How does Freud know that human behavior is significantly influenced by unconscious thoughts? Grünbaum poses this question most systematically in *The Foundations of Psychoanalysis: A Philosophical Critique,* published in 1984, although the book's main contentions had been aired in a series of papers that began appearing in philosophical journals during the late 1970s. By that time, Grünbaum, who was born in 1923, already had behind him a distinguished career as a philosopher of science. He was especially admired for his "magisterial" studies in the philosophy of time and space.[1] In contrast to

1. Robert S. Cohen, "Adolf Grünbaum: A Memoir," in *Physics, Philosophy and Psychoanalysis: Essays in Honor of Adolf Grünbaum,* R. S.

Sulloway and Masson, then, Grünbaum came to his engagement with Freud relatively late in life and with an impressive record of accomplishment in another field of inquiry.

The Foundations of Psychoanalysis has been widely hailed as the most substantial philosophical critique of Freud ever written. One might suspect the enthusiasm of so resolute an anti-Freudian as Frederick Crews, who greeted Grünbaum's book, in *The New Republic,* as "monumental" and "epoch-making." "After Grünbaum," wrote Crews, "the wholesale debunking of Freudian claims, both therapeutic and theoretic, will be not just thinkable but inescapable."[2] Yet even a critic of the book like the philosopher David Sachs acknowledged it as "an 'event' in philosophical criticism of psychoanalysis."[3] When, in 1986, the book was made the subject of "Open Peer Commentary" in the journal *The Behavioral and Brain Sciences,* forty-one of Grünbaum's colleagues paid tribute to his achievement. Robert R. Holt, professor of psychology at New York University, wrote that "the power and subtlety of the analysis and arguments Adolf Grünbaum presents in this book far surpass those of any previous philosophical evaluation of psychoanalysis," and Irwin Savodnik of UCLA called it "the most exhaustive and powerful critique of psychoanal-

---

Cohen and Larry Laudan, eds., Boston Studies in the Philosophy of Science, vol. 76 (Dordrecht, 1983), p. xii.

2. Frederick Crews, "The Future of an Illusion," *The New Republic,* January 21, 1985; repr. in Crews, *Skeptical Engagements* (New York, 1986), p. 81.

3. David Sachs, "In Fairness to Freud: A Critical Notice of *The Foundations of Psychoanalysis,* by Adolf Grünbaum," *The Philosophical Review* 98, no. 3 (July 1989), p. 350. Sachs's essay has been reprinted in *The Cambridge Companion to Freud,* Jerome Neu, ed. (Cambridge, 1991), pp. 309–38.

ysis to date."[4] Psychoanalysts were hardly less admiring—in sharp contrast to their response to Sulloway and especially Masson. The analysts Robert Wallerstein and Judd Marmor praised Grünbaum's incisiveness and his mastery of Freudian theory, while Marshall Edelson paid him the high compliment of writing an entire book to answer his criticisms.[5] Of all the attacks to which Freud has been subject in the past decade, Grünbaum's is undoubtedly the weightiest.

Although philosophical critiques of psychoanalysis have existed almost since the doctrine first made its appearance at the turn of the century, Grünbaum's analysis is distinguished from these earlier efforts by several features. Most notable are his extraordinary rigor and precision. Grünbaum is manifestly both very smart and very sophisticated, and his critique maintains an unprecedented level of dialectical intensity. At least for the philosophically untutored (to borrow one of Grünbaum's own favorite words), virtually every sentence must be carefully unpacked, so thick and unforgiving (although never obscure) is his habit of thought. At the same time, Grünbaum surpasses all previous philosophical critics of psychoanalysis in the breadth and suppleness of his knowledge of Freud's writings. This intimate relationship with the object of his criticism is closely linked to yet another characteristic of Grünbaum's work: its highly interesting ambivalence.

4. Robert R. Holt, "Some Reflections on Testing Psychoanalytic Hypotheses," and Irwin Savodnik, "Some Gaps in Grünbaum's Critique of Psychoanalysis," both in "Open Peer Commentary" on Adolf Grünbaum, "Précis of *The Foundations of Psychoanalysis: A Philosophical Critique*," *The Behavior and Brain Sciences* 9, no. 2 (1986), p. 242 and p. 257.

5. Marshall Edelson, *Hypothesis and Evidence in Psychoanalysis* (Chicago, 1984).

Strange as it may seem, much of Grünbaum's energy goes into defending Freud's philosophical astuteness. In part, this effort at building Freud up is a dialectical ploy—a disingenuous show of admiration that renders Grünbaum's *coup de grâce* all the more stunning when it is finally delivered. Yet the fact remains that Grünbaum reserves his most withering criticisms not for Freud himself but for those of Freud's followers who fail to measure up to the master's methodological standards, and, even more so, for Grünbaum's fellow philosophers: whether friendly to analysis (Jürgen Habermas, Paul Ricoeur) or hostile to it (Karl Popper, Frank Cioffi), they are invariably described as slovenly readers of Freud as well as poor logicians. This ambivalence renders Grünbaum's critique all the more compelling.

Yet despite his superior critical muscle, Grünbaum has not achieved the prominence of Sulloway or Masson, and I doubt that he will have as marked an influence on Freud's reputation as either of them. The explanation for Grünbaum's relative obscurity lies in the exceptional difficulty of his writing: *The Foundations of Psychoanalysis* is profoundly inaccessible. Grünbaum has only the most primitive sense of how to compose a book, taking up topics in no discernible order and seldom resisting the temptation to digress. A chapter of fifty pages is followed by one of three pages; internal subdivisions and titles provide little useful guidance to the intellectual proceedings. But the idiosyncrasies of the book's organization would be tolerable were its language less forbidding. Most bothersome is Grünbaum's addiction to a highly technical philosophical vocabulary. To a certain extent, of course, the use of this terminology reflects his commitment to intellectual precision. But a devotion to precision will not explain the ornate and pedantic rhetorical structures into which Grünbaum embeds his technical terms. Again and again, the reader must struggle to disentangle fearsome syntactical complexities. Here is a representative sample: "Duhem showed, before Habermas was born, that the presence of auxiliary hypotheses in the experimental testing of a major hypothesis in physics precludes a deductively conclusive refutation of the latter, despite the deductive validity of a *modus tollens* inference."[6] This sort of writing serves principally to inhibit comprehension. Reading *The Foundations of Psychoanalysis,* one can easily doubt that anything so disorganized and impenetrable could ever pose a serious threat to Freud.

Quite apart from its sheer inscrutability, Grünbaum's writing occasionally succumbs to disconcerting lapses in tone. With no warning he will plunge from the philosophic empyrean to the journalistic lowlands. Admittedly, this habit lends an intriguingly human touch to the book, although it also makes one wonder about Grünbaum's judgment. For example, consider his discussion of Freud's theory that paranoia results from repressed homosexuality. Grünbaum's general philosophical point is this: because Freud's theory invites the (clearly falsifiable) prediction that a decline in the repression of homosexuality ought to result in a corresponding decline in paranoia, it disproves Karl Popper's claim about the unfalsifiability of psychoanalytic propositions. But Grünbaum chooses to make his point in a most curious fashion:

The recently revealed likelihood that, in 1893, Tchaikovsky was blackmailed into suicide—under threat of exposure of a homosexual liaison—is a measure of the lethal power possessed by the

6. Adolf Grünbaum, *The Foundations of Psychoanalysis: A Philosophical Critique* (Berkeley, 1984), p. 41. Hereafter, page references to this work will appear in parentheses in the text.

ban on homosexuality in the Christian world less than a century ago. This suicide occurred at the pinnacle of his career, less than a week after the Saint Petersburg premiere of his celebrated *Pathétique* symphony. Yet, for nine decades the standard biographies of him attributed his death at the age of fifty-three to cholera, probably yet another manifestation of the prevailing taboo on homosexual behavior and on suicide as well. Since 1893, which was also the year of Breuer and Freud's momentous "Preliminary Communication," even prominent members of both sexes have publicly identified themselves as homosexuals despite the harassing agitation of Anita Bryant. Perhaps it is therefore not too early now to begin garnering appropriate statistics on the incidence of paranoia with a view to ascertaining in due course whether these epidemiologic data bear out the psychoanalytically expected decline. (38–39)

How did we get to Tchaikovsky and Anita Bryant? Such apparently gratuitous observations erupt into Grünbaum's otherwise relentlessly abstract discourse rather like neurotic symptoms, disturbing the philosophical peace. At the very least they bespeak a remarkable—albeit not unattractive—indifference to appearances. One begins to suspect that Adolf Grünbaum is a deeply eccentric man.

The sensibility on display in these pages is light-years removed from Freud's. Even his harshest critics agree that Freud was among the most lucid and least pedantic of writers. So far as I know, he was never guilty of the sorts of lapses in tone that give Grünbaum's book a sometimes surreal effect. The discrepancy might well be irrelevant. But so profound a difference in literary manner carries certain intellectual implications. One begins to worry that, for all his philosophical acuity and his knowledge of the psychoanalytic literature, Grünbaum cannot actually engage Freud. One fears, in other words, that because Freud and Grünbaum inhabit such manifestly alien rhetorical universes, the encounter between the two risks becoming an intellectual nonevent.

THE HERMENEUTIC FREUD

The first third of *The Foundations of Psychoanalysis* is devoted to the hermeneutic interpretation of Freud advanced by Jürgen Habermas and Paul Ricoeur. Grünbaum's massively detailed attack on these two philosophers, coming right at the start of his book, is rather disorienting for the unwary reader. Why, one is apt to wonder, does a book purporting to deal with the foundations of psychoanalysis begin so arbitrarily with this obscure and difficult philosophical disagreement? And why does its author inveigh so passionately and at such length against the interpretations offered by these two thinkers?

Typically, Grünbaum does not explain himself. But his decision to begin with Habermas and Ricoeur in fact makes perfect sense. Grünbaum plans to argue that psychoanalysis does not meet the standards of proof expected in the natural sciences—an enterprise Habermas and Ricoeur threaten to undermine from the start by getting Freud off the evidential hook. They have been leading voices in the campaign to loose psychoanalysis from its scientific roots and replant it, so to speak, in the more hospitable soil of the humanities. Their hermeneutic reinterpretation turns on the idea that psychoanalysis is not a science, even though Freud made the mistake of claiming it was. Rather, it is an interpretive discipline, more akin in its intellectual methods and goals to philosophy, history, and literature than to physics, chemistry, or biology. And because psychoanalysis is not a science, it obviously cannot be held to the standards of proof that obtain in science. To complain that Freud's ideas fail to measure up to the canons of inductivism demanded in the sciences (as opposed to the ways of knowing that prevail in the humanities) is to misunderstand what sort of knowledge psychoanalysis imparts.

Grünbaum views the hermeneutic approach as a fiendishly clever stratagem designed to save psychoanalysis from intellectual oblivion. He distrusts its easy appeal to a profession that has long found itself on the epistemological defensive, alluding darkly to the "desire to safeguard a lifetime professional investment in the practice of psychoanalytic treatment":[7]

Faced with the bleak import of skeptical indictments of their legacy, they [psychoanalysts] are intent on salvaging it in some form. Hence, some of them will be understandably receptive to a rationale that promises them absolution from their failure to validate the cardinal hypotheses of their clinical theory, a failure I demonstrate in depth . . . below. Be of stout heart, they are told, and take the radical *hermeneutic* turn. Freud, they learn, brought the incubus of validation on himself by his scientistic pretensions. Abjure his program of causal explanation, the more drastic hermeneuticians beckon them, and you will no longer be saddled with the harassing demand to justify Freud's causal hypotheses. (57)

Grünbaum regrets that a number of prominent analysts— such as George Klein, Roy Schafer, and Donald Spence— have thrown in their lot with the hermeneuticians. They argue, in Donald Spence's words, that psychoanalysis seeks not "historical truth" but "narrative truth," and they urge analysts to abandon the claim to offer objective expla-

---

7. Grünbaum, "Précis of *The Foundations of Psychoanalysis*," p. 220.

nations of human behavior in favor of more modest interpretive goals, such as providing the analysand with a coherent (though not necessarily accurate) account of his experience. Understandably, Grünbaum is eager to head off this intellectual retreat, because, if successful, it would render his inductivist critique of psychoanalysis otiose. Hence the savage attack on Habermas and Ricoeur with which he begins.

Grünbaum complains that the hermeneutic interpreters radically misrepresent Freud's views. In particular, Grünbaum objects to their effort to portray Freud as a helpless victim of nineteenth-century positivism, caught in the embrace of unreconstructed philosophical materialism. The hermeneutic interpreters err, Grünbaum insists, in thinking that Freud's claim to be a scientist rested on his continued faith in an outdated materialist ontology of mind—classically embodied in the Helmholtzian *Project for a Scientific Psychology*—whose residues, they argue, infected even his mature metapsychological conceptions. Rather, asserts Grünbaum, once Freud had abandoned the 1895 *Project,* he held to a strictly methodological or "epistemic" (6) notion of the scientific credentials of psychoanalysis: psychoanalysis was scientific because it arrived at general truths by way of induction, not because it had identified the fundamental material entities of the human mind. Accordingly, for Freud the most scientific part of psychoanalysis was its clinical theory—its explanations for various mental illnesses and its ideas about dreams and slips, all of which, Freud maintained, rested first and foremost on a "wealth of dependable observations" gathered from the couch.[8] In keeping with the inductive methods of science, the metapsychological constructs were a secondary

8. Freud, letter to Saul Rosenzweig, February 28, 1934, quoted by Peter Gay, *Freud: A Life for Our Time* (New York, 1988), p. 523n.

development, intended to account for those primary clinical findings. The metapsychology was frankly speculative, and, as Grünbaum shows, Freud was always ready to give it up if it came into conflict with clinical material. Thus, writing in 1925 about his metapsychological description of the mind in terms of "agencies" or "systems" (like the unconscious and the preconscious), Freud noted: "Such ideas as these are part of a speculative superstructure of psycho-analysis, any portion of which can be abandoned or changed without loss or regret the moment its inadequacy has been proved."[9] The hermeneutic revisionists, Grünbaum complains, erroneously treat the metapsychology not as "a speculative superstructure," which Freud truly deemed it to be, but as the discreditable philosophical base of his thought. They thereby fundamentally misconstrue the nature of Freud's commitment to science.

■   ■   ■

Jürgen Habermas is the hermeneutic interpreter whose version of psychoanalysis most offends Grünbaum. Habermas's principal discussion of psychoanalysis occurs in *Knowledge and Human Interests* (1968), where he argues that Freud was guilty of "scientistic self-misunderstanding" in thinking his discoveries were a contribution to science.[10] Habermas's case depends on showing that the essential features of psychoanalytic theory deviate from the intellectual procedures routinely found in the sciences. Grünbaum

9. Freud, *An Autobiographical Study,* in *The Standard Edition of the Complete Psychological Works of Sigmund Freud,* translated from the German under the general editorship of James Strachey (London, 1953–74), vol. XX, pp. 32–33.
10. Jürgen Habermas, *Knowledge and Human Interests,* trans. Jeremy J. Shapiro (New York, 1971), p. 246.

criticizes both ends of Habermas's dichotomy: psycho-analysis, Grünbaum insists, does not depart from the scientific norm (at least in its aspirations) as Habermas says it does, and science, for its part, turns out to be a rather different intellectual animal from the caricature conjured up by Habermas. Here Grünbaum draws on his profound knowledge of modern physics to suggest that Habermas is something of a scientific illiterate, whose pronouncements about what is and what is not scientific are based on massive ignorance of the intellectual practices actually employed by scientists.

According to Habermas, psychoanalysis differs most importantly from science in that it does not aspire to causal knowledge. Rather than trying to explain human behavior in terms of general causal laws, it aims to dissolve the causal nexus of the natural world. "In technical control over nature," Habermas writes,

we get nature to work for us through our knowledge of causal connections. Analytic insight, however, affects the causality of the unconscious as such. Psychoanalytic therapy is not based, like somatic medicine, which is "causal" in the narrower sense, on making use of known causal connections. Rather, it owes its efficacy to overcoming causal connections themselves.[11]

Habermas's thinking here is not easy to grasp. He apparently believes that an analytic cure actually destroys the causal tie between a repression and its neurotic symptom. Analysis, one might say, rescues the patient from the causal regime of nature. It lifts the patient out of the material world of causality into a more purely intellectual or spiritual realm where mundane causality is transcended. Psychoanalysis is, in effect, a doctrine of liberation.

11. Ibid., p. 271.

Grünbaum is eager to dispatch this conception, because his own critique of Freud will focus above all on Freud's failure to provide adequate evidence for the causal propositions at the heart of psychoanalytic theory. If Habermas is correct, Freud's theory does not advance causal propositions at all; on the contrary, the theory radically undermines the role of causality in human behavior. Grünbaum has little trouble showing that this notion is repeatedly contradicted in Freud's writings, which are saturated with causal claims. Indeed, they exhibit an almost compulsive search for causes—whether of neurotic symptoms, dreams, or slips. Grünbaum also argues that Habermas's claim is philosophically "incoherent": "Habermas slides from the therapeutic conquest of *effects* by the removal of their cause into the dissolution of the causal *linkage* between the pathogen and the neurosis. Overcoming an effect by undercutting its cause is hardly tantamount to dissolving the causal connection that links them" (11–12). In other words, psychoanalytic therapy does not abolish causal connections but instead makes use of them: the patient escapes his symptom by bringing to consciousness the repressed experience that gave rise to the symptom. Far from attempting to effect some mysterious liberation of human experience from the causal order, psychoanalysis traffics precisely in causal propositions—and in this regard it is indistinguishable from any natural science.

Another difference between psychoanalysis and science, in Habermas's account, is that the analyst does not enjoy the sovereign intellectual authority over his subject exercised by the natural scientist. The order of nature, which the scientist investigates, exists only as an object, and the scientist alone is the source of knowledge about its functioning. In analysis a very different situation obtains. Here the "object" of investigation is himself or herself a subject.

Indeed, in Habermas's view, the patient stands in a privileged relation to the knowledge generated under analysis: not only is the patient the active source of all the material out of which interpretations are fashioned, but the truth of those interpretations ultimately depends on the patient's embrace of them. "Analytic insights," Habermas writes, "possess validity for the analyst only after they have been accepted as knowledge by the analysand himself."[12] By insisting on the privileged epistemological position of the analysand, Habermas undermines any notion of the psychoanalyst as functioning like a physicist or chemist, who confidently determines the laws to which the objects of his study must submit. Instead, the analyst's constructions have the tentative or heuristic quality of interpretations in the humanities; as such they must be confirmed by the patient before they can be accepted as true. Once again, Habermas seeks to distance psychoanalysis from science by showing that it assumes a fundamentally different way of knowing, and hence a different method of validation.

Habermas's argument for the patient's epistemological sovereignty is perhaps less threatening to Grünbaum than his outright denial that psychoanalysis deals in causes. But it stands in opposition to one of Grünbaum's central complaints about analysis, namely, that its findings are subject to evidential contamination. In Grünbaum's view, the patient is a source not of truth but of error, a highly dubious authority, whose memory cannot be trusted and whose reliability is compromised by a desire to fulfill the analyst's expectations. Indeed, the "suggestible" patient is the weak link—the Achilles' heel—in Freud's intellectual system. Grünbaum consequently cannot tolerate Habermas's exaltation of that patient into the arbiter of

12. Ibid., p. 261.

analytic truth. He is thus eager to discredit the notion of the patient's unique intellectual authority.

Grünbaum can easily show that Freud awarded the analysand no such veto power over analytic interpretations. In fact Freud's prejudices were just the opposite: in the best medical tradition, he believed in the absolute intellectual superiority of the doctor to the patient. In several of the case histories Freud insists that his interpretations are correct even when the patient expressly rejects them— indeed, precisely *because* the patient rejects them. An especially clear-cut example is provided by the young lesbian subject of "The Psychogenesis of a Case of Homosexuality in a Woman" (1920), whose refusal of his analytic insights Freud attributes to a desire to punish him, as a surrogate for her father. The same prejudice is famously on display in the Dora case, where Freud shows an overweening contempt for the objections of his patient. More generally, the doctrine of the unconscious—the very heart of psychoanalysis—contravenes Habermas's notion that the patient enjoys unique intellectual authority. The entire logic of psychoanalysis, one might say, undermines the traditional pretensions of the individual to self-knowledge: the psychoanalytic self is largely ignorant of its desires and deluded about its intentions. Habermas's effort to restore to this self its traditional authority reveals a quaint loyalty to the ideals of the Enlightenment, but it is entirely foreign to the teachings of analysis.

Grünbaum goes on to argue that evidence from cognitive psychology supports Freud's skepticism about the patient's self-knowledge. Recent studies cast doubt on the ability of individuals to achieve genuine understanding of even their conscious motives. "When a subject attributes a causal relation to some of his own mental states, he does so—just like outside observers—by invoking theory-based causal schemata endorsed by the prevailing belief-system" (30). In other words, what passes for self-knowledge is often only the projection of one's current intellectual prejudices onto one's past. Habermas's insistence on the analysand's intellectual authority is thus contradicted not only by Freud's practice but also by the latest experimental findings, which show that the individual is a poor judge of what has caused him to behave or think the way he does. It follows that the relationship between the analyst and his subject (a person) is not categorically different from that between the scientist and *his* subject (the world of nature). Once again, Habermas's effort to create a conceptual opposition between psychoanalysis and science turns out to be misguided.

Finally, Habermas contends that analytic knowledge also differs from scientific knowledge in its radically historical character. The truths of psychoanalysis are time-bound and contingent, Habermas argues, while those of science are timeless and absolute. Grünbaum rejects this dichotomy just as vigorously as the others Habermas adduces. In this instance, however, Habermas's error stems not from a misunderstanding of Freud but from his ignorance of science. Many of the propositions of the natural sciences, Grünbaum maintains, are just as historical—as "contextual"—as the propositions of analysis. Rather boldly, Grünbaum chooses his examples not from biology or geology—which on first blush might seem the most historical of the sciences—but from physics. Thus he argues that the physical theory of classical electrodynamics is every bit as historical as is psychoanalytic theory: "At ANY ONE INSTANT, the electric and magnetic fields produced throughout infinite space by a charge moving with arbitrary acceleration depend on its own PARTICULAR ENTIRE INFINITE PAST KINEMATIC HISTORY!" (17). Grünbaum presents several other examples of this sort, which unfortunately convey the impression that he drastically misunderstands what Habermas means by "historical." Grünbaum seems to confuse "history"—the cumulative and meaningful realm of human experience—with "time"—the hermeneutically neutral movement of particles through space. Put another way, the "infinite past history" of an electric charge is hardly the same as the finite past of a human life. As Grünbaum himself observes, almost wistfully, "Some hermeneuticians may retort that these physical cases do not capture the relevant sense of 'history' " (19).

While one might sympathize with the objection that Habermas trades on "stone age physics" (20), making a virtue of scientific ignorance, there remains something wooden about Grünbaum's uninflected insistence that the human and natural realms are entirely comparable—that knowledge of human behavior can assume exactly the same form as knowledge of the behavior of magnetic particles. Habermas may exaggerate the difference between science and psychoanalysis, and he certainly misrepresents Freud's view of the matter, but Grünbaum's hard-hat examples remind one that the hermeneutic construction of psychoanalysis has a certain credibility. Put another way, if the hermeneuticians err in failing to see that psychoanalysis differs from literature, Grünbaum errs in failing to see that it also differs from physics. Psychoanalysis aims to be a science of the self, but ideas about the self can never achieve the rigor of ideas about nature. Analysis thus necessarily exists on the border between science and the humanities. As much as Freud himself wanted his theory to conform to the model of physics, chemistry, and biology, his human subjects forced him to make a number of intellectual compromises, all of which bring his ideas legitimately into the hermeneutic orbit.

■   ■   ■

Paul Ricoeur first presented his hermeneutic interpretation of psychoanalysis in *Freud and Philosophy* (1970), followed in due course by *Hermeneutics and the Human Sciences* (1981). Ricoeur's master theme is that psychoanalysis is not a science but a language—or, as Ricoeur puts it, psychoanalysis is a "semantics of desire."[13] Even more so than Habermas, Ricoeur seeks to bring Freud's ideas into conformity with the linguistic turn of recent intellectual history—the effort to understand virtually all aspects of human behavior in terms of language. As a result of this linguistic perspective, Ricoeur is led to limit the proper subject of psychoanalysis to the verbal communications of the patient in the analytic situation. Psychoanalysis, he writes, is "a work of speech with the patient."[14] All the facts of psychoanalysis are linguistic facts, to wit, the words actually uttered by the patient and the interpretations those words inspire. As Jacques Derrida has it, "There is nothing outside the text"[15]—in this case, nothing outside the text produced by the patient under analysis. Unlike the natural scientist, therefore, the psychoanalyst does not have access to a supposedly objective realm beyond the patient's story. "There are no 'facts' nor any observation of 'facts' in psychoanalysis," writes Ricoeur, "but rather the interpretation of a narrated history."[16]

13. Paul Ricoeur, *Freud and Philosophy: An Essay on Interpretation,* trans. Denis Savage (New Haven, 1970), p. 6.

14. Ibid., p. 369.

15. Jacques Derrida, *Of Grammatology,* trans. Gayatri Spivak (Baltimore, 1976), p. 163.

16. Paul Ricoeur, "Technique and Nontechnique in Interpretation," trans. Willis Domingo, in Ricoeur, *The Conflict of Interpretations,* ed. Don Ihde (Evanston, Ill., 1974), p. 186.

Ricoeur finds evidence for his restriction of psychoanalysis to the patient's "narrated history" in Freud's abandonment of the seduction theory: Freud rightly gave up any claim to identify an objective external experience as the source of the patient's illness, confining his attention instead to the patient's fantasies—a narrative rather than a historical reality—as revealed in the analytic session.

Ricoeur's limitation of the proper domain of analysis to the patient's utterances sends Grünbaum into paroxysms of philosophical castration anxiety. He protests against "this ideological surgery on the psychoanalytic corpus" (47), which he also describes as a "mutilation" (43), an "ontological amputation" (44), and an "emasculation" (60) of Freud's views. Grünbaum shows that Freud himself entertained no such "truncated" (43) conception of the analytic domain. In fact, Freud often turned his attention to the patient's nonverbal behavior (our fingers betray us, he said, even when our mouths don't), and he speculated freely about the psychological meaning of mute artifacts like statues and paintings. Similarly, Freud's substitution of fantasied for actual seductions in no way limits the scope of analysis to the patient's narration, any more than it relieves Freud of the burden, which he shares with any scientist who makes a causal assertion, of proving that imaginary seductions in fact have the pathological effects attributed to them. Most important of all, in Grünbaum's view, Freud clearly believed that his discoveries held true for individuals who had never been analyzed and thus never had occasion to produce a narrative account of their symptoms. In effect, Freud was convinced he had created a general psychology, one quite capable of universally valid statements about human behavior and motivation. He was hardly so modest as to limit his intellectual claims to whatever emerged directly from his patients' stories.

In keeping with the linguistic perspective on analysis, Ricoeur regards all analytic productions, including slips, dream symbols, and neurotic symptoms, as semantic structures. They are elements of a language, and their purpose, like that of ordinary language, is to convey meaning. Against this interpretation Grünbaum argues that Freud did not conceive of the "meaning" of symptoms or slips according to the communicative model of a language. Rather, the "meaning" of symptoms and slips refers to their "definite causal origin" (63). They resemble not linguistic forms but causal traces, like footprints in the sand: "The footprint is *not,* as such, a vehicle of communication; it is not a linguistic sign or symbol; it does *not* semantically stand for, denote, designate, or refer to the past pedal incursion" (64). Grünbaum illustrates this difference by way of the psychoanalytic theory of paranoia, which (as I have already indicated) especially fascinates him. When the paranoid expresses his repressed sexual desires through feelings of persecution, he is not—as the semantic theory would seem to imply—seeking to communicate the fact that he is a homosexual:

Paranoid *behavior* may well be a *vicarious outlet* for repressed homosexuality, but in no case is it a verbal label for it! Thus, as we saw, etiologically that behavior is the afflicted person's attempt to cope with the anxieties generated by his unconscious sexual urges, *not* his/her attempt to *communicate* these yearnings by means of persecutory delusions and behavior. (66)

Here as elsewhere, Grünbaum argues, Ricoeur's effort to treat psychoanalysis as a language, rather than a causal theory, stands at odds with Freud's own conception. It is another misguided attempt to rescue psychoanalysis from the clutches of science.

• ■ ■

Grünbaum ultimately judges the hermeneutic interpretation of Freud as unworthy of its subject. Habermas and Ricoeur represent "a nihilistic, if not frivolous, trivialization of Freud's entire clinical theory" (58). Moreover, Grünbaum predicts, the hermeneutic rescue operation will in fact lead to the ruin of psychoanalysis. "Far from serving as a new citadel for psychoanalytic apologetics," he warns, "the embrace of such hermeneuticians is, I submit, the kiss of death for the legacy that was to be saved" (58). Convinced that he has disposed of analysis's hermeneuticist friends, Grünbaum turns next to its positivist enemies, in particular the philosopher Karl Popper. Significantly, he finds Popper's criticism of Freud no more cogent than Habermas's or Ricoeur's defense of him.

KARL POPPER AND THE QUESTION OF FALSIFIABILITY

Grünbaum was a critic of Karl Popper before he became a critic of Freud. Indeed, it was through Popper that Grünbaum was drawn to Freud. "The first impetus for my inquiry into the intellectual merits of the psychoanalytic enterprise," he writes, "came from my doubts concerning Karl Popper's philosophy of science" (xii). The philosophy of science in question was the theory of falsifiability, which Popper proposed in place of inductivism as the essential measure of scientific knowledge. Popper saw the need for this supposedly more rigorous standard, he said, when he encountered intellectual systems like Marxism and psychoanalysis that claim to derive from observation—that is, from some form of inductive reasoning—yet obviously fall far short of true science. "My problem perhaps took the simple form, 'What is wrong with Marxism, psychoanalysis, and individual [Adlerian] psychology? Why are they so different from physical theories, from Newton's theory, and especially from the theory of relativity?'"[17] Popper's solution was the notion of falsifiability: these pseudosciences may base their ideas on observation, but, unlike true science, they advance propositions that are not open to the possibility of disproof. A scientific theory is a high-risk affair; it asserts things that have a real chance of being contradicted by as yet undisclosed facts. Indeed, science conducts its business so as to encourage the discovery of precisely such disconfirming facts. A pseudoscience, by contrast, is never in danger of this embarrassment. Its propositions are so designed as to be immune to contradictory evidence, because every imaginable state of affairs can somehow be reconciled with them. In Popper's view, the theories of Freud and Adler offer especially clear-cut examples of such nonfalsifiable (and hence unscientific) intellectual systems:

Neither Freud nor Adler excludes any particular person's acting in any particular way, whatever the outward circumstances. Whether a man sacrificed his life to rescue a drowning child (a case of sublimation) or whether he murdered the child by drowning him (a case of repression) could not possibly be predicted or excluded by Freud's theory; *the theory was compatible with everything that could happen.*[18]

17. Karl Popper, *Conjectures and Refutations* (London, 1963), p. 34.
18. Karl Popper, "Replies to My Critics," in *The Philosophy of Karl Popper,* vol. 2, Paul Arthur Schilpp, ed. (La Salle, Ill., 1974), p. 985.

Psychoanalysis was "simply non-testable, irrefutable. There was no conceivable human behaviour which would contradict" it. [19]

Grünbaum views this charge as astonishingly ignorant. In fact, Grünbaum professes amazement at Popper's "obliviousness to Freud's actual writings" (124). Instead of citing real instances of intellectual malfeasance, Popper rests his entire case on a hypothetical example (known as the drowning baby), which Grünbaum dismisses as "grossly contrived" (114). (It is more than contrived: the notion that intentionally drowning a baby might count as an instance of "repression" makes little psychoanalytic sense.) Grünbaum then proceeds to offer evidence, from the Freudian corpus, that controverts Popper's strictures. In both theory and practice, Grünbaum insists, Freud honored the criterion of falsifiability.

An early example is provided by "A Reply to Criticism of My Paper on Anxiety Neurosis" (1895), in which Freud defends his hypothesis that anxiety neuroses are caused by a contemporary disturbance in sexual life, such as masturbation or coitus interruptus. In the paper Freud admits that his theory would be discredited if his critics could produce a case of anxiety neurosis in the absence of sexual anomalies. "My theory can only be refuted," he writes, "when I have been shown phobias where sexual life is normal."[20] A Popperian might complain that Freud does not make this concession in the spirit of falsifiability; his "only" suggests a less than open mind about the likelihood of contrary instances. But the passage satisfies Grünbaum that Freud was prepared to play the scientific game by the

---

19. Popper, *Conjectures and Refutations*, p. 37.

20. Freud, "A Reply to Criticisms of My Paper on Anxiety Neurosis," *Standard Edition*, vol. III, p. 134.

rules—that he advanced empirically "risky" propositions. Freud's statement, Grünbaum writes, "would do any falsificationist proud" (120).

Grünbaum is even more impressed by the 1915 paper "A Case of Paranoia Running Counter to the Psycho-Analytic Theory of the Disease," whose very title seems to have a falsificationist ring about it. Here Freud discusses a seemingly paranoid woman in whom he finds no evidence of homosexuality. In other words, the case contradicts the psychoanalytic theory that paranoia is caused by repressed homosexual desire. Grünbaum admires the paper because in it Freud expressly recognizes the intellectual consequences of his negative finding: either he must give up his theory of paranoia, or he must contemplate the possibility that the woman is not in fact suffering from the disease. "Freud explicitly allowed that if the young woman *was* paranoid, then her case was a *refuting* instance of the etiology he had postulated for that disorder. Alternatively, he reckoned with the possibility that she was not paranoid" (109). Like Freud's much earlier "Reply to Criticisms of My Paper on Anxiety Neurosis," "A Case of Paranoia Running Counter to the Psycho-Analytic Theory of the Disease," Grünbaum argues, is admirably sensitive to the criterion of falsifiability.

Unfortunately for Grünbaum's latter illustration, Freud did not in fact abandon his hypothesis in the face of recalcitrant facts. Instead, he managed to wriggle off the methodological hook, and in a manner a Popperian would surely find incriminating. A second session with his patient turned up the gratifying evidence that she did indeed have an unconscious homosexual attachment to a woman under whom she worked: lo and behold, her paranoia had an orthodox analytic source after all. Thus, while the case may suggest a commendably rigorous theoretical commitment to the principle of falsifiability, in practice it shows Freud doing just what his Popperian critics find most objectionable about psychoanalysis: he generates new facts to make his patient's circumstances fit the theory.

According to Grünbaum, then, the papers of 1895 and 1915 demonstrate that Freud understood and accepted the logic of falsification. But Grünbaum also insists that Freud practiced what he preached: on several occasions Freud actually gave up ideas because they proved empirically insupportable. That is, he operated just as Popperian theory says a scientist ought to, abandoning theoretical positions when they were contradicted by the facts:

> Freud's successive modifications of many of his hypotheses throughout most of his life were hardly empirically unmotivated, capricious, or idiosyncratic. What reconstruction, I ask, would or could Popper give us of Freud's rationale for these repeated theory changes, and still cling to his charge of nonfalsifiability and/or to his charge that Freud was inhospitable to adverse evidence? (117)

The classic example of Freud's changing his mind when the facts so obliged him is, of course, his decision to abandon the seduction theory. Grünbaum frequently draws attention to the famous renunciation letter of September 21, 1897, in which, Grünbaum says, Freud confesses "how adverse evidence that he himself had uncovered drove him to repudiate his previously cherished seduction etiology of hysteria" (117). Given all the controversy over Freud's decision, this amounts to a rather simplistic account of the episode. Grünbaum leaves the impression that Freud had come upon new information that contradicted the seduction hypothesis, forcing him to renounce it. As we have seen, however, Freud's letter in fact mentions no new evidence. Rather, it draws attention to a consequence of the seduction theory that Freud now finds empirically doubtful, namely, that the real sexual abuse of children was as common as the incidence of hysteria would require it to be ("surely such widespread perversions against children are not very probable," he writes).[21] Had Freud actually cited some sort of new evidence—that, for example, his hysterics' stories of seduction had, in concrete instances, been contradicted by the testimony of adults—Jeffrey Masson would never have been able to mount his argument that Freud betrayed a discovery he knew to be true. The import of the seduction theory for Freud's reputation as a scientific methodologist is, I'm afraid, less clear than Grünbaum would like to think.

Whether or not Freud himself believed in or practiced science according to Popperian criteria, his writings, Grünbaum insists, are full of assertions that can in fact be shown to be falsifiable. Psychoanalytic theory repeatedly predicts circumstances whose failure to materialize must result in its disconfirmation. As we've noted, Grünbaum's favorite example of such an obviously falsifiable idea is the Freudian etiology of paranoia, which sets up a decidedly risky epidemiological prediction: "If repressed homosexuality is indeed the specific etiologic factor in paranoia, then the decline of the taboo on homosexuality in our society should be accompanied by a decreased incidence of male paranoia" (111). The theory also invites disconfirmation through historical or anthropological research, because it implies that paranoia will be relatively uncommon in societies, such as ancient Greece, less hostile to homosexuality.

21. Freud, *The Complete Letters of Sigmund Freud to Wilhelm Fliess, 1887–1907,* ed. and trans. Jeffrey Moussaieff Masson (Cambridge, Mass.: 1985), p. 264.

Finally, Grünbaum's strongest evidence against Popper is supplied by psychoanalytic ideas that have actually been proven false—the ultimate scientific compliment, one might say, in a Popperian universe. Here Grünbaum cites Seymour Fisher and Roger Greenberg's "monumental" book *The Scientific Credibility of Freud's Theories and Therapy* (1977), which summarizes a vast number of empirical studies and argues that, among other psychoanalytic propositions, Freud's theory of dreams "has been contradicted by many scientific observations."[22] Freud's ideas, in other words, both invite and receive empirical refutation. They are eminently falsifiable.

■   ■   ■

Grünbaum's vigorous defense of Freud against Popper begs for explanation. As with his polemic against Habermas and Ricoeur, the reader wonders why Grünbaum has allowed himself to get so exercised over a philosophical critic whose animadversions on Freud seem to have been both brief and superficial. Part of the reason has nothing to do with psychoanalysis per se. As a philosopher of science, Grünbaum's stock in trade has been the defense of classic Baconian inductivism, which he regards as the epistemological foundation of modern science. Indeed, his critique of psychoanalysis is framed as a defense of inductivism. Grünbaum agrees with Popper that psychoanalysis "does not come up to scientific standards" (106). But the

22. Adolf Grünbaum, "Is Freudian Psychoanalytic Theory Pseudo-Scientific by Karl Popper's Criterion of Demarcation?" *American Philosophical Quarterly* 16, no. 2 (April 1979), p. 137; Seymour Fisher and Roger P. Greenberg, *The Scientific Credibility of Freud's Theories and Therapy* (New York, 1977), p. 394.

fact that it nonetheless passes Popper's falsifiability test proves that the test itself is a poor means of distinguishing science from pseudoscience. The bulk of *The Foundations of Psychoanalysis* is given over to arguing that Freud's theory, despite its genuinely scientific aspirations, does not meet the traditional Baconian requirements. "Popper's application of his falsifiability criterion is too insensitive to exhibit the most *egregious* of the epistemic defects bedeviling" psychoanalysis, while the "time-honored inductive canons for the validation of causal claims have precisely that capability" (124–25). The Freudian case thus serves to vindicate the familiar inductivist understanding of science and discredit the Popperian challenger.

But Grünbaum's championing of Freud against Popper cannot be explained solely in terms of a long-standing philosophical commitment to inductivism: his heavily inflected language suggests that something else is going on. My own view is that Grünbaum is profoundly divided in his attitude toward Freud. Without doubt, his main purpose in *The Foundations of Psychoanalysis* is to prove that Freud's intellectual brainchild is, as Grünbaum says more than once, "fundamentally flawed" (xii, 94, 124, 128). Put bluntly, he is out to get psychoanalysis. In the course of prosecuting his case, however, Grünbaum seems to have grown remarkably fond of the object of his abuse. Thus his later writings, like *Foundations,* are much warmer in their enthusiasm than are his early papers. It is difficult to avoid psychoanalytic language in describing this phenomenon. There seems to be an element of deferred allegiance to the repudiated father, a perhaps guilty attempt to atone for intellectual aggressions. Grünbaum's ambivalence is the exact inverse of Frank Sulloway's. Where Sulloway pretends to reveal Freud's scientific originality while secretly holding him in contempt, Grünbaum sets out to dispute the scientific credentials of psychoanalysis but is unable to suppress a growing admiration for its creator. He seems truly angered by Karl Popper's disrespectful attitude toward Freud, who emerges from Grünbaum's pages as an intellectual giant, albeit a blemished one, and a scientific methodologist of the first order.

Grünbaum's writings are in fact studded with tributes to Freud. Sometimes this praise offers Freud no more than his historical due as a force in modern intellectual life: his thought is "momentous" (39), "pioneering" (148), "epoch-making" (10). But Grünbaum also insists on the power and profundity of Freud's ideas. No adjective comes more readily to Grünbaum's mind in connection with Freud than "brilliant" (13, 93, 135). Freud displays "a soaring mind" (189) and a "brilliant theoretical imagination" (278). The caliber of his arguments is "astronomically higher, and their often brilliant content incomparably more instructive" (93) than are the glosses of his hermeneutic critics. He is the author of a "monumental clinical theory of personality" (94). His thinking is "admirably rich and lucid" (168). Even more striking than these generic celebrations of Freud's intelligence is Grünbaum's repeated insistence on Freud's methodological acuity—in other words, his distinction in precisely that department of intellectual affairs where Popperians find him most wanting. Freud's reflections on the philosophy of science are "pregnant" (42), and his concerns with the contaminating effects of suggestion "always unflagging" (129). He displays a "keen appreciation of methodological pitfalls that are commonly laid at his door by critics" (168). Indeed, he must be acknowledged "a sophisticated scientific methodologist, far superior than is allowed by the appraisals of friendly critics like Fisher and Greenberg or Glymour, let alone by very severe critics like Eysenck" (128, and see 172). In other words, Freud is to be admired not simply as a daring theorist but also as a "meticulous" (135) and "careful" (169) practitioner. When Freud falls short of his own high methodological standards (as he inevitably does), Grünbaum records such failures more in sorrow than in anger. He seems disappointed that Freud's arguments are sometimes "unworthy" (141) of so incisive a scientific mind.

At the same time, Grünbaum's animus toward Popper is not just a matter of an inadequately repressed admiration for Freud. It also reflects Grünbaum's fear that the dismissal of psychoanalysis as "non-testable, irrefutable" will divert attention from Freud's real shortcomings. Popper's "indictment of the Freudian corpus as inherently untestable," Grünbaum writes, "fundamentally misdiagnosed its very genuine epistemic defects" (xii). In this respect, Grünbaum's hostility to Popper ultimately stems from the same source—or has the same rationale—as his hostility to Habermas and Ricoeur. Although Popper and the hermeneuticians hold diametrically opposed attitudes toward science—for Popper science is the greatest intellectual achievement in history, whereas for Habermas and Ricoeur science is an imperialistic threat to the interpretive understanding of human affairs—they agree, ironically, that psychoanalysis falls beyond the scientific pale. For the hermeneuticians, of course, this is a blessing, while for Popper it is a curse. But from Grünbaum's point of view, both parties threaten to excuse Freud's gravest defect as a thinker: his failure to supply adequate evidence for his ideas. Habermas and Ricoeur excuse this failure by arguing that the sort of hermeneutic knowledge psychoanalysis supplies does not require the same inductive support as do the truths of science. Popper, for his part, excuses it by arguing that the question of empirical evidence is beside the point when every conceivable state of affairs is compatible with analytic theory. Against both the apologetic left and the critical right, Grünbaum maintains that psychoanalysis is a science in aspiration, if not in fact. He wants to disprove Popper's claim that psychoanalysis is unfalsifiable precisely because he is eager to falsify it.

Grünbaum has little difficulty showing that Popper's case against Freud is slight and ill-informed. But Grünbaum's dismissal of the charge of nonfalsifiability overlooks a genuine intellectual weakness of psychoanalysis, one that Popper obviously sensed and gestured toward—however crudely—with his example of the drowning baby. I have in mind the "heads-I-win-tails-you-lose" style of argument that pervades psychoanalytic reasoning. (Freud himself acknowledged the problem in his late essay "Constructions in Analysis," where he responded to the charge that analysts construe the patient's "no" to mean "yes" whenever it serves their purpose.) Psychoanalytic theory provides its adepts with too many interpretative alternatives—too many choices—which often seem to function as intellectual escape routes when the evidence is unaccommodating. In particular, concepts like resistance, ambivalence, overdetermination, and reaction formation let the analyst have it both ways—or, as Popper would insist, have it any way whatsoever. Thus, when one of Freud's patients reported dreams that apparently revealed no hidden wish, Freud notoriously interpreted them as revealing the wish to disprove his dream theory! Clearly Popper was onto something when he charged that analysis is closed to the possibility of contradiction.

The answer to this line of criticism, put very generally, it that human beings are complex and the contingencies of life innumerable. A given action does not always have the same meaning, not even for a single individual. In terms of Popper's hypothetical example of the drowning baby, a person may repress an impulse in one instance while sublimating it in another, and the desire to save (or drown) a baby might be variously motivated. A psychological system must leave room to maneuver if it wishes to make sense of the vagaries of human experience. By contrast, a theory that always gives unambiguous answers—that provides the binary predictions Popper seems to want— will inevitably flatten out the human reality it seeks to esplain. Of course, the very flexibility of psychoanalytic theory means that the analyst must be exceptionally disciplined in its application, because the temptation to intellectual abuse is so great. In lesser hands, Freud's ideas too often invite the sort of bad intellectual manners that Popper complains of.

THE TALLY ARGUMENT

Having disposed of Habermas, Ricoeur, and Popper, Grünbaum arrives at the centerpiece of his critique: his claim to have discovered in Freud a hitherto ignored philosophical defense of psychoanalysis, which he christens the Tally Argument. Grünbaum divides his energy about equally between celebrating the Argument's virtues and exposing its weaknesses. His method is dialectical, or at least dramatic: he builds the Argument up so that its ultimate collapse will seem all the more ruinous. In effect, Grünbaum establishes Freud's methodological sophistication in order to use it against him, suggesting that Freud neglected standards of proof whose legitimacy he fully understood. Freud's shortcomings thereby seem willful rather than naive.

Grünbaum contends that the Tally Argument provides the philosophical justification for virtually all of Freud's psychoanalytic concepts. But in fact the Argument bears mainly on the idea of the unconscious. Its implications for that other great pillar of psychoanalysis, the theory of infantile sexuality, are at best indirect. Significantly, Freud's ideas about the beginnings of sexual life figure only marginally in Grünbaum's analysis. His focus on the unconscious to the neglect of infantile sexuality makes his treatment of Freud very unlike the critiques of Frank Sulloway and Jeffrey Masson, in which Freud's notions about the sexual lives of children are always the center of attention, while the unconscious is largely ignored.

As Grünbaum recognizes, Freud's theory of the unconscious is distinguished by two features. First, it holds that ideas we are unaware of exert a significant influence over our behavior. Neurotic symptoms provide the prime example of such influence. Second, the mechanism through which ideas become unconscious is repression. Originally conscious, these ideas are forced into the unconscious when they prove incompatible with conscious convictions. "The theory of repression," Freud says, "is the cornerstone on which the whole structure of psychoanalysis rests."[23] Thus the archetypal Freudian claim, whose credentials Grünbaum sets out to evaluate, asserts that a particular piece of behavior—typically a neurotic symptom—is caused by an unconscious idea, whose repression usually occurred some distance in the past.

If one asks Freud and other analysts what persuades them that repressed ideas actually have such consequences, they point over and over to the evidence gathered from clinical practice: their conviction, they say, derives above all from the observation of patients in analysis. "Most advocates" of psychoanalysis, Grünbaum writes, "regard

---

23. Freud, "On the History of the Psycho-Analytic Movement," *Standard Edition*, vol. XIV, p. 16.

the analyst's many observations of the patient's inter-actions with him in the treatment session as the source of findings that are simply *peerless,* not only heuristically but *also* probatively" (99–100). The clinical situation provides unique insights, in this view, both because a typical anal-ysis lasts for several years and because the analyst follows the patient's free associations wherever they may lead. Analysis thus allows for the accumulation of evidence about the patient's life that is unparalleled in its quantity, detail, and nuance.

Not only do analysts insist that evidence from the couch supplies a firm empirical base for psychoanalytic ideas, but they are deeply skeptical about the value of any other kind of evidence, in particular the experimental and epidemio-logical data so beloved of academic psychology. Such sta-tistical information, derived from a transitory laboratory setting, is, in their estimate, contrived and superficial and hence incapable of yielding the deep insights obtained in analysis. Freud himself set the pattern for the analytic ten-dency to belittle experimental evidence. When the psy-chologist Saul Rosenzweig sent Freud an account of exper-imental results that purportedly confirmed Freud's ideas, Freud responded: "I have examined your experimental studies for the verification of the psychoanalytic assertions with interest. I cannot put much value on these confirma-tions because the wealth of reliable observations on which these assertions rest make them independent of experi-mental verification. Still, it can do no harm."[24]

The clinical defense of psychoanalysis suffers one great philosophical weakness: the possibility that information gathered from patients under analysis cannot be trusted.

24. Freud, letter to Saul Rosenzweig, February 28, 1934, quoted by Grünbaum, *Foundations,* p. 101.

For some critics that information is unreliable because the
sample on which it rests—persons who seek analysis—is
unrepresentative. But a far weightier objection—and the
one to which virtually all of Grünbaum's attention is devoted—is that analytic patients are victims of suggestion.
The interpretations that emerge in analysis, critics charge,
are compromised by the analyst's theoretical expectations.
Far too often, the patient simply tells the analyst what the
analyst wants to hear. Because information from the couch
is so hopelessly tainted, it cannot be considered "probative."

Grünbaum argues that, contrary to general belief, Freud
was exquisitely sensitive to this criticism and went to great
trouble to refute it. The principal evidence lies in two in-
stallments from the *Introductory Lectures on Psychoanalysis,*
which Freud delivered to medical students at the University of Vienna during World War I. The first of these, on
"Transference," frankly acknowledges that suggestibility
poses a more serious threat to psychoanalysis than it does
to any other therapeutic procedure for the treatment of
mental illness. Analysis makes the emotional tie to the
doctor, the transference, absolutely central to the resolution of the patient's neurosis. The transference stems from
the recreation, in an analytic setting, of significant emotional relationships of childhood, with the doctor typically
assuming the role of parent. Analysis thus invests the doctor—already an authoritative figure in any therapeutic situation—with the added authority of a parental surrogate.
As a consequence, the patient is rendered even more vulnerable to the doctor's intellectual influence. The transference, writes Freud, "clothes the doctor with authority and
is transformed into belief in his communications and
explanations."[25] Thus, as "Freud knew all too well," the

25. Freud, *Introductory Lectures on Psycho-Analysis, Standard Edition,*
vol. XVI, p. 445.

notion of the transference virtually invites the criticism that clinical findings reflect not "true insightful self-discovery" (130) but the patient's compliance with the analyst's suggestions.

If Freud's lecture on "Transference" candidly acknowledges the extent of the problem, the next lecture, on "Analytic Therapy," provides what is for Grünbaum the most considered methodological defense of psychoanalysis ever written. This is the so-called Tally Argument, in which Freud "brilliantly, albeit unsuccessfully, came to grips with the full dimensions of the mortal challenge of suggestibility" (135). Grünbaum returns to the crucial passage over and over in his writings, and one can fairly say that his entire philosophical critique of psychoanalysis ultimately depends on his reading of it. The passage exhibits the sweet reasonableness so characteristic of Freud's expository works, in which he shows a masterly skill at anticipating his listeners' objections:

But you will now tell me that, no matter whether we call the motive force of our analysis transference or suggestion, there is a risk that the influencing of our patient may make the objective certainty of our findings doubtful. What is advantageous to our therapy is damaging to our researches. This is the objection that is most often raised against psycho-analysis, and it must be admitted that, though it is groundless, it cannot be rejected as unreasonable. If it were justified, psycho-analysis would be nothing more than a particularly well-disguised and particularly effective form of suggestive treatment and we should have to attach little weight to all that it tells us about what influences our lives, the dynamics of the mind or the unconscious. That is what our opponents believe; and in especial they think that we have "talked" the patients into everything relating to the importance of sexual experiences—or even into those experiences themselves—after such notions have grown up in our own depraved imagination. These accusations are contradicted more easily by an appeal to experience than by the help of theory. Anyone who has himself carried out psycho-analyses will have been able to convince himself on countless occasions that it is impossible to make suggestions to a patient in that way. The doctor has no difficulty, of course, in making him a supporter of some particular theory and in thus making him share some possible error of his own. In this respect the patient is behaving like anyone else—like a pupil—but this only affects his intelligence, not his illness. After all, his conflicts will only be successfully solved and his resistances overcome if the anticipatory ideas he is given tally with what is real in him. Whatever in the doctor's conjectures is inaccurate drops out in the course of analysis; it has to be withdrawn and replaced by something more correct.[26]

Grünbaum of course dubs this the Tally Argument after the crucial verb in the penultimate sentence: the patient's difficulties will be solved—his neurosis cured—only if the analyst's interpretations "tally with what is real in him." The passage, Grünbaum writes, contains Freud's "cardinal epistemological defense of the psychoanalytic method of clinical investigation and testing, a pivotal vindication whose import had gone completely unnoticed in the literature, as far as I know, until I called attention to its significance in two recent papers" (135).

Grünbaum proceeds to "tease out" and give more precise philosophical expression to the assumptions of the Tally Argument.[27] In essence, Grünbaum suggests, the Argument involves two propositions, whose "conjunction" (139) he calls the Necessary Condition Thesis, or NCT. The first proposition is that psychoanalysis alone provides insight into the unconscious causes of the pa-

---

26. Freud, *Introductory Lectures, SE,* vol. XVI, p. 452.
27. Grünbaum, "Précis of *The Foundations of Psychoanalysis,*" p. 221.

tient's illness: "Only the psychoanalytic method of interpretation and treatment can yield or mediate to the patient correct insight into the unconscious pathogens of his psychoneurosis" (139). The second proposition is that such insight is essential to the patient's cure: "The analysand's correct insight into the etiology of his affliction and into the unconscious dynamics of his character is, in turn, *causally necessary* for the therapeutic conquest of his neurosis" (139–40). Simply put, the truth of Freud's ideas is guaranteed by the success of his therapy: his theories are validated by the fact that patients are cured. (Freud does not, be it noted, claim that analysis *always* results in cures; more modestly, according to Grünbaum, Freud says that analytic insight is a necessary but not a sufficient cause of therapeutic success.) The Tally Argument protects analytic interpretations from the charge of suggestion because only if those interpretations are true, the Argument asserts, will the patient get well. Interpretations that do not reflect the patient's reality will not result in cures and, Freud asserts optimistically, will in fact wither away as the analysis proceeds. Grünbaum adds that just as individual cures assure Freud of the correctness of particular interpretations, so the cumulative therapeutic successes of analysis guarantee its general ideas: "Collectively, the successful outcomes of analyses . . . constitute *cogent* evidence for all that general psychoanalytic theory tells us about the influences of the unconscious dynamics of the mind on our lives" (140).

The Tally Argument, in Grünbaum's construction, has two further implications, although Freud expressly mentions neither. Both involve empirical matters, and, as one might expect, they contain the seeds of the Argument's downfall. The first is that the Argument implicitly rules out the possibility of spontaneous remissions—cures that happen without any kind of professional intervention.

This conclusion follows logically from the Necessary Condition Thesis, which asserts that only analysis can provide the insights needed to effect a cure: spontaneous remissions, whatever their cause, are not produced by the insights of analysts. (Freud's self-analysis might qualify as an exception, although "spontaneous remission" usually designates a return to health that results from nothing more strenuous than the ordinary business of living.) By the same logic, the Tally Argument commits Freud to the belief that analysis is therapeutically superior to all rival psychiatric methods, none of which, in Freud's view, delivers insight into the repressed causes of neurosis—the sine qua non of therapeutic success, according to the Necessary Condition Thesis. Thus the twin spectres of spontaneous remission and rival cures hang like threatening empirical clouds over the Tally defense. If neurotics get well without psychiatric help, or if they get well through the ministrations of a non-Freudian therapist, then the Tally defense collapses. As we shall see, the philosopher David Sachs accuses Grünbaum of overburdening the Tally passage when he makes it an argument not just against suggestibility but against spontaneous remission and rival cures as well.

Grünbaum believes that the Tally Argument constituted the deepest source of Freud's confidence in the truth of his ideas. It was "a veritable pillar" (163) of his doctrine and the ground for his "sovereign patronizing serenity" (170) in the face of charges that analytic "insights" were but spurious products of suggestion. It assured Freud, in a profound psychological way, that his method of clinical investigation was intellectually sound. Above all, the Argument gave Freud the unshakable conviction that clinical evidence was sufficient to validate his claims about the role of unconscious ideas in mental illness—that there was no need for recourse to statistical comparisons with untreated control groups. As Grünbaum portrays him, Freud always had the Tally defense hovering in the back of his mind as a kind of philosophical security blanket.

Grünbaum ignores certain obvious objections to this promotion of the Tally Argument. More than once he expresses surprise that no one before him seems to have recognized the Argument's significance. But, of course, this neglect could simply mean that the Argument possesses neither the cogency nor, more important, the centrality in Freud's thinking that Grünbaum claims for it. After all, Grünbaum's entire case comes down to his reading of a single sentence in the vast Freudian corpus, and that sentence occurs in what Freud himself regarded as a piece of popular writing—a kind of *haute vulgarisation*—in which he presented his ideas to a nonanalytic audience. If the Argument were as fundamental to Freud's thinking as Grünbaum says, Freud might have been expected to follow his normal practice of making it the subject of a technical paper or monograph. At the very least, he presumably would have offered a more systematic and extended discussion of its logic, rather than contenting himself with a single, terse sentence embedded in the middle of a university lecture (and introduced almost offhandedly with "after all"). One cannot escape the impression that Grünbaum has seized on a relatively casual remark and blown it up into a major intellectual event—making a philosophical mountain out of an expository molehill.

Grünbaum nowhere suggests, however, that this objection has crossed his mind. I don't know whether his silence is a sign of cunning or of simple insensitivity to matters of tone and proportion. Nonetheless, Grünbaum apparently feels the need to lend a broader textual resonance to his claims for the Tally defense. Accordingly, he combs Freud's writings for further passages that might be construed to reflect a similar line of reasoning. Perhaps the strongest support comes from the Little Hans case, in which Freud again defends his practice of providing the patient with "anticipatory ideas" ("Erwartungsvorstellungen") and, in contrast to the Tally passage, explicitly casts doubt on spontaneous remissions. "Slight disorders," Freud writes, "may perhaps be brought to an end by the subject's unaided efforts, but never a neurosis." To overcome a neurosis, "another person [i.e., the analyst] must be brought in, and in so far as that other person can be of assistance the neurosis will be curable."[28] Unfortunately for Grünbaum, the passage does not explicitly associate the analyst's "anticipatory ideas" with the charge of suggestibility: it contains part of the Tally defense, but not all of it. It thus fails to dispel the suspicion that the Tally Argument is Grünbaum's own artful concoction, which he has forced on Freud's innocent philosophical imagination.

Grünbaum hears echoes of the Tally Argument whenever Freud makes a remark (however general) that associates psychoanalytic theory with its therapeutic application. Thus the Argument lies behind Freud's assertion that in psychoanalysis "scientific research and therapeutic effort coincide" as well as his later claim that "in psycho-analysis there has existed from the very beginning an inseparable bond between cure and research."[29] Grünbaum professes to be "dumbfounded" (146) by contemporary analysts who would separate the theory from the therapy, as does Judd Marmor when he writes: "I suspect that it was

28. Freud, "Analysis of a Phobia in a Five-Year-Old Boy," *Standard Edition*, vol. X, p. 104.
29. Freud, "Two Encyclopedia Articles," *Standard Edition*, vol. XVIII, p. 236; Freud, *The Question of Lay Analysis, Standard Edition*, vol. XX, p. 256.

largely the historical accident that Freud was attempting to earn a living as a psychiatric practitioner that drove him to utilize his investigative tool simultaneously as a therapeutic instrument."[30] Grünbaum warns that such a separation of theory from therapy invites disaster for psychoanalysis, since it ignores Freud's profound understanding, as recorded in the Tally Argument, that the intellectual fortunes of analysis are inextricably linked to achieving cures.

Ironically, Grünbaum finds one of the earliest invocations of the Tally defense in Freud's 1896 paper on "The Aetiology of Hysteria"—the very paper that Jeffrey Masson celebrates as "Freud's most brilliant" because it contains his boldest assertion of the seduction theory.[31] The irony, of course, is that therapeutic success is here made to testify on behalf of an idea Freud would repudiate a year and a half later in the most controversial intellectual about-face of his career. Nonetheless, Grünbaum detects the Tally Argument at work in Freud's claim, in "The Aetiology of Hysteria," that the seduction hypothesis had been "confirmed" therapeutically:

If you submit my assertion that the aetiology of hysteria lies in sexual life to the strictest examination, you will find that it is supported by the fact that in some eighteen cases of hysteria I have been able to discover this connection in every single symptom, and, where the circumstances allowed, to confirm it by therapeutic success.[32]

30. Judd Marmor, "New Directions in Psychoanalytic Theory and Therapy," in *Modern Psychoanalysis,* Judd Marmor, ed. (New York, 1968), p. 6; quoted by Grünbaum, *Foundations,* p. 146.
31. Jeffrey Moussaieff Masson, *The Assault on Truth: Freud's Suppression of the Seduction Theory* (New York, 1984), p. xviii.
32. Freud, "The Aetiology of Hysteria," *Standard Edition,* vol. III, p. 199.

Grünbaum also maintains that the collapse of the seduction theory did not lessen Freud's confidence in the Tally Argument. Nor, in Grünbaum's opinion, should it have. To be sure, if Freud's hysterical patients had actually been cured by being given false insights into childhood events (seductions) that never occurred, the Necessary Condition Thesis would have been "strongly disconfirmed" (159). But Grünbaum infers—rather generously—that Freud must have come to regard at least some of those cures as bogus, perhaps because the patients in question suffered relapses. In support of this inference Grünbaum cites the famous renunciation letter of September 21, 1897, in which Freud points to therapeutic disappointment as a major reason for his loss of confidence in the seduction theory. (Freud speaks of "the absence of the complete successes on which I had counted.")[33] Thus, far from discrediting the Tally defense, the abandonment of the seduction hypothesis implies that Freud continued to rely on the assumption that cures are the guarantor of truth: he gave up the hypothesis precisely because of therapeutic failures. The seduction debacle, Grünbaum concludes, "provides no basis for judging Freud to have been intellectually dishonest when he explicitly enunciated NCT in 1909 [the Little Hans case] and 1917 [the "Analytic Therapy" lecture]" (159). But, one could object, while Freud may not have been dishonest, he was surely imprudent. Having confidently asserted in 1896 that therapeutic success confirmed his seduction hypothesis only to conclude the following year that at least some of those successes were bogus, Freud might sensibly have decided not to place so much trust in the evidence of cures. Certainly the

33. Freud, *Complete Letters to Fliess,* p. 264.

experience ought to have made him leery about invoking cures as testimony to the correctness of his views.

*   *   *

Grünbaum's master theme in *The Foundations of Psychoanalysis* is that the Tally Argument constituted a powerful defense of analytic ideas and that Freud rightly derived great comfort from it. Nonetheless, Grünbaum also insists that, for all its strengths, the Argument ultimately fails. Its failure is in fact his second major preoccupation, creating the strong suspicion that his original enthusiasm for the Argument was something of a setup. When Freud does not acknowledge that psychoanalysis is defenseless without the Tally Argument, his otherwise admirable methodological sophistication becomes grounds for questioning his integrity.

Grünbaum is surprisingly elusive about the exact reasons for the Argument's failure. He gives two versions of the story, without saying which he considers the more important. And should we find either of these accounts unconvincing or think that the damage is not irreparable, Grünbaum holds yet another version—the definitive one, I suspect—in reserve.

In the first version, the Tally Argument collapses not for logical or empirical reasons but because Freud himself abandoned it. Like Marx's capitalist, Freud in effect becomes his own gravedigger. This focus on Freud's attitude toward the Argument, rather than on its inherent intellectual weaknesses, confirms the impression that Grünbaum's perspective on Freud is as much psychological as philosophical. He is interested in the character of Freud's conviction—the source of his persuasion—not just in whether that conviction was justified.

The key to the Argument's fate, in Grünbaum's first version of its downfall, lies in the evolution of Freud's therapeutic views. All historians of psychoanalysis agree that Freud grew more pessimistic about analytic therapy during the final decades of his life—a pessimism fully in keeping with the darker atmosphere of his later thought, as reflected in such speculative works as *Beyond the Pleasure Principle* (1920) and *Civilization and Its Discontents* (1930). It was given its most melancholy expression in the 1937 essay "Analysis Terminable and Interminable," in which Freud reveals grave doubts about the thoroughness and durability of analytic cures. Analysis, the essay concedes, cannot guarantee that the patient won't suffer a recurrence of his affliction, any more than it can provide immunization against the outbreak of a different neurosis. Mental illness now appears to Freud more elusive and intractable than ever before. Analysis, accordingly, becomes "an interminable task."[34]

Grünbaum reads Freud's late therapeutic pessimism as an implicit disavowal of the Tally Argument. The Argument posits a radical dependence of analytic ideas on therapeutic success, but Freud's growing doubts about his ability to achieve genuine and lasting cures effectively stripped the Argument of its essential premise. "The import of this therapeutic pessimism is shattering" (160), Grünbaum writes. If analysis cannot produce cures, it forfeits its sole guarantee against the crippling charge of suggestibility. Freud thus gave up his only defense when he lost faith in analysis's healing powers.

The gloomy outlook of "Analysis Terminable and Interminable" represents, according to Grünbaum, the culmination of a therapeutic retreat that began over a decade earlier.

---

34. Freud, "Analysis Terminable and Interminable," *Standard Edition,* vol. XXIII, p. 249.

Although Grünbaum generally speaks of this retreat as a gradual process, he is inclined to regard the publication of *Inhibitions, Symptoms and Anxiety* in 1926 as a watershed: in it Freud expressly abandons one of the supposed pillars of the Tally defense, the denial of spontaneous remissions. "As a rule," Freud there writes, "our therapy must be content with bringing about more quickly, more reliably and with less expenditure of energy than would otherwise be the case the good result which in favourable circumstances would have occurred of itself."[35] Once he demoted analysis in this fashion—making it a mere expediter rather than the indispensable cause of the patient's recovery—Freud effectively gave up the Tally defense. "Unless analytic treatment is the paragon of the therapies as claimed in the Tally Argument," Grünbaum concludes, "Freud himself has acknowledged that he cannot be assured of the inherent scientific value of psychoanalysis" (172).

Without ever saying so forthrightly, Grünbaum constructs a history of Freud's methodological opinions, according to which Freud adopted the Tally Argument at the end of the nineteenth century (in his paper on "The Aetiology of Hysteria"), held to it for thirty years, and then abandoned it in 1926. Admittedly, the Argument received explicit formulation only in the Little Hans case of 1909 and the "Analytic Therapy" lecture of 1917. But Grünbaum implies that Freud nonetheless depended on it from 1896 to 1926—in other words, throughout the central three decades of his creative life.

This construction is superficially attractive, because many of Freud's disparaging remarks about therapy do in fact date from his later years. For instance, in 1926—the very year in which he admitted the reality of spontaneous

35. Freud, *Inhibitions, Symptoms and Anxiety, Standard Edition,* vol. XX, p. 154.

remissions—Freud wrote: "The future will probably attribute far greater importance to psycho-analysis as the science of the unconscious than as a therapeutic procedure."[36] That same year he also called himself "a supporter of the inherent value of psycho-analysis and its independence of its application to medicine."[37] And in the *New Introductory Lectures* of 1933 he remarked, only half-jokingly: "I do not think our cures can compete with those of Lourdes. There are so many more people who believe in the miracles of the Blessed Virgin than in the existence of the unconscious."[38] Clearly, as he reached the end of his life, Freud took a sober view of the therapeutic situation.

Nonetheless, Grünbaum's historical construction is highly dubious. In fact, it is a phony history. One can assemble a substantial body of evidence to show that doubts about analytic therapy are by no means confined to Freud's later thinking. "I have never been a therapeutic enthusiast," he rightly said of himself.[39] Nor are assertions about the independence of analytic ideas from their practical application unique to his final years. One of the most emphatic of such assertions occurs in the *locus classicus* of the Tally Argument, *The Introductory Lectures* of 1916–17, where Freud writes: "Even if psycho-analysis showed itself as unsuccessful in every other form of nervous and psychical disease as it does in delusions, it would still remain completely justified as an irreplaceable instrument of scientific research."[40] Grünbaum dismisses this embar-

---

36. Freud, "Psycho-Analysis," *Standard Edition*, vol. XX, p. 265.
37. Freud, *The Question of Lay Analysis, SE*, vol. XX, p. 254.
38. Freud, *New Introductory Lectures on Psycho-Analysis, Standard Edition*, vol. XXII, p. 152.
39. Ibid., p. 151.
40. Freud, *Introductory Lectures, SE*, vol. XVI, p. 255.

rassing denial of the link between science and therapy as "a gratuitous piece of salesmanship, unworthy of the Freud who gave us the Tally Argument" (141). But in fact, during the very years when he was supposedly devoted to the Tally defense, Freud displayed a remarkable willingness to associate psychoanalysis with therapeutic failure—most spectacularly in the famous case histories. Dora (1901) and the Wolf Man (1914) were therapeutic fiascos, yet Freud insisted they yielded valuable insights. Because analytic failure prolonged treatment, it had the ironic effect of aiding discovery. Even in what he regarded as his one unqualified success, the Rat Man case (1909), Freud wrote that "the scientific results of psycho-analysis are at present only a by-product of its therapeutic aims, and for that reason it is often just in those cases where treatment fails that most discoveries are made."[41]

Judged in its entirety, then, the evidence does not support the historical pattern Grünbaum claims to detect. Rather, it suggests that throughout his career Freud's view of the relation between therapy and science remained inconsistent: he seems to have been in the grips of a permanent ambivalence. Sometimes, allowing his hopes to get the better of him, Freud overstated both the therapeutic prospects and their significance for the truth of his ideas. At other times, his inherent conservatism or his annoyance with the excesses of enthusiasts such as Reich or Ferenczi led him to adopt a more circumspect view—to speak of the value of his ideas as independent of their practical consequences. Despite the undeniable dimming of his hopes in later years, Freud's career cannot be neatly divided into three decades of therapeutic optimism (thanks to the Tally

41. Freud, "Notes upon a Case of Obsessional Neurosis," *Standard Edition*, vol. X, p. 208n.

Argument) followed by thirteen years of despair—when, as Freud should have recognized, the Tally defense was discredited and analysis left in methodological shambles.

Grünbaum's abortive attempt to link Freud's notions about therapy and truth in an unambiguous historical pattern suggests that the Tally Argument may not have been the deep source of Freud's confidence in psychoanalysis after all. His undiminished belief in his ideas after 1926 seems to Grünbaum incomprehensible—an act of sheer willfulness in the face of the unambiguously negative implications of his own therapeutic doubts. But Freud's failure to draw these allegedly inescapable conclusions implies that in Freud's mind the connection between therapy and science—between cures and truth—was much looser than Grünbaum would have us believe. This in turn implies that the real source of Freud's conviction lay elsewhere and hence was undisturbed by the decline of his therapeutic hopes. Such is the conclusion reached by two of Grünbaum's severest philosophical critics, David Sachs and Frank Cioffi—the former a friend of analysis, the latter an inveterate enemy—who, as we shall see, argue that Freud's sublime confidence in his ideas had entirely different foundations. Not only for Freud himself but for many others who have found his ideas compelling, the intellectual attractions of psychoanalysis seem quite independent of its therapeutic claims.

Much of Grünbaum's effort, I have indicated, goes into contending that the Tally Argument was abandoned by its own maker. This dialectical critique—his first version of the Argument's demise—clearly holds great appeal for him. Because Grünbaum has labored so heroically to prove that the Tally Argument was the most powerful defense of psychoanalysis ever conceived, its dismantlement by Freud's own hand seems all the more devastating. It conjures up Wagnerian images of self-immolation, a kind of psychoanalytic *Götterdämmerung*.

But perhaps sensing that his portrayal of Freud's evolving therapeutic opinions might be open to challenge—and knowing full well that, in purely logical terms, Freud's *view* of the Tally Argument is irrelevant to its validity—Grünbaum offers a second version of the Argument's collapse. In this account the Argument comes to grief not because Freud betrayed it but because recent experimental studies have discredited one of its chief empirical supports, namely, the claim that psychoanalysis produces better results than its therapeutic rivals—of which, Grünbaum says, there are "at least well over 125" (161). In *The Foundations of Psychoanalysis* Grünbaum touches only briefly on these studies, but in his earlier papers they receive substantial attention and weigh heavily in his case against analysis.

The studies are remarkably similar. All were produced by teams of experimental psychologists, whose names litter Grünbaum's texts like so many international law firms: Meltzoff and Kornreich; Fisher and Greenberg; Bergin and Lambert; Rachman and Wilson; Smith, Glass, and Miller; Strupp, Hadley, and Gomes-Schwartz. They write books with titles like *Research in Psychotherapy, The Effects of Psychological Therapy, The Benefits of Psychotherapy,* and *Psychotherapy for Better or Worse,* which, appropriately, come to more or less the same conclusions. First, the studies suggest that any form of psychotherapy is preferable to no therapy at all, because the recovery rate for persons who seek therapy is higher (though not dramatically so) than the incidence of spontaneous remissions. Second, they find that, among psychotherapies, analysis works no better than its competitors, several of the studies even judging it inferior to behavioral therapy. Finally, they draw the inference that, because the results obtained by different therapies are indistinguishable, the benefits of psychotherapy most likely derive from some feature common to all therapies. Grünbaum likes to refer to this as the placebo effect: therapies work not for the reasons given by their proponents but because they share some inadvertent factor. In all likelihood, the operative common denominator is nothing more mysterious than the therapist's sympathetic ear.

The upshot of these findings, for Grünbaum, is that Freud's implicit claim for the superiority of psychoanalytic treatment turns out to be groundless; therefore, the Tally Argument is scuttled. In particular, if psychoanalytic cures are "placebogenic" (161), then Freud was simply wrong when he argued that neurotics get well only through analytic insight into their unconscious motives. This conclusion inspires Grünbaum to a rare exercise of philosophical wit: "The therapeutic achievements of psychoanalysis are *not* wrought after all by the patient's acquisition of self-knowledge, much to Socrates' sorrow" (161). As Grünbaum is careful to note, the recent experimental studies do not actually prove that psychoanalysis works by placebo effect, although the implication is very strong. The Necessary Condition Thesis of the Tally Argument, he concludes, has suffered an "empirical demise" (171), and the principal defense of Freud's ideas thus lies in ruins.

Grünbaum's emphasis on recent experimental studies, like his emphasis on Freud's late therapeutic pessimism, gives the impression that the Tally Argument may once have been valid but that it has since been twice discredited by historical developments. First Freud himself did it in when he lost confidence in analytic cures, and then, for good measure, it was done in again by empirical findings, which showed that analysis is no more effective than other psychotherapies. But, in truth, Grünbaum does not really believe in his own historical scenario. Ultimately, neither

Freud's change of heart nor the recent findings of experimental psychology invalidated the Tally Argument. Rather, the Argument was invalid from the start. Grünbaum's painstaking account of its historical rise and fall is disingenuous.

The Argument's fundamental defect was plain from the beginning. It makes an empirical assertion that must be backed up with evidence—but the evidence is not forthcoming, and even the need for it goes unacknowledged. The empirical assertion is that neurotics will get well only if they obtain insight into the unconscious causes of their neuroses: in Freud's own words, the patient's "conflicts will only be successfully solved and his resistances overcome if the anticipatory ideas he is given tally with what is real in him." Despite his initial pretense to take this reasoning seriously, Grünbaum obviously finds Freud's claim hollow unless it can be supported by statistical comparisons with neurotics who have *not* been given insight into the presumed unconscious causes of their neuroses. As evidence, analytic successes—even spectacular ones—by themselves mean nothing, because factors other than insight may be at work. That is, these successes may be placebo effects—attributable not to insight but to the analyst's solicitousness. One can cogently argue that analytic insights produce cures only by carrying out controlled experiment: such insights must be provided to some neurotics but withheld from others, and the results compared. In Grünbaum's view, then, Freud's ideas could never be vindicated by purely clinical evidence, as the Tally Argument seems to promise. They always stood in need of extraclinical confirmation. From the perspective of most psychoanalysts, of course, this demand for experimental controls represents a counsel of perfection; it sets a standard of proof that can never be met when the subject under investigation is as complex and elusive as an individual's psyche. In the study of human behavior, such certainty can be attained only if one is willing to limit inquiry to the banal and the trivial.

Although he does not say so, Grünbaum clearly thinks that the need for experimental controls should have been obvious to Freud when he advanced the Tally defense. Freud's later therapeutic pessimism and the recent findings of experimental psychologists are therefore, strictly speaking, philosophically irrelevant. One need not await actual empirical disconfirmation in order to pronounce an argument unsound. The Tally Argument, by Grünbaum's own inductivist criteria, was always unsound. Moreover, Freud would have been a much less astute methodologist than Grünbaum claims he was if he failed to recognize its unsoundness. Indeed, the Argument's obvious defects again make one doubt Grünbaum's entire case for its centrality in Freud's thinking. It appears a product more of Grünbaum's fertile imagination than of Freud's presumed philosophical rigor.

In his later writings on Freud, notably in *The Foundations of Psychoanalysis,* Grünbaum tends to obscure his own negative judgment of the Argument, presumably in order to promote his discovery of the Tally defense. But earlier he was uncompromising. Thus in 1978 he wrote:

Neither Freud nor other psychoanalysts have controlled for inadvertent placebo effects by means of appropriate research studies. And since the rival hypothesis of placebo effect thus stands unrefuted, such treatment successes as analysts may achieve beyond spontaneous remission cannot warrantedly be adduced as support for the therapeuticity of analysis *as such*.[42]

42. Adolf Grünbaum, "Is Psychoanalysis a Pseudo-Science?" *Zeitschrift für philosophische Forschung* 32, no. 1 (January–March 1978), p. 53.

In the same essay Grünbaum also expressly dismissed Freud's central assertion in the Tally passage: "There is no cogency in Freud's empirical claim that an analysis can be therapeutically successful *only* if the analyst's interpretations 'tally with what is real' in the patient."[43] Thus Grünbaum's elaborate demonstration, in *The Foundations of Psychoanalysis,* that the Tally Argument remained alive and well until it was sabotaged by Freud himself and subsequently by empirical studies is ultimately a charade. The Argument was dead in the philosophical water from the start. The only real mystery is why Grünbaum has expended such energy on it—first coaxing it out of Freud's reluctant text, then celebrating its supposed philosophical virtues, and finally composing a mythical trajectory for its rise and fall—when he obviously considered it "fatally flawed" from the outset.

DREAMS AND SLIPS

Freud arrived at his idea of the unconscious by way of the neuroses, and neurotic symptoms always remained for him the principal evidence for the influence of unconscious thoughts on human behavior. But very early in his psychoanalytic career Freud also sought support for his theory of unconscious motivation in two other phenomena: dreams and slips (or "parapraxes"). Dreams and slips became, respectively, the subjects of two of his most influential books: *The Interpretation of Dreams* (1900) and *The Psychopathology of Everyday Life* (1901). Freud returned to these topics over and over again whenever he wanted to argue the case for the unconscious.

43. Ibid.

Most discussions of Freud's ideas about dreams and slips fail to recognize that their primary function was always an evidentiary one. Freud himself was responsible for this misunderstanding, because with regard to both dreams and slips he advanced a provocatively universalist hypothesis, thereby drawing attention away from his more modest intellectual goal of providing evidence for the unconscious. Freud insisted that all dreams could be interpreted as the fulfillment of unconscious wishes, just as all slips (at least all significant ones) were caused by unconscious impulses. But for purposes of establishing the reality of the unconscious, these universalist claims were logically unnecessary. All Freud needed to prove was that *some* dreams and slips can be explained only by the assumption of unconscious motivation.

Much of the critical literature on Freud's theory of dreams and slips argues that, in many instances, these phenomena can be accounted for more readily in other ways and that Freud's universalist hypotheses are therefore wrong. Grünbaum cites a good deal of this literature and endorses its general conclusions. He is particularly impressed by Sebastiano Timpanaro's contention, in *The Freudian Slip,* that parapraxes allow of a variety of linguistic explanations. He also gives an uncritical account of the views of R. W. McCarley and J. A. Hobson, who maintain that the theory of dreams as wish fulfillments has been discredited by neurophysiological findings. But Grünbaum shrewdly recognizes that disproving Freud's explicit hypotheses does not get to the heart of the matter. Even if dreams and slips do not always have the specific purpose Freud assigns them, they can still offer evidence for the influence of unconscious motives on human behavior. If Grünbaum is to sustain his case that clinical material alone cannot underwrite psychoanalytic ideas, he must show that dreams and slips fail to supply Freud with cogent reasons for believing in the unconscious.

Substantial portions of Grünbaum's writings on psychoanalysis are devoted to precisely this endeavor. In essence, Grünbaum contends that dreams and slips do not provide genuinely autonomous evidence for the unconscious. Rather, the argument from dreams and slips is dependent on the historically prior and intellectually more fundamental argument from the neuroses. Or, as Grünbaum likes to put it, the theory of dreams and the theory of slips are "epistemically parasitic" (167) on the theory of neurotic symptoms.

Grümbaum justifies this subordination of dreams and slips to symptoms by an appeal to Freud's notion that both dreams and slips are analogous to the neuroses. In a sense, Freud suggests, dreams and slips are manifestations, in normal experience, of the same psychic processes that lead to the development of symptoms in neurotics. Like symptoms, they are compromise formations, in which an unconscious impulse finds expression by assuming a strategic disguise. Hence they are appropriately thought of as "mini-neuroses." Freud returns to this comparison repeatedly. "Dreams," he writes, "are constructed like a neurotic symptom: they are compromises between the demands of a repressed impulse and the resistance of a censoring force in the ego."[44]

Grünbaum holds Freud to the letter of his analogy, pursuing its implications with a vengeance. The dream and slip theories, Grünbaum insists, are in fact merely extrapolations from the theory of the neuroses. They are, so to speak, the theory of the neuroses writ small. The claim that dreams and slips are caused by unconscious ideas

44. Freud, *An Autobiographical Study, SE,* vol. XX, p. 45.

therefore ultimately derives its legitimacy from the claim that neurotic symptoms are so caused. This means that, as intellectual parasites on his theory of the neuroses, Freud's ideas about dreams and slips also must rely on the Tally defense for their methodological validation: they are believable only to the extent that Freud can back up his conception of the neuroses with cures. And because the Tally defense has been discredited, Grünbaum concludes, Freud's ideas about dreams and slips have been robbed of their essential intellectual support, however indirect that support might seem. The failure to produce cures thus sinks the entire psychoanalytic ship, as the evidence of dreams and slips is washed away along with that for Freud's neurotic etiologies.

Grünbaum drives this analogical critique to even further lengths. He argues that the repression theories of dreams and slips are actually "misextrapolations" (194) from the repression theory of the neuroses. The analogy is imperfect, he maintains, because it lacks an essential component of the theory of neurotic symptoms: the claim that the "disorder" can be alleviated by bringing its repressed cause to consciousness. In the case of dreams and slips, there is nothing to correspond to the therapeutic payoff that supposedly confirms Freud's conception of the neuroses, namely, the elimination of the symptom. Grünbaum even suggests what such a payoff might look like if Freud had only seen the analogical necessity for it. In the case of dreams, making the dreamer aware of his unconscious motives ought to have the "therapeutic" effect of causing him to dream less, perhaps ultimately not at all. With slips, a knowledge of their unconscious source should enable the "patient" to overcome the habit of committing such errors. Freud is taken to task for failing to advance these claims, thus depriving the argument that dreams and slips are caused by unconscious motives of even the "prima facie therapeutic support" (194) that lends plausibility to the psychoanalytic theory of the neuroses. Without confirmation by something analogous to cures, the assertion that dreams and slips testify to the influence of the unconscious is, in Grünbaum's view, entirely empty.

Freud himself clearly never intended his analogy to be taken so literally or pushed to such surrealistic extremes. The analogy with symptoms was meant primarily as a heuristic device, intended to shed light on his ideas about dreams and slips by drawing attention to certain resemblances with his findings about the neuroses. In other words, the analogy was not the central epistemological bulwark that Grünbaum imagines. Freud obviously felt that the evidence for the unconscious provided by dreams and slips was persuasive on its own terms. It spoke directly; it did not depend on some circuitous justification by way of neurotic cures. Grünbaum is of course aware of this conviction, and, accordingly, he is at pains to show that Freud's way of defending his ideas about dreams and slips does not pass philosophical muster.

When Freud argues that a slip or a dream originates in an unconscious idea, he appeals to two kinds of evidence. The first is thematic affinity: he identifies a substantive likeness between the slip or the dream on the one hand and the unconscious idea on the other. Second, Freud points to free association. If the dreamer or the person who commits the slip allows his mind to travel undisturbed along the chain of associations that the dream or slip gives rise to, he will eventually be led to the motivating idea.

Grünbaum illustrates Freud's dependence on both thematic affinity and free association—as well as their liabilities—with an example that Freud himself discusses at the beginning of *The Psychopathology of Everyday Life,* the so-called *aliquis* slip. A young Jewish man expresses his anger about anti-Semitism by quoting Freud the line from the *Aeneid* in which Dido invites posterity to wreak vengeance on Aeneas: *Exoriare aliquis nostris ex ossibus ultor* ("Let someone arise from our bones as an avenger").[45] But the young man misremembers the line: he leaves out the word *aliquis* ("someone"). In order to determine the unconscious meaning of the slip, Freud asks the man to relate whatever comes into his mind in connection with the missing word. The man obliges by producing a series of associations. *Aliquis* first divides into *a* and *liquis*. *Liquis* then gives rise to *Reliquien* ("relics"), *liquefying, fluidity,* and *fluid. Reliquien* in turn leads to religious associations, notably with Saint Augustine and Saint Januarius (both of whom, Freud observes, have to do with the calendar). Saint Januarius returns the young man's associations to the earlier notion of liquefying, because the saint's blood, kept in a phial in a Neapolitan church, is said to liquefy miraculously on a particular holy day. The thought of Saint Januarius's liquefying blood (in Naples) produces the final association and, according to Freud, the unconscious idea that inspired the original lapse: the young man is reminded of his Italian mistress and in particular of his fear that her periods may have stopped. Freud congratulates his interlocutor: "You've made use of the miracle of St. Januarius to manufacture a brilliant allusion to women's periods." "And you really mean to say that it was this anxious expectation that made me unable to produce an unimportant word like *aliquis?*" asks the skeptical young man. "It seems to me undeniable," Freud responds.[46]

45. Freud, *The Psychopathology of Everyday Life, Standard Edition,* vol. VI, p. 9.
46. Ibid., p. 11.

The stream of the young man's associations is united by certain thematic affinities, of which the calendar and the blood that flows on a particular day are the most obvious. The original forgetting of *aliquis* is bound to its unconscious cause by the overarching theme of descent: the young man's repressed fear that his mistress might be pregnant has interfered with his ability to produce a correct version of his wish for descendants who will avenge the wrongs of the Jews. To be precise, it has blocked out his ability to remember the very word that alludes to the avenging descendant, *aliquis*. Freud explains the underlying logic of the slip as follows:

> The speaker had been deploring the fact that the present generation of his people was deprived of its full rights; a new generation, he prophesied like Dido, would inflict vengeance on the oppressors. He had in this way expressed his wish for descendants. At this moment a contrary thought intruded, "Have you really so keen a wish for descendants? That is not so. How embarrassed you would be if you were to get news just now that you were to expect descendants from the quarter you know of. No: no descendants—however much we need them for vengeance."[47]

Readers are apt to respond variously to Freud's explanation. For some it will seem overwrought: surely nothing so complicated is needed to account for the simple inability to remember a word in a quotation, especially a quotation in a foreign language. The fact that the young man forgot *aliquis* seems less remarkable—and thus less in need of explanation—than the fact that he remembered the rest of the line. For others, however, the ingenious sequence of associations, the uncanny echo of descendants desired and undesired, and, above all, the frisson of the ultimate revela-

47. Ibid., p. 14.

tion, in which high-minded indignation is done in by a dirty erotic secret, will seem undeniably beguiling. Freud, they will conclude, is onto something.

Grünbaum does his best to discourage the latter reaction by showing that it is open to severe philosophical objections. Neither thematic affinity nor free association, Grünbaum argues, carries the evidential weight necessary to justify such a causal assertion. He grants, for the sake of argument, Freud's assumption that the associations are genuinely free, that is, that they have not been contaminated by the analyst's proddings or expectations—although Grünbaum thinks there is reason to doubt this. Still, even assuming that the "meandering associations starting out from the restored memory of *aliquis*" (192) are spontaneous, they simply do not represent cogent grounds for thinking that the young man's unconscious worry about his mistress's pregnancy *caused* him to forget the word *aliquis*. Put another way, although one might argue that *aliquis* launched the string of associations that brought forth the man's repressed anxiety, one cannot reverse the causal sequence and claim that the repressed anxiety caused the original forgetting:

Let it be granted that [the] chain of associations from his corrected parapraxis issued causally in the disclosure of the repressed anxiety afflicting him, *and* that this unconscious fear of pregnancy had been clamoring for overt expression. How, then, does this assumed motive serve to explain even probabilistically why [he] suffered any memory loss at all, let alone why he forgot *aliquis?* (197)

The inadequacy of free associations for establishing causes is illustrated for Grünbaum by the problem of how the analyst decides where to end the associative sequence.

After all, the associations could be extended indefinitely, with a view to turning up yet deeper unconscious motives. What determines that one association rather than another is the true source of the slip? Grünbaum rejects any appeal to confirmation by the person committing the slip, who may, of course, testify to the reality of a particular fear or desire but who is no more expert than the rest of us concerning "the alleged *causal nexus* between the given fear and the slip" (208).

Ultimately, Grünbaum insists, to argue that free association can identify causes is to fall victim to the error of *post hoc ergo propter hoc:* the temporal fact that the revelation of the supposed source occurs after the slip does not prove that the slip was in fact caused by that "source." Freud's "epistemic tribute to free associations," Grünbaum complains, "rests on nothing but a glaring causal fallacy" (186). "To endow the unconscious with cunning, uncanny powers of intrusion upon conscious actions is only to baptize the causal fallacy by giving it an honorific name" (192). Nor can Freud's defenders fall back on the argument that Freud at least has offered an explanation for slips, whereas such errors have generally been ignored or considered inexplicable—in violation of the scientific principle that nothing in the world is uncaused. On the contrary, Grünbaum responds, Sebastiano Timpanaro and others have provided alternative explanations for slips that beg fewer questions. Moreover, similar psycholinguistic explanations were available to Freud when he wrote *The Psychopathology of Everyday Life,* and Grünbaum judges Freud's dismissal of those competing theories particularly weak. "Not even the tortures of the thumbscrew or of the rack," Grünbaum concludes rather picturesquely, "should persuade a rational being that free associations can *certify* pathogens or other causes!" (186).

As to thematic affinity, the notion is far too elastic, Grünbaum argues, to provide free association with the sort of discipline that might rescue it from the charge of *post hoc ergo propter hoc*. With sufficient ingenuity one can generate unlimited thematic echoes, especially if the stream of associations is not prematurely interrupted. "For any emerging repression," Grünbaum writes, "it will be possible to find some thematic thread, however farfetched, such that there will be *some* topical kinship with the given lapse" (199). He clearly thinks that the thematic affinity linking *aliquis* with the feared pregnancy—the play on wanted and unwanted descendants—is an example of just such a farfetched connection. To illustrate the excessive elasticity of thematic affinity—as well as the related problem of where to terminate the sequence of associations— Grünbaum constructs a hypothetical extension of Freud's interview with the forgetful young man (whom he calls AJ for "Austrian Jew") and offers his own alternative explanation for the slip:

Suppose that Freud had allowed AJ to continue well past the disclosure of the pregnancy fear. Perhaps it would then have emerged that AJ's parents had taught him early that the Romans had crucified Jesus, but that Christians had then unfairly blamed the Jews for deicide. It might furthermore have emerged that AJ had repressed his ensuing hatred of the Romans when Virgil, Horace, and other Roman poets were shown great respect in his Austrian educational environment. . . . Would AJ's hypothesized repression of his hatred for the Romans not have had greater thematic "suitability as a determinant" of his *aliquis* slip than his anxiety about the pregnancy, even though the former assumedly emerged only later in the associative chain? After all, Virgil was a Roman, and AJ was citing the line from the *Aeneid* to express his conscious resentment of Christian anti-Semitism.

What a golden opportunity to punish the unconsciously resented Romans simultaneously by spoiling Virgil's line! Although the repressed hatred for the Romans is, of course, purely hypothetical in the case of AJ, it does lend poignancy to the complaint of selection bias, which is given substance generally by the thematic elasticity of the associations I have emphasized. (209–10)

One suspects that Freud would have responded, "Yes, but of course the man produced no such associations." Still, the problem of using thematic affinity as a means of exercising intellectual control over free associations is genuine. The difference between Freud's account and Grünbaum's is ultimately aesthetic: Freud's story is a good one, while Grünbaum's falls flat. Indeed, the example lends support to Habermas's and Ricoeur's argument that psychoanalytic interpretation has more in common with literature than with science. In the matter of dreams and slips, Grünbaum would doubtless not only accept this verdict but argue that it makes his point: while thematic affinity may be fine for poets and novelists, it cannot be trusted as a guide to causes.

Because of the intellectual shortcomings of free association and thematic affinity, Freud's theory of slips and his theory of dreams are thrown back on the theory of the neuroses for their epistemological salvation. But, as we have already seen, Grünbaum believes that this recourse is in vain. The analogy with the neuroses fails because it is imperfectly drawn—it lacks a therapeutic payoff—and in any event the cardinal defense of the theory of the neuroses, the Tally Argument, has itself been discredited. Thus the argument from dreams and slips can neither stand on its own nor find support from its crippled conceptual neighbor.

GRÜNBAUM'S CRITICS

Grünbaum has elicited at least three significant responses. The analyst Marshall Edelson, who is a professor of psychiatry at Yale, devoted an entire book—*Hypothesis and Evidence in Psychoanalysis* (1984)—to answering his attack. More recently, two philosophers, David Sachs and Frank Cioffi, have published shorter but nonetheless incisive critiques of Grünbaum's writings on analysis. Sachs is a defender of analysis, while Cioffi is a staunch opponent, yet, remarkably, they agree about where Grünbaum goes wrong.

Of the three, Marshall Edelson is the most sympathetic to Grünbaum. In fact, Edelson is in many ways an admirer, who thinks that analysts must take Grünbaum's "formidable argument" very seriously.[48] Edelson's main concern is not with Freud but with the future of psychoanalysis. He fears that if Grünbaum's objections go unanswered, the outlook for the profession is bleak. Young scientists and scholars will not want to pursue careers in the service of a tradition that has been intellectually discredited. Accordingly, the purpose of Edelson's book is to argue that, despite Grünbaum's weighty criticisms, analytic ideas can still be defended with clinical evidence.

Edelson accepts Grünbaum's definition of the problem. He is not particularly interested in the Tally Argument and the supposed historical reasons for its collapse, but he concurs that the fundamental issue in the defense of analysis is therapeutic success. Freud's ideas ultimately depend on the claim that analytic insights produce cures, although Edelson argues for a more modulated conception of "cure" than the rather mechanical notion of the removal of

48. Marshall Edelson, *Hypothesis and Evidence,* p. 121.

symptoms. Also like Grünbaum, Edelson rejects the effort to salvage analysis by separating theory from therapy—the ideas from their practical application—just as he rejects the hermeneutic escape route proposed by analysts like Roy Schafer and Donald Spence. For better or worse, psychoanalysis is committed to giving the patient a truthful, not just a narratively coherent, account of his circumstances, and it is distinguished from all other psychotherapies by its belief that such truthful insight alone is the key to psychic health.

Most important, Edelson agrees with Grünbaum that the great weakness of analysis has been its failure to provide its clinical findings with the necessary intellectual controls. Analysts are under the misapprehension that they can establish the truth of their ideas simply by piling up instances of therapeutic success. But Grünbaum has shown that therapeutic successes by themselves prove nothing. One must also eliminate (or at least reduce) the possibility that those successes can be explained otherwise than through analytic insight. That is, one must guard against their being placebo effects—the result of some inadvertent factor in the analytic situation, such as the analysand's intellectual confidence in the analyst or the peculiar emotional tie between doctor and patient. Edelson thus implicitly endorses my view that the Tally Argument fails not for the historical reasons proffered by Grünbaum—because Freud himself abandoned it or because recent experimental findings contravene it—but because it was inadequate from the start. It always begged the question of how to eliminate alternative explanations.

Edelson nonetheless criticizes Grünbaum's conclusion that one can eliminate rival explanations only through experimental control studies—that is, statistical comparisons between patients who have undergone analytic treatment and otherwise identical populations who have not been given insight into their unconscious motives. Edelson strongly defends the skepticism that analysts, beginning with Freud himself, have always felt about such studies. The effort to verify analytic ideas through experimental comparisons is bound to fail—not, as Grünbaum would imply, because analytic ideas are insupportable, but because the experiments can never be refined enough to measure the complex and nuanced matters explored under analysis. To demand comparative studies in which all relevant variables are controlled so as to rule out every conceivable alternative explanation is to offer "a counsel of perfection," which analysts have rightly rejected.[49]

Fortunately, Edelson argues, there is another way of obtaining the necessary controls, one that avoids the "breathtakingly nontrivial defects" of group studies.[50] This alternative is to introduce controls within the clinical framework itself. To be exact, Edelson urges substituting time controls for group controls: information gathered from a single subject at different moments during the analysis can take the place of comparative data from an experimental group. The analyst can compare "time slices of the subject"—notably, slices taken before and after a particular interpretation has been given to the patient.[51] To the extent that other factors have been held constant, the analyst will be able to rule out rival explanations for any changes that have occurred in the patient. In this manner the individual patient can serve as his own "historical" control, and single-subject research can acquire the probative quality of group-comparison research. This proposal for intraclinical testing is the heart of Edelson's response to Grünbaum: temporal comparisons can lend clinical case

49. Ibid., p. 125.   50. Ibid., p. 63.   51. Ibid., p. 66.

studies something of the intellectual texture of group-comparison studies.

Edelson insists that Grünbaum himself gives his blessings to such a "time-series design" or "multiple baseline design" in his discussion of the cases in *Studies on Hysteria,* especially that of Anna O.[52] Grünbaum in fact greatly admires the Anna O. case, because it shows that Freud was sensitive to the danger of placebo effect. In answer to the charge that Anna O.'s symptoms were lifted not by recovering their traumatic origins but through suggestion, Freud and Breuer cite the peculiar manner in which her symptoms disappeared: they vanished separately and independently, each one at the very moment its historical source was recalled. If Anna O.'s cure had resulted merely from suggestion—from the more or less constant influence of the doctor's attentions—no such temporal pattern should have emerged. As Grünbaum concludes, approvingly: "The separate symptom removals are made to carry the vital probative burden of discrediting the threatening rival hypothesis of placebo effect, wrought by mere suggestion" (179).

There is merit, then, in Edelson's contention that the Anna O. case anticipates the sort of time-controlled inquiry that Edelson hopes will rescue psychoanalysis. But he overestimates Grünbaum's enthusiasm for the case. True, Grünbaum views it as a move in the right direction: having duly recognized the threat posed by the placebo argument, Freud and Breuer tried to respond to it by emphasizing the separate removal of individual symptoms. But this defense remains for Grünbaum ultimately unsatisfactory. The sequential lifting of symptoms could still be a placebo effect, because Anna O. must have known that

52. Ibid., pp. 68, 124.

Breuer hoped to uncover a thematically appropriate memory whenever he focused her attention on the first appearance of one of her symptoms. In other words, she may still have been obliging the doctor's strongly felt expectations. Even when symptoms disappear one by one, therefore, the only way to establish that their removal has resulted from insight rather than suggestion is through comparisons with "a suitable control group whose repressions are *not* lifted" (180). If Anna O. is a prototype for the time-slice method Edelson advocates, the method fails to measure up to Grünbaum's standards.

Edelson argues that the idea of comparing different moments in a single analysis is more than just a suggestion for the future. Psychoanalytic hypotheses not only can be, but already have been, successfully tested in the clinical setting on at least two occasions. Edelson's book culminates in his discussion of these two cases, which offer what he considers a "decisive refutation" of Grünbaum.[53] I fear, however, that the cases make rather a poor climax: *Hypothesis and Evidence in Psychoanalysis* is long on foreplay but short on action. One of the cases is merely a reconstruction, by Clark Glymour, of Freud's Rat Man study, in which Glymour argues that Freud might have been seen as using a "bootstrap strategy" to test and reject rival hypotheses.[54] It proves nothing beyond good intentions. Apparently, then, the sole instance in which the time-slice method has actually been put to the test is Lester Luborsky's case of "Miss X" (1974). By comparing different moments in her analysis, Luborsky shows that Miss X suffered episodes of forgetting whenever her emotional involvement with the analyst grew especially intense. Luborsky establishes this connection by pairing passages—or, as he prefers to say,

53. Ibid., p. 122.   54. Ibid., p. 147.

"contexts"—from her analytic sessions. As Edelson explains it, "each pair of contexts, differing with respect to whether momentary forgetting has or has not occurred, has been matched . . . so that the contexts can otherwise in crucial respects be regarded as equivalent."[55]

Unfortunately, whatever the merits of this experiment, it is a slender empirical reed on which to rest the argument for a purely clinical defense of psychoanalysis. Grünbaum justly complains that the Miss X case does not even address—let alone substantiate—any of Freud's significant causal hypotheses. In particular, it has no bearing on the essential Freudian claim that insight into a patient's unconscious motives is essential to therapeutic success. If anything, it tends to prove just the opposite, namely, that patients respond not to insight but to the emotional influence of the analyst—which Grünbaum, of course, would categorize as a placebo effect. If Luborsky's Miss X is the best that Edelson has to offer, the prospects for the intraclinical confirmation of analytic ideas must be pronounced exceedingly faint.

In Grünbaum's view, Edelson's defense of intraclinical testing is worse than unpersuasive: it is intellectually irresponsible. It holds out a false hope and thus encourages further delaying tactics, when in fact analysts desperately need to recognize the inadequacy of purely clinical evidence and set about devising appropriate experimental control studies. "It is now ninety years since the publication of *Studies on Hysteria*. The hour is late, and the bell is tolling."[56]

55. Ibid., p. 146.
56. Adolf Grünbaum, "Cognitive Flaws in the Psychoanalytic Method" (1985), p. 23. Unpublished manuscript courtesy of Professor Grünbaum.

■   ■   ■

Marshall Edelson's mistake, I would suggest, is to have accepted Grünbaum's ground rules. Once you embrace the premise that everything hinges on cures, it is difficult to escape the demand for experimental controls. David Sachs and Frank Cioffi both avoid this mistake. They challenge the fundamental assumption that therapeutic success was the source of Freud's confidence in his ideas. Grünbaum errs, they maintain, in arguing that psychoanalysis lives or dies with its ability to produce cures.

David Sachs attacks Grünbaum along two fronts. First, Sachs demonstrates that the Tally Argument is a product of Grünbaum's aggressive misreading of the passage in the "Analytic Therapy" lecture from which the argument is extracted. Grünbaum burdens the passage, Sachs insists, with claims it simply does not make. More important, Sachs argues that Freud's ideas rest on a much broader evidential base than Grünbaum allows. They do not depend exclusively on clinical data, and even less on clinical data illustrating therapeutic success. Grünbaum's conception of the "foundations" of psychoanalysis is thus shown to be excessively narrow.

According to Sachs, Freud's real purpose in the Tally passage is quite modest: he is concerned with answering the charge that analysis works entirely by suggestion. "What it says is tantamount to the following: unless the suggestions an analyst makes to his patient correspond to facts about him, an understanding of his conflicts will not be attained, and his resistances will not be defeated."[57] The passage contains nothing to justify the two further contentions with which Grünbaum saddles it: that cures never

57. Sachs, "In Fairness to Freud," p. 351.

occur spontaneously and that nonanalytic therapies are ineffective. Grünbaum simply puts words in Freud's mouth when he characterizes the passage as a "bold assertion of the *causal indispensability* of psychoanalytic insight for the conquest of the patient's psychoneurosis" (139). In effect, Sachs shows that the Tally Argument, properly speaking, doesn't really exist. It is a figment of Grünbaum's overwrought philosophical imagination.

Moreover, Freud would never have argued that analytic insight is indispensable to achieving cures, because, as Sachs documents, Freud always recognized that neurotics may recover either on their own or through the aid of other therapies. In the "Analytic Therapy" lecture itself, Freud recalled the "complete and permanent" cures he had sometimes achieved, in the 1890s, using the pre-analytic technique of hypnotic suggestion.[58] Freud also speculated that neuroses might one day succumb to purely chemical treatment—which would obviously mean without benefit of analytic insight. On the matter of spontaneous remissions, he acknowledged in 1913 that all the disorders successfully treated by analysis were also "occasionally subject to spontaneous recovery."[59] Grünbaum's insinuation of the "causal indispensability" claim into the Tally passage is thus contradicted by clear evidence that Freud knew all along about both spontaneous remission and rival cures. Furthermore, Freud held that analysis could provide correct views even when it was powerless to relieve the patient's complaint, notably in the understanding of the psychoses. Dementia praecox and paranoia were immune to analytic therapy, yet Freud confidently insisted that they

58. Freud, *Introductory Lectures, SE,* vol. XVI, p. 449.
59. Freud, "The Claims of Psycho-Analysis to Scientific Interest," *Standard Edition,* vol. XIII, p. 165.

yielded to analytic explanation. His ideas were reliable, he felt, even when they were therapeutically unavailing.

Sachs's demonstration that Freud neither formulated nor believed in the Tally Argument points to what is surely the central mystery of Grünbaum's critique: why he goes to such lengths to create this philosophical mirage, which he even equips with a mythic (and tragic) history. It would be both petty and foolish to suggest that Grünbaum is motivated by base academic instinct, the desire to claim a new textual discovery: he seems too caught up in his philosophical enterprise to be concerned with scoring scholarly points. More likely, as Sachs suggests, Grünbaum has chosen to employ an inflationary and deflationary tactic in his effort to discredit psychoanalysis. First he creates the impression that all Freud's ideas depend on therapeutic claims (the inflationary opening move); then he shows that those claims are unwarranted, which leads in turn to the inevitable conclusion that the original ideas are without support (the deflationary goal). Because Grünbaum feels so confident he can demolish the therapeutic pretensions of analysis, he is driven to sweep the whole analytic operation into the therapeutic bin. The Tally Argument serves this purpose ideally. It puts the assertion that analytic ideas depend on analytic cures into Freud's own mouth—where, however, it clearly does not belong.

More telling than Grünbaum's misconstrual of the Tally passage is, in Sachs's view, his neglect of the wide variety of nonclinical material on which Freud based his ideas. Many of Freud's writings, Sachs reminds us, are devoted to showing that analytic ideas find support in such diverse nonclinical phenomena as sexual behavior, jokes, religious ceremonies, mythology, folklore, literature, sculpture, and painting. Not all this extraclinical evidence is equally impressive, but that it did much to inspire

Freud's conviction seems undeniable. The same breadth of intellectual reference also contributes powerfully to Freud's ability to attract adherents. Grünbaum, however, ignores it, arbitrarily allowing only clinical evidence—indeed only clinical evidence of therapeutic upshot—to bear any weight in Freud's calculations.

Sachs is particularly offended by Grünbaum's treatment of the two most important nonclinical sources Freud relies on: dreams and slips. Many of the dreams and at least some of the slips Freud discusses of course originate in a clinical setting: they are produced by his patients, often in association with their neurotic symptoms. But a substantial portion of the dreams and the vast majority of the slips are extraclinical: they come, as Freud's title indicates, from "everyday life." Sachs argues that Grünbaum's attempt to finesse their importance by calling them "misextrapolations" from the theory of the neuroses (and thus clinical, as it were, only by courtesy) bizarrely distorts Freud's own understanding of them.

Above all, Sachs criticizes Grünbaum's complete neglect of the particular category of slips that provides the best evidence for the unconscious, so-called compound or accumulated parapraxes, in which two or more errors cooperate in fulfilling the same wish. Compound parapraxes often serve the purpose of what Sachs calls "tendentious forgetting"—forgetting that has a patently self-interested motive.[60] One of Freud's examples involves a woman living in Basel, who unconsciously resented a friend's recent marriage. When the friend, "Selma X. of Berlin," visited Basel on her honeymoon, the woman managed to forget an afternoon rendezvous with her. Then at the very hour of the rendezvous, the woman was forced into an "uncon-

60. Sachs, "In Fairness to Freud," p. 366.

scious safeguarding" of her first parapraxis through the commission of a second.[61] Engaged in a conversation about the recent marriage of the famous coloratura soprano Selma Kurz, she ventured some critical remarks about the marriage. But, to her embarrassment, she was unable to think of the singer's first name, though ordinarily she knew it very well and had heard Kurz sing many times. That evening, with the woman's friend now safely departed from Basel, the famous singer again came up in conversation, "and without any difficulty the lady produced the name '*Selma* Kurz.' 'Oh dear!' she at once exclaimed, 'it's just struck me—I've completely forgotten I had an appointment with my friend Selma this afternoon.' "[62] Timpanaro's linguistic theory sheds no light on this ingenious conspiracy of forgetting, whereas its logic becomes transparent given Freud's hypothesis of an unconscious wish that pursues its objective first one way and then another. Grünbaum, Sachs complains, nowhere mentions such combined parapraxes, even though Freud believed they offered the most convincing evidence for his theory of unconscious motivation.

Sachs sees an exactly parallel neglect of nonclinical evidence in Grünbaum's slighting of the psychoanalytic theory of dream symbolism. Why does Grünbaum downplay it so? The answer seems obvious: Freud insists that he learned the unconscious meaning of dream symbols "from fairy tales and myths, from buffoonery and jokes, from folklore (that is, from knowledge about popular manners and customs, sayings and songs) and from poetic and colloquial linguistic usage."[63] In other words, all his sources

---

61. Freud, *The Psychopathology of Everyday Life, SE*, vol. VI, p. 34.
62. Ibid., p. 35.
63. Freud, *Introductory Lectures, SE*, vol. XV, pp. 158–59.

were nonclinical—and, Freud adds, "if we go into these sources in detail, we shall find so many parallels to dream-symbolism that we cannot fail to be convinced of our interpretations."[64] Freud's conviction in this crucial matter of dream symbolism—which figures prominently in the interpretation of neurotic symptoms, slips, and literary works as well—finds its "epistemic basis" entirely outside the clinic.[65] His patients' free associations, of which Grünbaum is so contemptuous, play no role whatsoever, and the question of therapeutic success (the sine qua non of analytic conviction, according to the Tally Argument) is even more irrelevant. Once again, Grünbaum refuses to provide a comprehensive and balanced account of the evidence on which Freud relied. Grünbaum is able to transform psychoanalysis into a purely clinical doctrine only by severely distorting Freud's actual intellectual practices.

· ■ ·

Much of Frank Cioffi's critique of Grünbaum closely resembles David Sachs's. Cioffi, too, complains that Grünbaum greatly overestimates Freud's reliance on cures to guarantee his ideas. In particular, Cioffi insists that Freud could never have advanced the Tally Argument as a plausible defense of psychoanalysis. At the heart of the Argument, in Grünbaum's construction, stands the claim that analytic therapy is superior to all its rivals. But, according to Cioffi, Freud knew perfectly well that he was in no position to make such a claim, because it implied that he had undertaken a comparative study of other therapies and found their results inferior to his own—

64. Ibid., p. 159.   65. Sachs, "In Fairness to Freud," p. 364.

which of course he hadn't. Quite illogically, the Tally Argument portrays Freud as deriving comfort from a defense that any minimally rational person would dismiss as patently flimsy.

Freud, then, would have had no grounds to believe that the Argument, as Grünbaum construes it, was true. Even worse, in Cioffi's view, he would have had good reason to think it false, at least in its central premise that analytic insight is indispensable to cures. Unlike Sachs, Cioffi does not stress the clear evidence that Freud always recognized both spontaneous remission and the success of rival therapies. Instead, Cioffi hones in on Freud's own earlier claim to have achieved cures even when he was relying on his erroneous seduction theory: Freud himself pretended to cure neurotics *before* the discovery of the Oedipus complex, and thus before he could possibly provide his patients with "veridical" insight into the unconscious causes of their illness. Hence the contention that analytic insight is indispensable to cures—Grünbaum's Necessary Condition Thesis—had been contradicted by Freud's own experience as a therapist.

Cioffi's case against Grünbaum does not rest solely on an appeal to Freud's intelligence and his presumed aversion to contradicting himself. Cioffi also shows that Freud's confidence in his ideas was largely independent of their therapeutic consequences. Much of this evidence is already familiar from David Sachs's critique: Freud often supported his theories with material drawn from outside the clinic; he believed that his insights were valid even when, as with the psychoses, there was no hope of a cure; in the famous case histories he remained confident of his interpretations despite therapeutic disaster. Cioffi is particularly struck that Freud expressed not the slightest doubts that his analysis of the Wolf Man was correct even after the patient again became deranged. In all this the pattern is unmistakable: Freud's convictions did not depend on cures.

The real source of Freud's confidence, Cioffi argues, lay elsewhere. Freud believed in his interpretations, and in the theoretical views on which they rested, above all because of their narrative coherence—their "ability to confer intelligibility on the data."[66] Grünbaum refers to this as the argument from "inductive consilience" (275): the harmonious convergence of an interpretive element with other pieces of evidence to form a psychological whole. But Grünbaum insists that Freud resorted to this defense only at the very end of his life, after he had lost faith in the Tally Argument. In Cioffi's view, by contrast, narrative coherence was always the deep source of Freud's conviction. The stories Freud constructed to explain his patients' behavior appealed to him in the manner of a jigsaw puzzle. Indeed, both early and late in his career, Freud invoked precisely this analogy to convey the attraction of his interpretations. In the famous 1896 paper on "The Aetiology of Hysteria," he defended the scenes of infantile seduction in terms of their perfect fit with "the whole of the rest of the case history":

It is exactly like putting together a child's picture-puzzle: after many attempts, we become absolutely certain in the end which piece belongs in the empty gap; for only that one piece fills out the picture and at the same time allows its irregular edges to be fitted into the edges of the other pieces in such a manner as to leave no free space and to entail no overlapping. In the same way, the contents of the infantile scenes turn out to be indispens-

---

66. Frank Cioffi, "Did Freud Rely on the Tally Argument to Meet the Argument from Suggestibility?" in "Open Peer Commentary" on Grünbaum, "Précis of *The Foundations of Psychoanalysis*," p. 230.

able supplements to the associative and logical framework of the neurosis, whose insertion makes its course of development for the first time evident, or even, as we might often say, self-evident.[67]

Over a quarter century later the analogy reappears in "Remarks on the Theory and Practice of Dream Interpretation" to explain the analyst's faith in his interpretations. "What makes [the analyst] certain in the end," Freud writes, "is precisely the complication of the problem before him, which is like the solution of a jig-saw puzzle."[68] Such avowals, Cioffi asserts, reveal the secret of Freud's persuasion: they appeal not to cures but to coherence. In effect, very much like the hermeneutic revisionists, Cioffi identifies what might fairly be called the aesthetic power of Freud's ideas as the source of his confidence. Freud believed in his interpretations because they brought order to material that otherwise remained chaotic.

If one hopes to rout psychoanalysis—as Cioffi clearly does—one must, he argues, attack the reasoning on which it actually relies. And because narrative coherence was Freud's ultimate court of appeal, the critic of analysis must show that Freud's narratives do not in fact possess the intelligibility he claimed for them—that they "fail to meet the standards of plausible story telling (vague as these are) current in good historical, biographical, or forensic practice."[69] Grünbaum's exclusive focus on cures is therefore "a great strategic error."[70] His heavy philosophical

---

67. Freud, "The Aetiology of Hysteria," *SE*, vol. III, p. 205.
68. Freud, "Remarks on the Theory and Practice of Dream Interpretation," *Standard Edition*, vol. XIX, p. 116.
69. Cioffi, "Did Freud Rely on the Tally Argument?" p. 231.
70. Ibid.

artillery is wasted obliterating a defensive formation of little consequence, while the real enemy—the argument from consilience—escapes unscathed to continue its depredations.

Much of Cioffi's energy goes to arguing that *The Foundations of Psychoanalysis* is largely beside the point. But in at least one regard Cioffi considers the book more than innocuous: he profoundly objects to Grünbaum's effort to rehabilitate Freud's reputation as a scientific methodologist. Cioffi is especially annoyed by the suggestion that Freud responded hospitably to adverse findings. Against Karl Popper, Grünbaum of course maintains that Freud not only advanced falsifiable propositions but actually withdrew ideas if they were discredited empirically. "As a rule," writes Grünbaum, Freud's "repeated modifications of his theories were clearly motivated by evidence."[71] The abandonment of the seduction theory is the most famous case in point.

Cioffi will have none of this. Much more typical of Freud's intellectual practice than any inclination to revise his ideas in the face of contradictory evidence was his tendency to rearrange the data—in a word, to lie. Freud was especially adept at inducing his patients to manufacture information that confirmed his theories. He never let mere facts get in the way of an idea.

Ultimately, then, Cioffi views Grünbaum's writings on pyschoanalysis as an effort to exonerate Freud—to show that Freud possessed the empirical scruples of a true scien-

71. Grünbaum, "Is Freudian Psychoanalytic Theory Pseudo-Scientific by Karl Popper's Criterion of Demarcation?" p. 135; quoted by Frank Cioffi in " 'Exegetical Myth-Making' in Grünbaum's Indictment of Popper and Exoneration of Freud," in *Mind, Psychoanalysis and Science*, Peter Clark and Crispin Wright, eds. (Oxford, 1988), p. 61.

tist, even though in practice he often fell short of his own standards. In Cioffi's view, however, Freud was not a failed empiricist but a sham empiricist. Grünbaum is thus guilty of giving comfort to the enemy and of disarming the unwary. Under the guise of a ruthless philosophical critique, his book in fact restores Freud to scientific respectability. No friend of science, Cioffi concludes, can fail to regret it.

Grünbaum responds to Cioffi by citing again the many passages in which Freud either affirms the therapeutic superiority of analysis or points to analytic cures as confirmation of his ideas. Thus the disagreement between Grünbaum and Cioffi finally comes down to how one weighs these passages against others in which Freud backs off from his therapeutic claims or insists on the validity of his interpretations regardless of their practical consequences. More generally, it is a question of how one measures the relative importance of the argument from cures against the argument from narrative coherence. In my own view, Cioffi is much nearer the truth than is Grünbaum. Freud was perfectly happy to cite the evidence of cures whenever it would lend credibility to his claims. Yet he clearly never felt bound by it. Cures were a kind of bonus. They were certainly welcome, but they were not the cornerstone of his conviction. Freud's faith in his ideas went undisturbed even when cures failed to materialize.

Perhaps even more important, the therapeutic argument has played only a minor role in the broad appeal of psychoanalysis. Freud did not become one of the most influential thinkers of the twentieth century because he convinced the world that he had found a cure for mental illness. As Cioffi suggests, Freud's ability to persuade can be attributed largely to the distinctive character of his interpretations. Although the issue is more complex than

Cioffi recognizes, the notion of narrative coherence rightly affirms that the secret of Freud's success is an intellectual rather than a therapeutic matter. Grünbaum's massive philosophical attack is thus curiously irrelevant. Whether one feels (as I am inclined to) that Grünbaum wins the therapeutic argument or (with Marshall Edelson) that he loses it, the heart of Freud's appeal, as both Frank Cioffi and David Sachs show, lies elsewhere. He seduces us as a thinker, not as a doctor.

FREUD AND THE EMPIRICIST TRADITION

In the end, what are we to make of Adolf Grünbaum's critique of Freud? I've tried to suggest something of the difficulty of evaluating it. Perhaps the central problem—beyond its sheer density of expression and general disorganization—is Grünbaum's curiously inconsistent attitude toward Freud. On the one hand, there is the impassioned defense of Freud's methodological acuity and the scathing dismissal of his ill-informed and philosophically inept critics. On the other hand, there is the repeated complaint that Freud's creation is "fundamentally flawed" because it fails to measure up to the inductivist standards of modern science—standards whose legitimacy, Grünbaum argues, Freud himself not only fully understood but embraced.

As we have seen, Grünbaum's critique hinges on his construction of the Tally Argument and its supposed demise. But, despite extraordinary ingenuity and special pleading, Grünbaum is unable to show that the Argument figured centrally in Freud's thinking. Without question, this failure is the most disabling fault in Grünbaum's entire treatment of Freud. I am inclined to agree with David Sachs that the Tally Argument as such never existed in

Freud's own mind—certainly not in the elaborate, self-conscious form that Grünbaum gives it. Hence the question of the Argument's validity is essentially moot, as is the question of whether its demise is attributable to Freud's abandonment of it or to disconfirming evidence produced by recent experimental studies or (as I believe, and as Grünbaum himself argued in 1978) to a simple error of logic in the Argument's formulation.

The evidence that the Tally Argument provided the sustaining intellectual justification for Freud's ideas from 1896 to 1926, the central decades of his career, is even less persuasive. Rather, the Argument seems to have been more of a passing thought, tossed out almost nonchalantly in the "Analytic Therapy" lecture and perhaps hinted at elsewhere (in the passage Grünbaum cites from the Little Hans case, for example), but never thought through systematically or relied upon consistently. No amount of textual bullying can force Freud's random and contradictory statements about the relation between his ideas and their therapeutic effect into conformity with the methodological principles supposedly enunciated in the Tally Argument. Likewise, both David Sachs and Frank Cioffi are certainly right when they maintain that Freud's confidence in his ideas derived in large part not from cures—not, in fact, from clinical evidence at all—but from his interpretation of such disparate nonclinical phenomena as dreams, slips, jokes, fairy tales, and works of art. Neither Freud himself nor, just as important, those who have been persuaded by his ideas rest their conviction on the ability of psychoanalysis to cure the mentally ill. Rather, that conviction has much more to do with the peculiar charm of the ideas themselves and with their power to illuminate a wide array of psychological and cultural behavior.

In short, the central thesis of Grünbaum's critique is poorly sustained. His arduously constructed (and deconstructed) image of Freud as a methodological sophisticate gone wrong ultimately collapses under its own weight and sheer improbability. In this respect, it is very much like Frank Sulloway's image of Freud as a crypto-biologist—again a product of great textual ingenuity but no less mythical than the Freud of Grünbaum's Tally Argument. Just as Sulloway tries to persuade us that, beneath his psychological cloak, Freud was a clandestine Darwinian, a precursor of the sociobiologist Edward O. Wilson, so Grünbaum insists that Freud, in his heart of hearts, was as self-conscious a philosopher of science as Francis Bacon or John Stuart Mill and a far better scientific methodologist than anti-Freudians like Karl Popper or Hans Eysenck have cared to recognize. But the evidence of Freud's writings provides no better support for Grünbaum than it does for Sulloway. Rather, Grünbaum has created a Freud after his own philosophical fancy. For all the industry and intelligence he has invested in his critique, its actual payoff is remarkably meager.

■　　■　　■

Grünbaum's judgment of Freud as a scientist contrasts interestingly with Sulloway's. On first blush, one might expect Grünbaum and Sulloway to adopt similar positions. After all, both approach Freud from a scientific perspective, Grünbaum as a philosopher of science, Sulloway as a historian of science. But instead they offer radically opposite views of Freud's scientific credentials. Sulloway's long book contains not so much as a word to suggest that Freud falls short of the empirical standards of modern science. On the contrary, Sulloway speaks of Freud as a scientific genius of the first order. Why, one wonders, is Sulloway unconcerned with the methodological shortcomings that inspire Grünbaum's obsessive elaboration of the Tally Argument and its unhappy fate?

The answer lies in the disparate conceptions of science that Grünbaum and Sulloway entertain. When Grünbaum speaks of science, he has in mind classical physics, the subject of his earlier work in the philosophy of science. Thus, when Grünbaum says that psychoanalysis is "fundamentally flawed," he means that it does not meet the evidential standards routinely expected in physics. By way of contrast, the science against which Sulloway measures Freud is historical biology, which necessarily has a more indulgent conception of proof—a more latitudinarian notion of what is authentically scientific—than is generally tolerated in physics. Because Darwin is Sulloway's model, Sulloway finds Freud's intellectual procedures far less heterodox than does Grünbaum. In historical biology the demand for laboratory comparisons and group control studies to justify causal assertions is, if anything, even more a counsel of perfection than it is in psychoanalysis. Darwin's science is at once empirical and hermeneutic: it works by deciphering clues—such as the fossil remains of extinct species—in order to reveal a hidden reality, namely, the workings of natural selection. Freud proceeds in exactly the same fashion when he deciphers the evidence of dreams, slips, and neurotic symptoms to reveal the hidden reality of the unconscious.

The sharp contrast between Grünbaum's and Sulloway's judgments of Freud as scientist is a potent reminder that "science" encompasses a wide range of intellectual practices. Science is in fact a continuum, with psychoanalysis occupying an honored place toward the Darwinian end. Such is the view taken by I. Bernard Cohen in his magisterial and authoritative study *Revolution in Science,* which treats Freud, alongside Darwin, as a major scientific innovator.

■   ■   ■

Grünbaum is best understood, I believe, as the latest and most sophisticated spokesman for the long-standing empiricist hostility to psychoanalysis. More generally, he is a representative of the well-established tradition of analytical philosophy—especially popular in Britain and North America but also boasting important adepts in Freud's own Vienna—that takes a dim view of the speculative and metaphysical habits of Continental thinkers. This affinity is obscured by Grünbaum's squabble with Karl Popper, who has been one of the leading voices of analytical philosophy in the twentieth century. But despite their disagreement about whether Freud comes to grief for inductivist or falsificationist reasons, Grünbaum and Popper share the same basic philosophical prejudices. For both of them, psychoanalysis fails because, unlike science, it is not genuinely empirical. Grünbaum differs from Popper mainly in being much cleverer and much better informed about the enemy.

Seen in this perspective, Grünbaum's critique of Freud has a historical flavor quite distinct from that of the nearly simultaneous critiques of Frank Sulloway and Jeffrey Masson. What is most striking about Sulloway and Masson is their clear dependence on intellectual and, in the case of Masson, social developments of the past two decades. Sulloway's Freud obviously presupposes the rise of sociobiology, or, more generally, what Carl Degler has called the

"return of biology" in the 1970s.[72] Masson's Freud is a
product of our newfound consciousness about child abuse
in the 1980s. Grünbaum, by contrast, can be linked to no
significant intellectual movement of the immediate past. If
anything, he is at odds with the prevailing philosophical
temper of recent times, when the linguistic turn and the
enthusiasm for French imports like deconstruction have
made Grünbaum's hard-nosed empiricism seem decidedly
old-fashioned. Hence my claim that his critique of Freud
should be viewed as the end product of the astringent
philosophical tradition that has dominated British and
American philosophy for most of the century and whose
roots in English intellectual history reach back into the
classical and medieval eras. This accounts for Grünbaum's
profound hostility to Jürgen Habermas and Paul Ricoeur,
both of whom speak for the Continental philosophical tradition so opposed to the radical empiricism (Habermas
and Ricoeur would say positivism) espoused by Grünbaum, and both of whom, of course, argue that Freud belongs firmly in the more capacious and intellectually sup-
ple school of interpretation that has flourished on the
Continent.

■   ■   ■

Above all else, Grünbaum's critique serves to heighten
our awareness of Freud's tense and richly dialectical relation to the ideals of modern science. By placing the Tally
Argument at the center of Freud's thinking, Grünbaum
points up Freud's commitment to those ideals: the belief
in observation, the demand that generalizations be sup-

---

72. Carl Degler, *In Search of Human Nature: The Decline and Revival
of Darwinism in American Social Thought* (New York, 1991), p. ix.

ported by a large number of individual instances, the recognition that a single contrary instance can discredit such generalizations, and the need to eliminate alternative explanations for one's findings. In this respect, Grünbaum, like Sulloway, offers a valuable reminder of Freud's profound identification with the scientific tradition, as well as a useful corrective to the misguided efforts of hermeneutic interpreters like Habermas and Ricoeur to obscure that identification. Freud, Grünbaum shows us, puts up enormous resistance to being treated as an artist rather than a scientist.

At the same time, Grünbaum's equal insistence on the failure of the Tally Argument draws our attention to the opposite but no less important truth that Freud also stands at odds with the scientific tradition. Freud refuses to trim his imagination to suit the strict empirical and skeptical canons of modern science. Like the great artists, he knows that the deep and important truths about human experience are complex, ambiguous, and, alas, often obscure. Perhaps unwittingly, Grünbaum thus enriches our sense of the paradox of Freud's thought—its aspiration to be a science like any other and its simultaneous refusal to settle for the kinds of quantifiable insights that can be readily verified through laboratory comparisons and group control studies (such as have been pursued by American academic psychology, thereby guaranteeing its aridity and its irrelevance to modern intellectual life). The Freud who emerges from Grünbaum's critique is decidedly more exigent and empirical than his hermeneutic students like to allow, but he still insists that knowledge of human beings will always remain interpretive: it cannot be made to resemble the kind of knowledge we have about the physical universe. Of course, Grünbaum wants to push Freud further in the scientific direction than Freud can comfortably tolerate without sacrificing his distinctive intellectual achievement. But precisely Grünbaum's failure to prove his case testifies eloquently to Freud's refusal to budge from the rich interstices of art and science. Freud remains a border thinker, neither fish nor fowl, always at risk of seeming caught in a hopeless contradiction and destined to be fought over perpetually by the representatives of the two great intellectual traditions that have dominated modern culture.

Conclusion: Freud and Intellectual History

Frank Sulloway, Jeffrey Masson, and Adolf Grünbaum, I have argued, are the most formidable of Freud's recent critics. But the main conclusion to which my analysis of their writings points is that their criticisms are poorly founded and seem unlikely to have an enduring effect on our image of Freud. None of the three makes his case. Ultimately each of them fails for empirical reasons.

There is some irony in this state of affairs, because all three critics boast of their commitment to empiricism: they are, they tell us, devoted to the facts, to the documentary record, and to confounding unsupported and tendentious views. Yet, in the event, they are unable to sustain their interpretations of Freud with a persuasive reading of the available evidence. Frank Sulloway maintains that Freud's thought was dominated by a set of evolutionary ideas, derived from Darwin and mediated by way of Wilhelm Fliess. But Sulloway's case for the centrality of those notions in Freud's thinking depends on the extravagant promotion of a few selected passages in his letters and writings, and Sulloway conveniently ignores the overwhelming contrary evidence that psychological, rather than biological, ideas stood at the heart of the psychoanalytic revolution. Jeffrey Masson's reinterpretation lives or dies with the proposition that Freud abandoned the seduction theory because he could not bear the professional disapproval and personal isolation it brought him. But Masson fails to supply plausible, let alone convincing, evidence for this contention, and he consistently misrepresents Freud's views about the reality of seduction and its relation to mental illness. Perhaps most ironic of all, Adolf Grünbaum also comes to empirical grief in the central assertion of his interpretation. His claim that Freud defended his ideas with the Tally Argument is simply not borne out by Freud's writings, and Grünbaum's account of the Argument's historical collapse is equally lacking in textual support.

All three critics construct versions of Freud that pointedly ignore his actual intellectual achievement. Instead, they offer us alternative Freuds, to whom they assign very different real or imagined accomplishments. Thus Frank Sulloway devotes great ingenuity to conjuring up a Freud who invented not psychoanalysis as we know it but a secret evolutionary doctrine (Sulloway's "crypto-biology"), thereby transforming Freud into Darwin's principal heir and a forerunner of Edward O. Wilson. Jeffrey Masson, for his part, composes an entirely hypothetical career for Freud—his true calling, had he only recognized it—as a crusader against the sexual abuse of children. In this rendering of the story, psychoanalysis turns out to be not Freud's claim to greatness but the measure of his failure: it is the intellectual encoding of his retreat from the insight on which his historic career should have been founded— in short, an elaborate lie. Adolf Grünbaum's Freud is no less mythical than Masson's. In Grünbaum's hands, Freud becomes not a sexual reformer but a scientific methodologist comparable to Bacon or Mill, a sophisticated theorist who should have backed up his theories with the sort of group control studies that he knew to be necessary for their validation.

Quite apart from their imaginary character, all three versions assign Freud a career that, however admirable, is distinctly lesser than the one he chose for himself. Whether we picture him succeeding to Darwin's mantle or directing a campaign against child abuse or becoming a prominent experimental psychologist, these achievements pale in comparison to the profound intellectual revolution Freud in fact initiated. To the historian of ideas, the critics fail utterly to take the measure of their man. Like it or not, Freud virtually invented a new way of thinking about the self. If we hope to do him justice, we must recognize that his accomplishment—judged in terms of richness, breadth, and imagination—has been equaled by only a handful of figures in the history of thought, figures like Augustine, Newton, and Marx. It is precisely this Freud who disappears from sight in the interpretations of his recent critics. Reading Sulloway, Masson, or Grünbaum, one could never understand why Freud has exercised such a potent hold on the modern imagination.

Unless I am seriously mistaken, however, Freud's recent critics will do him no lasting damage. At most they have delayed the inevitable process by which he will settle into his rightful place in intellectual history as a thinker of the first magnitude. Indeed, the very latest scholarly studies of Freud suggest that the anti-Freudian moment may already have begun to pass. Peter Gay's major new biography, *Freud: A Life for Our Time* (1988), reaffirms the view of Freud's intellectual achievement and personal integrity presented by Ernest Jones over three decades ago. One might object that, despite his subtitle, Gay largely ignores the recent critics of psychoanalysis, dismissing them with a few choice adjectives in his bibliographical essay. But Gay's mastery of the archival and secondary literature on Freud is unique, and his portrait accordingly carries great authority. Even more suggestive of a revival in Freud's stock are books by two younger scholars, Jonathan Lear's *Love and Its Place in Nature: A Philosophical Interpretation of Freudian Psychoanalysis* and Mark Edmundson's *Towards Reading Freud*, both published in 1990. Lear is a philosopher and Edmundson a literary critic, and although they offer contrasting readings of Freud, they agree about his stature. Lear places him in the mainstream of Western philosophical thought, an heir to Socrates, and the most important modern theorist of the individual. For Edmundson he belongs in the great tradition of imaginative writers whose principal subject has been the self: Shakespeare, Milton, Wordsworth, and Emerson. A comparable estimate is implicit in *Freud's Moses* (1991) by Yosef Hayim Yerushalmi, who argues that psychoanalysis must be understood as a secularization of the moral and intellectual heritage of Judaism.

Michel Foucault has called Freud a "founder of discursivity," meaning by that someone who has created a new way of speaking, "an endless possibility of discourse."[1] Harold Bloom asserts, "No twentieth-century writer—not even Proust or Joyce or Kafka—rivals Freud's position as the central imagination of our age."[2] Freud has fundamentally altered the way we think. He has changed our intellectual manners, often without our even being aware of it. For most of us Freud has become a habit of mind—a

1. Michel Foucault, "What is an Author?" in Foucault, *The Foucault Reader,* ed. Paul Rabinow (New York, 1984), p. 114.
2. Harold Bloom, "Freud, the Greatest Modern Writer," *The New York Times Book Review,* March 23, 1986, p. 27.

bad habit, his critics would be quick to urge, but a habit now too deeply ingrained to be broken. He is the major source of our modern inclination to look for meanings beneath the surface of behavior—to be always on the alert for the "real" (and presumably hidden) significance of our actions. He also inspires our belief that the mysteries of the present will become more transparent if we can trace them to their origins in the past, perhaps even in the very earliest past we can remember (or, more likely, *not* remember). And, finally, he has created our heightened sensitivity to the erotic, above all to its presence in arenas, notably the family, where previous generations had neglected to look for it. Exactly the Freud who has so invaded our minds is dramatically absent in the writings of his recent detractors. With a poet's wisdom, W. H. Auden more accurately captured Freud's historical stature in a poem commemorating his death in September 1939:

> To us he is no more a person
> Now but a whole climate of opinion.

Index

Compositor: BookMasters, Inc.
Text: 11/13 Bembo
Display: Bembo
Printer: Haddon Craftsmen
Binder: Haddon Craftsmen